P9-DFD-819

THRESHOLDS OF REALITY

Kennikat Press
National University Publications
Literary Criticism Series

General Editor
John E. Becker
Fairleigh Dickinson University

Lois Hughson

THRESHOLDS OF REALITY

George Santayana and Modernist Poetics

National University Publications
KENNIKAT PRESS // 1977
Port Washington, N. Y. // London

Excerpts of poetry and prose are reprinted by permission as follows: Ezra Pound, *The Cantos,* © 1934 by Ezra Pound, New Directions Publishing Corp.; "Burnt Norton," "The Dry Salvages," "Little Gidding," and "East Coker" in *Four Quarters* by T. S. Eliot, © 1943 by T. S. Eliot, "Burnt Norton" © 1971 by Esme Valerie Eliot, Harcourt Brace Jovanovich, Inc.: "Peter Quince at the Clavier," "Notes Toward a Supreme Fiction," "An Ordinary Evening in New Haven," "Credences of Summer," "The Man with the Blue Guitar," "The Rock," and "The Auroras of Autumn," in *The Palm at the End of the Mind* by Wallace Stevens, © 1967, 1969, and 1971 by Holly Stevens, Alfred A. Knopf, Inc.; *The Necessary Angel* by Wallace Stevens, © 1942, 1944, 1947, 1949, and 1951 by Wallace Stevens, Alfred A. Knopf, Inc.; "Adagia" in *Opus Posthumus* by Wallace Stevens, © 1957 by Elsie Stevens and Holly Stevens, Alfred A. Knopf, Inc.: "The Statues," "Under Ben Bulben," "The Circus Animals' Desertion," and "Lapis Lazuli," ©1940 by Georgie Yeats, renewed 1968 by Bertha Georgie Yeats, Michael Butler Yeats and Anne Yeats; "Vacillation" and "A Dialogue of Self and Soul," © 1933 by Macmillan Publishing Co., Inc., renewed 1961 by Bertha Georgie Yeats; "The Tower" and "Among School Children," © 1928 by Macmillan Publishing Co., Inc., renewed 1956 by Georgie Yeats, all in *Collected Poems* of William Butler Yeats, Macmillan Publishing Co., Inc.; *Letters of William Butler Yeats,* edited by Allan Wade, © 1953, 1954 by Anne Butler Yeats; *Wheels and Butterflies* by William Butler Yeats, © 1934 by Macmillan Publishing Co., Inc., renewed 1962 by Bertha Georgie Yeats; *A Vision* by William Butler Yeats, © 1937 by W. B. Yeats, renewed 1965 by Bertha Georgie Yeats and Anne Butler Yeats, Macmillan Publishing Co., Inc.; *The Letters of George Santayana,* edited by Daniel Cory, *Persons and Places, My Host the World, Scepticism* and *Animal Faith* and *Character and Opinion in the United States,* all by George Santayana, Charles Scribner's Sons; "The Uses of Despair: Sources of Creative Energy in George Santayana" by Lois Hughson in *American Quarterly,* © 1971 by Trustees of the University of Pennsylvania; *The Sacred Wood* by T. S. Eliot, Methuen & Co. Ltd

Copyright © 1977 by Kennikat Press Corp. All rights reserved. No part of this publication may be reproduced, stored in a retrieval system, or transmitted, in any form or by any means, electronic, mechanical, photocopying, recording, or otherwise, without the prior written permission of the publisher.

Manufactured in the United States of America

Published by
Kennikat Press Corp.
Port Washington, N. Y./London

Library of Congress Cataloging in Publication Data

Hughson, Lois.
   Thresholds of reality.

   (National university publications) (Literary criticism series)
   Includes index.
     1. Santayana, George, 1863–1952–Knowledge–Literature. 2. Santayana, George, 1863–1952–Poetic works. I. Title.
PS2773.H8   811'.5'2   76-44012
ISBN 0-8046-9154-1

To Howard

Contents

PREFACE. . . . . *ix*

CHAPTER I. THE LYRIC POETRY *3*

CHAPTER II. *LUCIFER:* The LIMITS of SCEPTICISM *35*

CHAPTER III. The SENSE of BEAUTY. *54*

CHAPTER IV. The PRIMACY of the IMAGINATION. *89*

CHAPTER V. YEATS and HIS ENCHANTED STONE. *116*

CHAPTER VI. ELIOT'S REFINING FIRE *139*

CHAPTER VII. STEVENS and the SUFFICIENCY of REALITY. *158*

INDEX. *177*

Preface

We have arrived at that stage in our relationship with modernist poetry when we can no longer take its claims for itself for granted. The extent of its debt to the past, not the distant past it was always willing to acknowledge, but the immediate past, the generation which fathered it, claims our attention more and more. Encouraged by our newly rediscovered sense of history and cultural context, we seek sources and continuities where we once delighted in disruptions and originality. Who are the figures, we now ask, themselves not modernists, who enabled modernism to be? Not forerunners, alien to their own time, but figures who fully embody their own moment and in solving its problems prepare the next. Behind those two great spokesmen for modernist poetry's aims and means, T. S. Eliot and Wallace Stevens, looms the figure of George Santayana, a formidable bridge from the late Anglo-American Victorian world to modernist literary culture, his presence not yet acknowledged, his dimensions not yet measured. His influence on Eliot and Stevens is palpable to the attentive reader of their writings about literature and his own, although only Stevens has shown a sense of debt.

But beyond this is the equally important but less tangible significance of what Santayana stood for and articulated in those thirty years at Harvard between the early 1880s and 1912 when he resigned and left America for Europe. The fruit of those American years nourished Eliot and Stevens and are there to show us how modernist poetry came not merely out of earlier poetry or literary traditions, for to say this would be to perpetuate the modernist myth that poems are bred by other poems, but came out of particular cultural contexts. Furthermore, those years show us the fertile conjunction of particular needs of particular men with widely felt needs in that culture. When such men find solutions for the problems their own lives set them, they act for the culture. Or, in another perspective, the culture acts through them for it both sets problems and offers certain kinds of solutions. George Santayana was such a representative figure for the transitional period of the 1880s and 1890s.

His full career reached the 1950s. In the more than sixty years of his productive life there was scarcely a literary genre he left untried, while in his philosophy he ranged from Platonism and naturalism to what he aptly called literary psychology. His roots were deep in traditional culture as the nineteenth century conceived of it and were fed by both American and European sources. He is a legitimate heir of Emerson and Matthew Arnold alike. His capacity to transmit and transform the tradition he inherited was born of his personal need to express and redeem the devastating sense of loss and deprivation at the core of his sense of life. What might have been profoundly crippling in his earliest experience he was able to convert in his psychic economy to a source of sustained and far-reaching creativity. That conversion is the core of this study.

His poetry was the first phase of his continuing effort to conceive a world of values which could succeed the disintegrating nineteenth-century intellectual order and at the same time constitute a realm in which he would enjoy compensation for the gratification experience denied him. The lyrics and odes are full of the naturalism and rejection of traditional religion typical of the last decades of the nineteenth century when a generation was coming to maturity aghast at the chaos for which Henry Adams sought a law of acceleration. For Santayana, these attitudes were inextricable from the feelings of rage and impotence generated by his early separation from his mother and the three years he lived in Spain with his father before he joined her in America. He dealt with those feelings of rage and impotence as a large segment of the culture was to deal with their own—by a surrender of the demand for direct emotional gratification through action in the real world and a redirection of his energies toward fulfillment in a realm of art where belief cannot lead to betrayal or loss.

In *The Sense of Beauty* Santayana developed his naturalistic, relativistic concept of esthetic experience in a way that was determined both by existing cultural conditions, such as the dominance of the visual mode in nineteenth-century art, and by his feelings about his father, a failed painter. It was an esthetic that enabled him to keep experience at a safe distance and yet symbolically make it a part of himself and thereby within his control. The criticism of romanticism in art, a major feature of both *The Sense of Beauty* and *Interpretations of Poetry and Religion,* relied on the classicism that was part of nineteenth-century intellectual tradition, but a classicism freshly allied with both science and estheticism to support a symbolic theory of knowledge and of literary form. It expressed Santayana's drive to dominate and give form to immediate experience in the face of which he felt reduced to the impotence of his childhood.

Finally, in *Interpretations of Poetry and Religion,* he asserted the primacy of the imagination in every intellectual sphere. The creation of poetry itself became the explicit paradigm for every individual's creation of the world from the flux of his immediate experience. Here was announced the theme of much of the poetry and fiction of the early twentieth century: the poet as a maker, both of meaning and myth, who descends into the chaos underlying convention to emerge with materials for a world of his own making, a world symbolic of his experience but removed from it. For Santayana it meant the triumph in art of the significance of experience over its immediacy or extension and further constituted the realization of that realm where the self might recover the freedom and potency it lacked in the life of action.

These theories did, in fact, mark a great release of creative energy in Santayana's career, as they did for modern literature when poets increasingly came to see themselves as makers and art displaced action as a way of dominating experience. For Santayana it meant great surrenders in his personal life. Yet, as he felt himself so strongly, he was giving up only those things which were in any case unattainable. They were surrenders fundamentally so enabling and liberating that, although he was always to feel alien in the United States and eventually chose exile in Europe, he possessed an intellectual serenity and breadth that were to sustain his creative life into his eightieth year.

I have tried to demonstrate in three major modernists a similar relationship between a fragmented experience and a powerful and productive imagination. The chapters on Yeats, Eliot, and Stevens are in no sense meant to be comprehensive studies of their poetry. My aim was to follow through their work just this displacement of action by imagination and the extent to which their poetry acted out Santayana's hopes and theories. It seems to me particularly important to analyze the shifting relationship of power and art in Yeats just because his development was independent of, yet parallel in important ways to, Santayana's. If the claim for the centrality of Santayana's critical theories is just and if his experience does show how the energy of the modernist period came to replace the extensive lethargy of the late nineteenth century, then they should explain a major figure free of his direct influence. Furthermore, Santayana makes a context for Yeats's development not ordinarily perceived. Santayana was always a moralist; behind his vision of an imagination which both surrendered and repossessed the world was a drive to identify that part, as he put it, that might be loved. He recognized force;

he admitted all its claims, but he refused to worship it. He rendered unto necessity all that belonged to it but was moved always by the tears of things. Responding to so many of the same literary and personal problems in the same terms, Yeats was never so clear in his allegiances.

Eliot and Stevens, on the other hand, provide the working out in their poetry of those theories of Santayana that they largely restate in their prose. Unlike Yeats and Santayana, they are not figures of transition and carriers of change and new solutions; they are figures of fulfillment. Critically they no longer really break new ground. They have been given a place to stand and a perspective in which to view their literary problems. They do not forge a new critical vocabulary; they have been given a language to speak. The aim of my analysis in this study is to indicate what in their work is the language Santayana has provided them with, the extent to which their subjects are shaped by that language, and, finally, the way that language, forged in Santayana's own confrontations with experience, continued to be adequate to their own because their experience in important ways repeats his. Their achievement lights up the degree to which Santayana was a representative cultural figure, while his work enables us to see better the foundations of their art as well as its relationship to general intellectual changes.

My interest in cultural continuities and disruptions and the way literature grows out of cultural contexts was fostered in general by my years as both student and teacher at Columbia University and in particular by the example and encouragement of Quentin Anderson and Steven Marcus.

THRESHOLDS OF REALITY

The real is only the base. But it is the base.

Wallace Stevens, *Opus Posthumus*

The Lyric Poetry

George Santayana was the child of a second marriage. When he was five years old, his mother left him to fulfill her vow to bring up the children of her first husband in his native Boston, while George and his father remained in Spain. When Santayana was eight, his father, oddly convinced that the Protestant New England milieu with which his Spanish wife was connected through her first marriage would provide wider social options for his Catholic son, brought George to Boston to rejoin his mother. After one cold winter, the father returned to Spain alone, not to see his son again for ten years. The young Santayana was not effectually reunited with his mother emotionally, and he never felt himself an accepted part of the society for which so much had been sacrificed.

After such an extraordinary preparation for life, it is not surprising that Santayana felt himself born into the world of Matthew Arnold's poetry, where ignorant armies clashed by night and a man might wander "between two worlds, one dead, / The other powerless to be born." In that image his private history and the intellectual currents of his society came powerfully together. Under that sign he began to write his poetry, the first stage in a long and fruitful effort to express, master, and redeem the loss and deprivation at the core of his sense of life. It was the beginning of the long building of that world which could not bring itself to life. Its basis was naturalism; its method, the exploration of the ways in which life becomes conscious of itself and nature generates value; its justification, the reconciliation of spirit to its impotence and, in Santayana's view, its consequent liberation.

As an individual he would make this new world the world of his own art, where the gratification denied him by experience would be his, however transformed. As a public figure sensitive to the elements of nine-teenth-century culture available for readjustment of intellectual perspectives, he would contribute through his criticism to the new world of twentieth-century culture that conceived of itself as modern. For Santayana's psychic organization and the stratagems by which he endured or solved his emotional conflicts were expressed in an intellectual life extraordinarily representative of the changes in attitudes and concepts that marked the transition from the nineteenth to the twentieth century.

Santayana's earliest achievement in poetry was the first sonnet sequence, developed over a decade beginning in 1882 and appearing finally in his 1894 collection, *Sonnets and Other Verses.* He had written verse as a schoolboy, winning the Boston Latin School Prize in 1880 with a poem called "Day and Night," which he thought well enough of to revise as late as 1888 but never published. At the end of his life he remembered the well-known "O world, thou choosest not the better part" as his earliest sonnet. He spoke of it in his memoirs as an expression of the urgent need for faith he experienced early in life, which was never satisfied through Catholicism and finally issued in the concept of animal faith he worked out in his mature philosophy. It was a mistake in memory, for he seems to have written at least two sonnets of that sequence earlier, a mistake that emphasizes the continuity he felt in his own career as well as the persistence of the needs and conflicts that lay beneath.

This sonnet, however, which he remembered as his earliest, was one of his most popular, anthologized not only in standard collections like *The Oxford Book of American Verse,* but in the more specialized pages of *World's Great Religious Poetry* and *The Homiletic Review.* It is not a very good poem, and it is not, in the sense many of its approving readers took it to be, a religious one. Santayana judged it fairly himself in a letter to William Lyon Phelps: "... although the words are too much spaced, thinly scattered over an empty waste, like the scrub oaks over a ploughed field which in Spain are called a wood, yet the whole is perfectly limpid, and I can imagine that emitted in a rotund voice in a hushed religious atmosphere (do people still cough in the Yale Chapel?) it might have a good effect .... I hope our combined exhortation will encourage your young people to have faith—in themselves!"[1]

Part of the fun of this comment lies in the awareness of Santayana, probably not shared by Phelps, that as a young poet, no more than as a mature philosopher, was he concerned with encouraging received religious ideas or institutions. The sequence in which it ultimately figured as number three was distinguished by a central theme which ran counter to the popular reading of the sonnet: acceptance of the natural order was ultimately man's only source of comfort. The sequence is a farewell to child-hood and a putting away of childish things, among them Christianity. The poems contain the earliest expression of convictions that were to issue in his maturity in the vigor of this passage in a letter to William James:

Religion in particular was *found out* more than two hundred years ago, and it seems to me intolerable that we should still be condemned to ignore the fact and to give the parson and the "idealist" a monopoly of indigna-tion and of contemptuous dogmatism. It is they not we who are the pest; . . . What did Emerson know or care about the passionate insanities and political disasters which religion, for instance, has so often been another name for? He could give that name to his last personal intuition, and ig-nore what it stands for and what it expresses in the world. It is the latter that absorbs me . . . .[2]

Santayana almost always used the ordinary language of the educated man, even in his later technical philosophic writing. He was to achieve enor-mous range and color in its use, but at the outset of his career he was especially bound in his verse by conventional poetic diction. In fact, he was clearly, even at the beginning, freer and more supple in his prose. The freshness and originality in the sonnets lie mainly in the images and con-cepts; the language is disappointing and in its very conventionality, mis-leading. This conventionality was at the root of the general misreading of the poem. When he was looking for a term for the essentially irrational be-lief man has in the independent existence of his environment, he chose *animal* faith. In that way he hoped not to be understood, in the way his "earliest sonnet" was, "to advocate religious illusions feebly appended to science . . . ."[3]

It is easy to see, reading the sonnet apart from its sequence, how San-tayana's meaning was distorted.

> O world, thou choosest not the better part!
> It is not wisdom to be only wise,
> And on the inward wisdom close the eyes,
> But it is wisdom to believe the heart.
> Columbus found a world, and had no chart,
> Save one that faith deciphered in the skies;
> To trust the soul's invincible surmise
> Was all his science and his only art.
> Our knowledge is a torch of smoky pine
> That lights the pathway but one step ahead
> Across a void of mystery and dread.
> Bid, then, the tender light of faith to shine
> By which alone the mortal heart is led
> Unto the thinking of the thought divine.[4]

Here was a poem which told an audience accustomed to a degraded Emersonianism and a sentimentalized Christianity what it thought it knew and could not so well express. Using the very language of "ideality," of the genteel tradition at whose expense he was later to win fame, it seemed to reinforce the same gulf the tradition emphasized between the rough and tumble of an exploitative society and the rarified realm of truth, faith, sentiment, and art. There are some hints here of the direction in which Santayana will move away from a kind of Emersonianism, in the terms of the last opposition. The mortal heart "thinks" the thought divine. It is not passive, intuitive, but active, constructive. The heart itself is "mortal," not one with the thought. The association of the "thought divine" and the "void of mystery and dread" has some of the Christian air of the Word bringing the world out of chaos, but it also points to Santayana's future ideas about the way the mind creates the world out of flux. But these are merely hints to the initiated; the vocabulary alone—faith, soul, divine, vision—reinforces a conventional understanding of the poem based on the superiority of religious faith to worldly science and art, or on an Emersonian faith in the self.

However, the other poems in the sequence, two of them apparently written before this, the rest after, were an opportunity for Santayana to work out more clearly for himself, in terms more congenial and accurate, the attitudes and convictions taking shape in his mind. The sequence is not about the loss of faith; it presupposes that loss and is concerned rather with the state of mind of the poet, intensely self-conscious, isolated, full of a sense of loss, slowly becoming aware of the sources of comfort and adequacy available to him.

The first sonnet marks the descent from "the piteous height" at which the poet's "sad youth worshipped." (This, according to a notebook of 1890, was actually his earliest sonnet.[5])

> I sought on earth a garden of delight
> Or island altar to the Sea and Air,
> Where gentle music were accounted prayer,
> And reason, veiled, performed the happy rite.
> My sad youth worshipped at the piteous height
> Where God vouchsafed the death of man to share;
> His love made mortal sorrow light to bear,
> But his deep wounds put joy to shamèd flight.
> And though his arms, outstretched upon the tree,
> Were beautiful and pleaded my embrace,
> My sins were loth to look upon his face.
> So came I down from Golgotha to thee,
> Eternal Mother; let the sun and sea
> Heal me, and keep me in thy dwelling-place. (p. 3)

The poet has returned to earth to let nature heal him and keep him. What, then, are the causes of his renunciation of Christianity? The suffering of Christ and his own sins; the one separating him from joy, the other from spiritual love. That is a very serious criticism of revealed religion, and rather uncommon. For it means that the poet will seek in the use of reason and in natural processes those very satisfactions that religion often advises us must be sought beyond reason. But it was not at all the irrationality of Christianity that had disillusioned him. He had never thought it rational. He tells us elsewhere that he never had "any unquestioning faith in any dogma, and was never a practicing Catholic."[6] In his autobiography he contrasts his own position with that of his sister, Susana: "She thought religion a matter of fact . . . . Now I was aware, at first instinctively and soon quite clearly on historical and psychological grounds, that religion and all philosophy of that kind were *invented.* It was all conceived and worked out inwardly, imaginatively, for moral reasons . . . ."[7]

Another source of his attitude toward religion was the opinion of his parents. His mother was a Deist; in her belief God was too great to take particular care of man, and churches, credos, and rites were inventions of the clergy to extend their power. Santayana's father was not a Deist, but he shared his wife's opinions on the clergy and other institutions of the church. Santayana had learned Catholic prayers and the catechism as a social practice in the years he spent in Spain with his father as a young child, but he knew his parents believed all religion mere imaginings of man, with the implication that the works of the human imagination were bad. In contrast, the young Santayana believed that as works of the human imagination they were good, in fact the only thing good to be found, while the whole world was "ashes in the mouth."[8] Unlike his parents, he wrote, "I was quite sure that life was not worth living; for if religion was false everything was worthless, and almost everything, if religion was true. In this youthful pessimism I was hardly more foolish than so many amateur medievalists and religious aesthetes of my generation. I saw the same alternative between Catholicism and complete disillusion, but I was never afraid of disillusion and I have chosen it."[9]

Santayana believed that the poetic account of experience was fuller and truer to the complexity of the experience than prose discourse about it. "I sought on earth a garden of delight" does include elements that the memoirs omit. In the moment of disillusionment which the sonnet describes, the hope of joy and spiritual love is not really given up; the embrace of naturalism affirms reason and health. It is neither a surrender to despair nor to instincts and moral passivity.

This poem is not among the best of the sequence. It has a bland, easy quality not suited to the experience dealt with. Essentially this experience is over with; it is too easily contained. The creative energy of the sequence comes from another source: the effort to be healed and to find a new footing for his life, to come to terms with things from a new perspective and make sense of them. Sonnet V is a clear expression of that struggle. It plays with the meanings of sight and vision, dream and truth, waking and sleeping, so as to convey the confusion of meaning that dominates the early stages of his disillusionment.

> Dreamt I to-day the dream of yesternight,
> Sleep ever feigning one evolving theme, —
> Of my two lives which should I call the dream?
> Which action vanity? which vision sight?
> Some greater waking must pronounce aright,
> If aught abideth of the things that seem,
> And with both currents swell the flooded stream
> Into an ocean infinite of light.
> Even such a dream I dream, and know full well
> My waking passeth like a midnight spell,
> But know not if my dreaming breaketh through
> Into the deeps of heaven and of hell.
> I know but this of all I would I knew:
> Truth is a dream, unless my dream is true. (p. 7)

The first line establishes the distinction and confusion of two kinds of experience, but dreaming and waking will not be easily assigned to day or night. Reality remains uncertain. The poet awaits the "greater waking" which will clarify that sight. For if the things in waking life are only relatively less fleeting than in dream, then how are they essentially different? All action, then, is vanity. But the greater waking will not banish the dream. Both currents, reality and dream, will carry the flooded stream of his consciousness to a knowledge of truth. Yet the confusion is not dispelled. In the sestet this very image of waking as enlightenment is the content of his dream, while his real waking has the brevity and unreality of an interruption of sleep in the middle of the night, or, in another sense of "midnight spell," an interlude of bewitchment. Unless the poet's dream of an ultimate distinction between the fleeting forms of imagination and the enduring aspects of reality can be realized, then truth itself has no reality. This is the central anguish that surrounds the efforts of reason to reorder experience in a new perspective.

The succeeding sonnets of the sequence explore the possibilities of psychic reorganization. In VI, "Love not as do the flesh-imprisoned men," there is already the awareness that, if anything is to be kept from the ceaseless flow of experience, it cannot be kept in actual physical possession:

"But love thou nothing thou wouldst love the less / If henceforth ever hidden from thy ken" (p. 8). In VII, "I would I might forget that I am I," he sees death as a liberation of the spirit, potentially the master but impotently locked within him, while he is "doomed to know his aching heart alone" (p. 9). He cannot yet see how that spirit can be freed in life. Stoicism seems to offer the best consolation along with the promise that "Having known grief, all will be well with thee, / Ay, and thy second slumber will be deep" (p. 11). He surrenders the hope for joy on earth. In the first sonnet he searched for a garden of delight; now he asks,

> Doth the sun therefore burn, that I may bask?
> Or do the tirèd earth and tireless sea,
> That toil not for their pleasure, toil for me?
> Amid the world's long striving, wherefore ask
> What reasons were, or what rewards shall be?
> The covenant God gave us is a task. (p. 12)

God here is not the Christian God he had given up but a useful symbol for what he calls earlier in the poem "the force / That gives direction and hath given birth." For the Christian promise of salvation is simply not a possibility for him. Sonnet XI, "Deem not, because you see me in the press," is a curious combination of apologetic refusal to affirm the Christian myth and stoic detachment.

> Deem not, because you see me in the press
> Of this world's children run my fated race,
> That I blaspheme against a proffered grace,
> Or leave unlearned the love of holiness.
> I honour not that sanctity the less
> Whose aureole illumines not my face,
> But dare not tread the secret, holy place
> To which the priest and prophet have access.
> For some are born to be beatified
> By anguish, and by grievous penance done;
> And some, to furnish forth the age's pride,
> And to be praised of men beneath the sun;
> And some are born to stand perplexed aside
> From so much sorrow—of whom I am one. (p. 13)

He will not avoid his "fated race," yet he feels himself one of those "born to stand perplexed aside / From so much sorrow."

This sonnet embodies the strategic detachment Santayana was never to forsake. It was a natural outgrowth of his early emotional life and his social experience. He believed that his family history was "consonant with his philosophy and may have helped to form it."[10] On that occasion he was referring to the homelessness of his family. His father had been a colonial civil servant; his mother had had no permanent home as a child. She married an American in the Philippines, who left her a widow with three children whom she promised to educate as Americans. Her second husband was Santayana's father, and until Santayana was three, they all lived together in Spain. At that time his older half-brother, Robert Sturgis, was sent to America to school, and two years later his mother followed with her two Sturgis daughters; he remained behind with his father.

This physical desertion, however, must have been essentially the confirmation of an abandonment already experienced. Santayana creates in his autobiography an image of his mother as a woman profoundly indifferent to the world, cold, reserved, regarding all things calmly from a distance, "preserving her dignity and also her leisure" (*Persons and Places*, p. 53). This truth of her personality was so clear to Santayana and seemed so central to her life that he explains it in terms of a crisis produced by the only great sorrow in her life, the death of her first son as a child not yet two. "It made a radical revolution in her heart. It established there a reign of silent despair, permanent, devastating, ruffled perhaps by fresh events on the surface, but always dark and heavy beneath, like the depths of the sea" (p. 46). Although Santayana was reunited with his mother before he was nine, there was never any intimacy between them. He speaks of his sister, Susana, twelve years his senior, as inspiring all the love and closeness usually reserved for one's mother. He tells us, finally, that the crisis over the death of his mother's first child was a "veritable conversion," in which she surrendered earthly demands and attachments and in which "she retained her judgments and her standards, but without hope" (p. 51). He is confident that these must have been her feelings, he assures us, because "at about the same age" he had a similar conversion, which "rendered external things indifferent."

This essentially mythic explanation for his mother's behavior leads us to the emotional center of his creative life. That the portrait of his mother is a dramatic creation, composed of both his direct experiences with her and suppositions about the significance of her behavior that he had no way of confirming, seems clear. It is an attempt to explain her otherwise monstrous abandonment of him and her later willingness to separate herself and her young son from his father.

It is itself a variation on the theme that runs through all his creative effort: the loss of love, reacted to first with despair, then with renunciation, and finally with detachment. The personages of this fable are a mother and her son, the very actors in his real experience. The ultimate com-

10

fort of the fable lies in the fact that in it, death itself, that final fact of human life, is the cause of his abandonment. Loss of his mother's love need not be ascribed to her will or to his unworthiness; it rests finally beyond them both, on the nature of things. It was nobody's *fault* that his infant half-brother died. In the way he connects his mother's crisis with his own change of heart, or "metanoia," as he calls it, is a further indication of his effort to make her behavior to him natural. In his own case, "there were no outer events to occasion it, except the sheer passage of time, the end of youth and friendship, the sense of being harnessed for life like a beast of burden" (p. 51). This is how he describes his own experience in the chapter of his autobiography devoted to his mother. The end of youth and friendship and the sense of being harnessed seem to him to be the consequences of the passage of time. Nothing *happened*; it was life itself, unavoidable, that did this to a man. Again, loss is a part of the process of living. He has felt it himself. There is nothing monstrous or unnatural about his mother. He can be indifferent to her but filial. He need not hate her. But out of what an abyss of despair does a man of thirty, for that was his age at the time of his own emotional crisis, see the sheer passage of time as bringing naturally enough the loss of friendship and the sense of being a beast of burden! The price of denying his own rage involves the denial of the vast range of possibilities life offers a man of thirty. He cannot see mature sexual relationships or intellectual fulfillment or any other satisfactions of adulthood before him; he sees only loss and frustration. In fact, his metanoia, involving though it did extensive denials in his emotional life, also marked a great freeing of energies in his poetry and his criticism. It was as much an affirmation of the kind of intellectual life he was capable of, as a renunciation of the interpersonal and social fulfillment he recognized as beyond him.

There is another section of *Persons and Places* that indicates both the pain of the separation from his mother and the direction in which it turned his thinking and colored his conception of the world. The chapter called "Early Memories" begins by commenting on the dreamlike quality of his earliest recollections and perhaps their greater pertinence for being dreams rather then true memories because "they would show how my young mind grew, what objects impressed it, and on what themes it played its first variations" (p. 116). It ends with the reflection that what he had learned at Avila through his Spanish catechism in the three years he was separated from his mother was the conception of "the omnificent power and eternal truth" which he "reasserted," as he puts it, in his own philosophy in the notions of the realms of being in which man is powerless (p. 129). What the child was clearly learning in devastating measure in those years was his own helplessness.

The reminiscences lying between these observations are of repeated separations. The memory he thinks may have been his first is of his mother showing him a star as she puts him to bed, telling him that Pepin, her dead first-born, was behind that star. It is followed by the departure of Robert for America, the subsequent departure of his mother and half-sisters, the death of a cousin after the birth of a still-born child, the loss of attention from the aunt who had cared for him but now felt driven to devote herself to her son-in-law and his young daughters from a previous marriage (an interesting echo of his mother's compulsion), and finally the mental deterioration of his uncle. Before he left with his father to rejoin his mother in America, the household he had been entrusted to was completely destroyed.

He was profoundly aware of the significance of these events to him:

That crowded, strained, disunited and tragic family life remains for me the type of what life really is, something confused, hideous, and useless. I do not hate it or rebel against it, as people do who think they have been wronged. It caused me no suffering; I was a child carried along as in a baby-carriage through the crowd of strangers; I was neither much bothered nor seriously neglected; and my eyes and ears became accustomed to the unvarnished truth of the world, neither selected for my instruction nor hidden from me for my benefit. (p. 119)

Nevertheless, it is clear that Santayana's understanding of the meaning of these experiences is intellectual only. He denies any suffering on their account. The movement of mind apparent here is very much like that shown in his picture of his mother. The tragedy of his family is seen as the tragedy of life itself. It is unavoidable. There is no recourse. This inevitability makes it easier to deny the pain of the sensitive young boy actually at the mercy of pathologically poor judgment in the inadequate adults on whom he depended. But that he sees the events of that distorted household as the type of all experience goes a long way toward explaining the emotional sources of Santayana's unwillingness to affirm experience for its own sake and to throw all his energies into activities meant to isolate and affirm what is of value in experience only. To surrender oneself to experience, especially to feeling, was to be overwhelmed by it. If one confined himself to those aspects which could be understood, he was safe.

The climax of the chapter is an account of the birth of his cousin's still-born child. Like the account of his mother's crisis, which ends with a conversion in which she carries on her life but "without hope," an experience and phrase leading directly, as we shall see, to the five sonnets of the first sequence that resolve the poet's conflict and dissipate his despair, this episode ends with reflections that reverberate in his later philosophic career.

The account of Antonita's labor begins with a parenthetical observation that her room had been his mother's, back to back with his own, "but with no communication" (p. 125). The birth was long overdue and difficult. Before he is taken away from the apartment, he sees the dead child in a small wooden box, "lying naked, pale yellowish green." It appeared, he tells us, "most beautiful" to him, "not a ghastly object that ought to have been hidden from me, but as the most beautiful of statues, something too beautiful to be alive" (p. 125). And he goes on to develop the response to this sight, which, as in all his other childhood memories, caused him no pain.

And it has suggested to me a theory, doubtless fanciful, yet which I can't think wholly insignificant, concerning the formation of living things. They are all formed in the dark, automatically, protected from interference by what is called experience: experience which indeed would be impossible if there were not first a definite creature to receive it and to react upon it in ways consonant with its inherited nature. This nature has asserted itself in a seed, in an egg, in a womb, where the world couldn't disturb its perfect evolution. Flowers and butterflies come perfect to the light, and many animals are never more beautiful, pure, and courageous than when they first confront the world. But man, and other unhappy mammals, are born helpless and half-shapeless, like unbaked dough; they have not yet become what they are meant to be. The receptacle that held them could not feed them long enough, or allow them to attain their full size and strength. They must therefore be cast out into the glare and the cold, to be defeated by a thousand accidents, derailed, distorted, taught and trained to be enemies to themselves, and to prevent themselves from ever existing. No doubt they manage to survive for a time, halt, blind and misshapen; and sometimes the suppressions or mutilations of what they meant to be adapt them to special environments and give them technical knowledge of many a thing that, if they had been free, they might never have noticed, or observed only poetically, in a careless and lordly way. . . . I say to myself, therefore, that Antonita's child was so exceptionally beautiful and would doubtless have been exceptionally brave and intelligent, because he had profited longer than is usual by the opportunity to grow undisturbed, as all children grow in their sleep; but this advantage, allowed to butterflies and flowers, and to some wild animals, is forbidden to mankind, and he paid for it by his life, and by that of his mother. (pp. 125-26)

This is a significant theory indeed, organized around his early sense of abandonment and reflecting his mature attitudes and life decisions. Surely he is the child who could not be kept safe with his mother until he attained his full size and strength, he who is aware of being cast out into the cold to be defeated by life, while contemplating the beautiful dead child who is beyond suffering. But there is no safe place to grow into what one is meant to be. Again death intervenes, for this advantage is "forbidden" by nature to mankind. Experience is thus conceived as mutilation, and there-fore to be avoided. Antonita's child was exceptionally beautiful and, he imagines unjustifiably, would have been exceptionally brave and intelligent because he had stayed longer with his mother, but this delay in birth, seen as an advantage to the child, is paid for by his death and that of his mother. So we return again to the inevitability of the separation between San-tayana and his mother, and to the naturalness of these events, this time in the Darwinian terms of selection and adaptation in a warlike environment. For the pain and desolation which cannot be admitted to in the heart of the young Santayana, or the mature one, can be clearly regarded in the world about him.

We are again here in the prime source of the despair which caused San-tayana in his adolescence to see life as "ashes in the mouth" and to see the age of thirty as the time of loss of all those things in life he valued, few as they were; the despair which kept him, like Henry James, who was also obsessed with the effort to convert loss into gain, from being able to make that affirmation of life which marriage signified. Against the dangers of union and attachment he employed the tactics of detachment, of perpetual exile, of emotional noncommitment, those very features he discerns in his mother's emotional life. Intellectually, against the terrors of experience, he was to invoke the safety of knowledge and art.

It is against this background that we must see the major events of his life: his eagerness to be financially independent, to be free of a professor's obligations; his failure to form close lasting relationships with women, a sense of distance in even the most lasting friendships with men; his outspo-ken unwillingness to choose a permanent home, to surround himself with things and servants. It is against this background that we should consider his account of the major spiritual experience that he refers to in the dis-cussion of his mother's life and that he describes at length in the chapter, "A Change of Heart," appearing in the last volume of memoirs, *My Host the World.*

We have seen how he had claimed in his first mention of his change of heart that nothing really happened to bring it about, only the passage of time. This phrase, now that we have seen some of the things time passing has brought about for Santayana, takes on a sinister connotation. In fact, there were outer events to occasion his transformation, serious and reson-ant ones. First, his sister had married just the year before. She was forty-one and living in Spain, where she felt at home socially and religiously, for she was devoutly Catholic. Her husband was a widower with six child-ren whom Santayana tells us very little about except for anecdotes charac-terizing his selfishness and his insensitivity to his children's needs.

These anecdotes appear in a chapter about life in Avila. We hear about the significance of Susana's marriage in the chapter on the change of heart. There is nothing that makes clearer the shaping, dramatic imagination that is at work in the autobiographies than the varying factual detail Santayana selects depending on the shape and significance of the chapter he is writing. In the chapter "A Change of Heart," the subject of marriage is introduced with a quotation from Swinburne: "Marriage and death and division make barren our lives."[11] In quoting, he refers to Swinburne as a "coxcomb"; he is highly aware of the quote's paradoxical quality. And that is the quality he is trying to explain in his feelings about Susana's marriage, which are displeasing and disheartening far out of proportion to the actual effect the marriage has on his life. It is an occasion for him of an experience of barrenness and division, although actually he sees that he is not being divided from Susana; he will, in fact, have a new home in Avila to visit at a time when his father is ailing physically and close to death. He is reminded of how he felt when Susana entered a convent some years before, when the sense of spiritual sympathy more than outweighed the actual, almost complete physical separation. He can explain his feeling only in terms of an inability on her part to live out her religion, as he lived out his philosophy. (This is an indication, by the way, that even at that time, much before he was thirty, he was already formulating the philosophy that was to deal with his sense of loss, with significance, as we shall see, for his first sonnet sequence.) He identifies this inability as the gulf between them; she chose to live in Spain where she could use religion as a social support and perhaps as a substitute for happiness that she could never find with a selfish widower and his six children. To the disinterested observer, this widower and his family seem the most likely explanation for his feeling, but Santayana himself finally ascribes his desolation to disillusionment with her and with Catholicism, which he now sees as "worldliness transferred to a future world and thereby doubly falsified" (p. 10). And so he is led to affirm only the esoteric aspect of Catholicism and of every religion or philosophy that "terminates in the same inward liberation and peace that ancient sages attained under all religions or under none" (p. 11).

Here, then, was a reawakening of all the old experience of abandonment. Writing to Daniel Cory about the lady of the second sonnet sequence, which he says was the outgrowth of his metanoia, he speaks of his sister as "certainly the most important influence in my life, psychologically my mother, and one might almost say, my wife."[12] Furthermore, the connection between it and his striving toward spiritual liberation is unmistakable.

Only months after this marriage, Santayana's father died, calling up for him "a lurid image of what my life in the world was likely to be: solitary, obscure, trivial, and wasted" (*My Host the World*, p. 9). While he as-

15

sociated the affirmation of the esoteric aspects of Catholicism with the emotional separation from Susana, in connection with his father's death, it is Beatrice's advice to Dante that he quotes: "Drop (false hopes) the seed of tears, and listen"; ascribing to it the meaning he attaches to his own second sonnet sequence: "Listen to reason. If the joys of youth and the vision of perfect love have faded from your world, will you allow any baser thing to fetter you there? Let your heart rather follow its true object where that object is gone, into eternity" (p. 9).

These two streams of feeling and thought were brought together forcibly and augmented for him by the death of a young friend, Warwick Potter, whom he had come to think of as a younger brother and a part of himself. So he tells us in another section (*Persons and Places*, p. 109). However, in "A Change of Heart," he minimizes his attachment to him. "Although he was a general favorite and a long procession of us walked behind the bier at his funeral, there was after all nothing extraordinary about him." In fact, Santayana was "surprised by the effect that the news of his death" had upon him (*My Host the World*, p. 8). Another reaction out of proportion to the event. Again the impulse is to deny the dimension of his loss and so minimize the suffering. When he says with only partial accuracy "the cause of my emotion was in myself," then he can maintain a certain dominance over circumstances; he is not altogether a passive victim. Yet to have lost a younger brother and a part of oneself is no small loss and would ordinarily provoke no small grief. But Santayana must depersonalize this experience too, in order to bear it; without falsifying it, he gives it intellectual form and a generalized, rational content:

I was brimming over with the sense of parting, of being divided by fortune where at heart there was no division. I found myself, unwittingly and irreparably, separated from Spain, from England, from my youth and from my religion. It was not good simple Warwick alone that inspired my verses about him. It was the thought of everything that was escaping me: the Good in all the modes of it that I might have caught a glimpse of and lost. (p. 8)

Santayana chose to speak of his change of heart in terms of a metanoia, a term usually used, he remarks, for a religious conversion, rather than a philosophic one. The use of it is a dramatic technique to give cohesion and impact to an experience that was actually spread over a period of time even in its most crucial events, the deaths of Warwick Potter and his father, and the marriage of his sister. There was another aspect to his metanoia that he recognized himself as a long time building, tracing it back in one place to his first trip to Germany in 1887, after his graduation from Harvard, in another to his twentieth year, and finally finding that it had been native and congenital in him. The metanoia he speaks of as occurring when he was thirty and occasioning the second sonnet sequence was also the "gradual transformation of . . . his religious sentiments" that resulted in *Interpretations of Poetry and Religion* in 1900 (p. 4), the insight that came to him in Germany in the eighties that contributed to the first sonnet sequence, and, in fact, was so rooted in his earliest experiences in his family, as we have seen, that he felt it as inborn.

This fourth stream of thought contributing to his metanoia gathered strength in Germany in the form of a reaction to a poem of Goethe and was to be the resolution of the problem he was occupied with in the first sonnet sequence, a resolution contemporaneous with the trip to Germany. He had already written the earlier sonnets in the first sequence whose subjects, as we have seen, were his conflict and despair over a world where nothing endured. After his return to Harvard to teach philosophy, he published in 1892, in one issue of the *Harvard Monthly,* the five sonnets that resolve his conflict and bring comfort out of desolation.

What happened in 1887 when he went to Germany was that he recognized in Goethe's drinking song "Vanitas! Vanitatum vanitas!" his own "vital philosophy." It began:

> Ich hab' mein Sach auf Nichts gestellt . . .
> Drum ist's so wohl mir in der Welt.

And ended:

> Nun hab' ich mein Sach auf Nichts gestellt
> Und mein gehort die ganze Welt. (pp. 4-5)

Here he recognized the strategy of his own spirit trying to find something to keep in a world where possession seemed impossible and loving was dangerous. If he had to give up having things, he could never be deprived of knowing them, of having ideas of them:

The whole world belongs to me implicitly when I have given it all up, and am wedded to nothing particular in it; but for the same reason no part of it properly belongs to me as a possession, but all only in idea. Materially I might be the most insignificant of worms; spiritually I should be the spectator of all time and all existence. (p. 5)

He saw clearly enough looking back on his life from his seventies how the implications of this philosophy would be expressed emotionally in his later sonnets and years afterward in his philosophy when he "freed 'essences' from the psychological net in which we catch them" (p. 5). But it was already taking form in his earliest sonnets and in a context which makes them more interesting to a twentieth-century reader than the later sonnets can be, dependent as they are on the convention of Platonic love. Furthermore this philosophy functions in these early sonnets in a way that is characteristic of Santayana's intellectual life. It is an idealism in the service of naturalism. It is a renunciation that leads back to the world, not away from it. Its greatest success will be a double celebration of both the sources of spirit in the natural world and its liberation from the limits of that world.

The thread of this "vital philosophy" leads us back, then, from his emotional life to his poetry. In a sonnet probably written before he read the Goethe poem and before he could see his way out of the despair he felt over living without faith, he wrote "But love thou nothing thou wouldst love the less / If henceforth ever hidden from thy ken" (p. 8). The difficulty was how to do that. "The world is not a myth, to be clarified by a little literary criticism," he wrote later, considering the mechanism of renunciation (*My Host the World*, p. 6). The first step is to give up expectations; like Strether in *The Ambassadors,* to recognize that the important thing is to get nothing for oneself. This is another form of Santayana's mother's behavior, a way of living, as he says of her, without giving up standards and judgments but "without hope." This is the other thread that leads back from the core of his emotional life to his creative effort. The tone of those sonnets we have already considered which offer stoicism as the only refuge is the same tone of coldness and despair that dominates the portrait of his mother. But the theme echoes differently in sonnet XIII: "Sweet are the days we wander with no hope / Along life's labyrinthine trodden way" (p. 15). For there is another possibility in giving up hope, one which does not leave a man lonely and empty. This is the possibility explored in the five sonnets published together after the German trip but before the metanoia. In sonnet XIV there is a new way of looking at the self—it is not necessarily a prison; it may be a haven:

> There may be chaos still around the world,
> This little world that in my thinking lies;
> For mine own bosom is the paradise
> Where all my life's fair visions are unfurled.
> Within my nature's shell I slumber curled,
> Unmindful of the changing outer skies,
> Where now, perchance, some new-born Eros flies,
> Or some old Cronos from his throne is hurled.
> I heed them not; or if the subtle night
> Haunt me with deities I never saw,

I soon mine eyelid's drowsy curtain draw
To hide their myriad faces from my sight.
They threat in vain; the whirlwind cannot awe
A happy snow-flake dancing in the flaw. (p. 16)

Change still rules; everything given is still taken away. But it no
longer threatens him; he feels a completeness in himself that cannot be disturbed by the chaos around him, just as in the last lines of the poem "the
whirlwind cannot awe / A happy snow-flake dancing in the flaw." The
snowflake image encompasses an important relationship. The poet's being
is not separate from the chaos of the natural world: the snowflake is complete in itself, sufficient, but a part of the storm about it, in fact, a creature
of the storm. Equally important is the discovery of the paradise within,
the world of his own thought, where all his "fair visions are unfurled." He
is a creature of the storm, but in the world of the imagination he is masterful and free, and profoundly gratified. Yet this gratification, in turn, is
possible only because of the beauty of the natural world on which he
depends.

It is to this double reality that the dreamer of sonnet V awakes, the
dreamer who asked, "Of my two lives which should I call the dream? /
Which action vanity? which vision sight?" He begins to see the answer to
his question "if aught abideth of the things that seem." Sonnet XVII refers
back to that confusion of waking and dreaming:

There was a time when in the teeth of fate
I flung the challenge of the spirit's right;
The child, the dreamer of that visioned night,
Woke, and was humbled into man's estate.
A slave I am; on sun and moon I wait,
Who heed not that I live upon their light.
They flood my heart with love, and quench my hate.
O subtle Beauty, sweet persuasive worth
That didst the love of being first inspire,
We do thee homage both in death and birth.
Thirsting for thee, we die in thy great dearth,
Or borrow breath of infinite desire
To chase thine image through the haunted earth. (p. 19)

The poet's utter dependency on nature is affirmed, but nature's indifference and contempt have finally been compensated for by her beauty.
Through the experience of beauty, the love which he had given up returns
to him. When he has renounced everything, relinquished all claims, he is
able to see the one value that nature cannot withhold from him for he
takes it with his mind alone. The lines inspired by this awareness are never-

theless elegaic rather than triumphant. The beauty is subtle, evasive; it haunts the earth. The love it inspires, he writes in sonnet XVI, is "a sad love, like an eternal prayer, / And knows no keen delight, no faint surcease."

> A thousand beauties that have never been
> Haunt me with hope and tempt me to pursue;
> The gods, methinks, dwell just behind the blue;
> The satyrs at my coming fled the green.
> The flitting shadows of the grove between
> The dryads' eyes were winking, and I knew
> The wings of sacred Eros as he flew
> And left me to the love of things not seen.
> 'Tis a sad love, like an eternal prayer,
> And knows no keen delight, no faint surcease.
> Yet from the seasons hath the earth increase,
> And heaven shines as if the gods were there.
> Had Dian passed there could no deeper peace
> Embalm the purple stretches of the air. (p. 18)

The sadness comes from the feeling that beauty seems to promise some further revelation of value or power, and it is difficult for Santayana to give up the hope of that revelation. Another source for the sadness is the fear, kept at bay here, that the revelation promised by beauty will turn out to be the necessary surrender of power in the world of spirit. Furthermore, the sadness is an implicit reflection of the surrender of the hope for direct fulfillment of instinctual drives. The desire that spirit enjoy power as well as delight is explored later in *Lucifer*. So the sonnets here, dealing with reconciliation, use images of divinity, even as the movement of the poem is to banish divinity. For example, sonnet XVI begins:

> A thousand beauties that have never been
> Haunt me with hope and tempt me to pursue;
> The gods, methinks, dwell just behind the blue;

Although it ends:

> Yet from the seasons hath the earth increase,
> And heaven shines as if the gods were there.
> Had Dian passed there could no deeper peace
> Embalm the purple stretches of the air. (p. 18)

Again, in XVIII, he writes, "Blaspheme not love, ye lovers, nor dispraise," for "love is God" and brings forth the beauty that consoles us (p. 20). This is an inversion of the original relationship—that beauty brings him love. Once having been reconciled with nature through the experience of beauty, the quality of that experience becomes very important to him. If it is to be the foundation of his emotional life, he has to understand its implications. He feels it to be a source of value; he has, of course, been supported in this intuition by the movement of nineteenth-century thought. But he must understand it, how much it really promises him, at what cost it will compensate him for almost overwhelming losses already sustained.

For Santayana, then, there were two major aspects of his reconciliation, one spiritual, the other psychological. He wanted to explore both the spiritual satisfactions he could hope for from beauty and the sources for the experience of beauty within man as a natural organism. The second sonnet sequence issued from the first effort; *The Sense of Beauty* (1896), from the second.

"Above the battlements of heaven rise" is a symbolic exploration of the new ground Santayana hopes to occupy. It is not the "garden of delight" he sought in the first sonnet, although he will return to that image in the final lines of the sequence. Our eyes are directed upward after the long downward gaze away from Golgotha. They are raised now to quite a different vision of truth. While the suffering and sin in the Christian vision came from what was mortal and natural in man, the basis of this vision is what is deathless. Once man ceases to hope for anything from experience, he not only sees the beauty of nature as in sonnet XVII, where the poet says of the sun and the moon: "They flood my heart with love, and quench my hate"; he also sees the whole process of his life in a new perspective. Here the realm of art and spirit receive their first embodiment:

> Above the battlements of heaven rise
> The glittering domes of the gods' golden dwelling,
> Whence, like a constellation, passion-quelling,
> The truth of all things feeds immortal eyes.
> There all forgotten dreams of paradise
> From the deep caves of memory upwelling,
> All tender joys beyond our dim foretelling
> Are ever bright beneath the flooded skies.
> There we live o'er, amid angelic powers,
> Our lives without remorse, as if not ours,
> And others' lives with love, as if our own;
> For we behold, from those eternal towers,
> The deathless beauty of all winged hours,
> And have our being in their truth alone. (p. 21)

Here is the realm Santayana first caught a glimpse of in Goethe, where the whole world can belong to him in idea. The imagination earlier

ST. PETER'S COLLEGE LIBRARY
JERSEY CITY, NJ

rendered passive and impotent by its inability to distinguish truth from dream has aroused itself to constructive activity. It has reordered life, and, no longer caught in an impossible task of separating its inner life from the outer processes that surround and sustain it, it affirms the truth of its new perspective, which is the perspective not only of spirit but of art.

Since its subject is this perspective, the poem's suitable organizing images are those of sight. Since the poem is also about the conversion of loss into gain, and death into life, it progresses with the help of pairs of opposites which exchange identities through the change of perspective in the poet. The realm is initially presented as a kind of Olympus from which truth, in its brightness, distance, and detachment, like the stars, "passion-quelling," feeds immortal eyes. This is the first statement of the connection between truth and eternity in terms of its relation with seeing. On an emotional level the visual, that which is taken in by the eyes, is of pre-eminent value in Santayana's life. On the intellectual and metaphoric level, the perspective of eternity compensates for loss; the line, "the truth of all things feeds immortal eyes," reveals the role seeing plays as an emotional equivalent for primary oral gratification. Behind this metaphor in which truth becomes a food, playing its enormously fertile role in Santayana's conception of the realm of art, lies the pressing need for closeness to his mother and gratification by her which was early frustrated. By the symbolic ingestion of sight, he could internalize what he was forever separated from, be fed, and control what was actually beyond his control, all by the same act. Then, finally, that ancient childhood rage over his abandonment and separation would be stilled. For this reason, "the truth of all things," like a constellation, is "passion-quelling."

In the second quatrain, all goods that are hidden by the past or the future, "dreams of paradise" from our memories or "joys beyond our dim foretelling,"—hopes, desires, the dark of the caves and the dim of the future—are all to be "ever bright." The temporal sequence of life gives way to the simultaneity of eternity. The sensory image of the eighth line is a restatement of the abstract fourth line. In this bright light we can be relieved of the remorse that comes from personal responsibility, by seeing our lives as if they were not ours, and we can gain love by seeing other lives as if they were. In each case benefit comes from detachment from the self, from dispossession. We are prepared for the final pair of opposites: "deathless beauty" and "wingèd hours," and at the last—stasis. We have lost our individual lives with their memory, desire, and remorse, but we share in the immortal aspect of mortality—its truth, with all the symbolic gratification it embodies.

The imaginative compensation Santayana has created in this sonnet balances the ever-present lament in him for the transience of all things and sustains a large measure of serenity. While the poet's attitude at the beginning of the sequence was an averted gaze directed at a desolate and empty earth, the spiritual stance at the conclusion is upward gazing, yet permitting an affirmation of his roots in nature which can again be seen as full of promise and sustenance, "as if the gods were there." He evokes the gods again in the last sonnet, for his attachment to the Greek myths came from their embodiment of the power and fertility that lay in natural processes as well as their embodiment of the beauty which was the bridge between those processes and man's spirit:

> The soul is not on earth an alien thing
> That hath her life's rich sources otherwhere;
> She is a parcel of the sacred air.
> She takes her being from the breath of Spring,
> The glance of Phoebus is her fount of light,
> And her long sleep a draught of primal night. (p. 22)

Santayana's other lyrics of this period, like the first sonnet sequence, are dominated by the attitudes of naturalism and the assertions of the consolations of beauty. They reflect the nineteenth-century retreat from supernaturalism to estheticism, but their estheticism is modified by their naturalism into quite an individual sense of things. Beauty does not justify the ways of God to Santayana. The natural order remains what it is. It may be transcended, but never transfigured by the experience of beauty. The great Victorians were likely to see nature as a kind of Old Testament to be fulfilled by a New Testament of love, as in Tennyson, or of love and art as in Browning, or of art alone as in Ruskin and then Pater. This was one of the sources of Santayana's irritation with Emerson. Much as he concurred in Emerson's spiritual detachment, he was horrified by the bland face Emerson could turn to suffering. In Santayana's view, man was not to be saved by beauty any more than by philosophy. When Santayana talks about moral truths underlying Christian myth, he is more interested in the symbolic meaning of eternal damnation than in that of salvation, for damnation meant to him the utter finality of evil and suffering. Tennyson could obliterate his own vision of evolution by a vision of mystic reunion in love. For Santayana, as he was to write later, "to the heart that has felt it and that is the true judge, every loss is irretrievable and every joy indestructible" (*Letters*, p. 14).

In 1887 Santayana wrote to a friend:

Do you suppose the slow, painful, nasty, bloody process by which things in this world grow, is worth having for the sake of the perfection of a moment? Did you come into this world because you thought it worth while? No more do you stay in it because you do. The idea of demanding that things should be worth doing is a human impertinence. (p. 17)

There is no revelation waiting for man to make it all worthwhile. That conviction separates Santayana both from the Victorians and the esthetes. In his view, man is not to be removed from the natural process. So while his education, sense of tradition, and love of the ancients united him with high Victorian culture as well as with its decadent postscripts, it was a more austere sense of classic culture he carried with him, unsoftened by a sentimental version of Christianity; it was a sense of classicism that was both a source and a confirmation of his own thoroughgoing naturalism. His classicism never conflicted, as Freud's did not, with his materialism and admiration of science, for he saw modern science as the continuation of the Greek. So he wrote, also in the eighties:

Thus you will arrive at the moderately true description of the facts which consists in saying that men must act in pursuit of something of which they may have no idea and which they may never attain. Whether this uncertain something is a sensation or an action will be of no consequence. The difference between the hedonists and the naturalists will thus be reduced to an original difference in their observations. If a man believes that men usually know what they are about, he will like the hedonists; if he thinks men usually don't, he will like the naturalists. I like the naturalists. (*Letters*, p. 13)

In 1895, the year following Santayana's metanoia, he composed the second sonnet sequence, which he tells us was the direct expression of his spiritual crisis. In describing it he compares it to a dark night of the soul, ending in the realization that as a spirit he was not narrowly himself but "pure spirit, to whom all selves are mere vapours, to be endured courageously and no less courageously dismissed and wiped away. The truth of life could be seen only in the shadow of death; living and dying were simultaneous and inseparable" (*My Host the World*, p. 13). But after that dark night came the compensatory revelation. The world could be enjoyed if it were not coveted. Like Buddha, he saw that the root of suffering was desire. Therefore he was to live with as few possessions as possible and live freely among ideas. "To possess things and persons in idea is the only pure good to be got out of them; to possess them physically or legally is a burden and a snare" (p. 13).

The danger of possessing persons physically or legally, of continuing relationships with people he loved was the painful lesson of his childhood. He understands very well that to want this is an instinctual part of him which he is denying because it is too costly. He readily identifies as "spirit" the part which develops needs opposed to instinctual ones, and he recognizes that this liberation is a boon only for the spirit, not for what he calls "nature or life." "Life and nature," he writes, "do not ask to be saved from themselves; they ask only to run on at full tilt. It is the spirit that asks to be saved from that insane predicament" (p. 14).

For life and nature to run on, that is, for instinctual needs to be gratified, is too threatening to the spirit; it is seen as insanity. Santayana cannot conceive any less radical solution to this conflict than to identify completely with the spirit and renounce the instinctual needs, at least in their original form. There are forms in which he can fulfill them—"possess" them, in "idea." This process of sublimation did not go on without enormous self-awareness in Santayana. First of all, he was conscious of the importance of what was being given up: "Yet spirit is an emanation of life, and is more truly and naturally happy in the first phases of its career than in its final salvation" (*My Host the World*, p. 15). This final salvation was ordinarily reserved for the last phase in a man's life. In the Hindu tradition a man married, raised a family, and did his work in the world before he retired to the forest to seek enlightenment. Santayana does not remark on the particular sacrifice of instinct dictated by the choice of spirit in a man of thirty.

His awareness of the process of sublimation is also revealed in his choice of Platonic love poetry as the vehicle for this experience. Why, after all, did he feel an appropriateness not altogether justifiable? Platonic love sonnets traditionally celebrated the love of one good and beautiful lady so great that it opened the heart of the lover to the love of all beauty and all good and finally led him to love of the perfect beauty and goodness of God. The emphasis was equally on the beauty of the lady and on her inaccessibility so that usually the lover's only reward was the contemplation of her beauty and his own spiritual education. There are other aspects to the tradition. The poet is always faithful and never gives up hope of the lady's ultimate favors no matter what the frustrations, nor does he cease the celebration of her physical loveliness and his own physical and emotional suffering, cheerfully though it may have been undergone in the service of his love. These aspects are not so clearly in mind when Santayana writes of Platonic love poetry. In his essay on some Italian poets of the tradition, he speaks at length of the idealizing process in Dante's treatment of Beatrice and in Guido Cavalcanti's treatment of Giovanna. Yet while Beatrice does become Dante's spiritual guide, Guido Cavalcanti's love for other ladies does not mean Giovanna has been removed from his desire to be only a type of all beauty and all love for him. If he could possess her, he would—and have no need of other ladies. He does not prefer her inaccessibility as Santayana does in "Let my lips touch thy lips."

What Santayana thinks of when he thinks of Platonic love poetry is the frustration of physical love and the consequent spiritual education of the lover. In his essay, he adds a brief discussion of Plato in which he describes the idea of Platonic love as essentially an account of the mastering of experience and its conversion to spiritual use. This is also the significance of his metanoia. And that is why he believed the Platonic love sonnet an adequate vehicle for his spiritual experience. They coincided at a very important point—their source of energy: instinctual drives, not simply sexual, but all the primary drives to possess, devour, dominate, and transform which, when fulfilled, are our most profound gratifications.

He is aware, then, of what is at stake when the spirit is freed. He will write throughout the next decade about the ways sexuality affects man's other responses to life. In retrospect, as an old man writing about the sonnets and the experience they render, he is concerned with understanding what happens to the energies that are denied. He tells us that the key to the sequence lies in the line, "A perfect love is founded on despair,"[13] for the impossibility of fulfillment adds tragedy to lyric delight and transforms love into "a rapture in adoration" which seemed to him its perfection. What happens then to the psyche when "physical, social, or egotistical claims" that were "instinctive" in it are denied?

The passion of love, sublimated, does not become bloodless, or free from bodily trepidation, as charity and philanthropy are. It is essentially the spiritual flame of a carnal fire that has turned all its fuel into light. The psyche is not thereby atrophied; on the contrary, the range of its reactions has been enlarged. It has learned to vibrate harmoniously to many things at once in a peace which is an orchestration of transcended sorrows. (*My Host the World*, p. 15)

The key image here is the flame of carnal fire that has turned all its fuel into light. The psyche has not atrophied, in the sense that it continues to be active in another way, but it does give up a certain kind of activity it was meant for. It gives up the sphere of doing for the sphere of knowing. Again, in the essay on the Italian love poets, he tells us, "Nothing is more characteristic of the platonic mind than a complete indifference to the continuation of experience and an exclusive interest in its comprehension."[14] At the same time it is important to emphasize that Santayana is speaking of an indifference to the continuance of experience, not to experience itself. For this was another reason for his sharp disagreement with idealism. He stressed throughout his career his conviction that ideas referred back to some undeniable, though directly unknowable, reality. Man's action in that reality took place in the realm of matter, irrationally, on the basis of instinct and environmental stimulus. That action was then the source of all his ideas about the environment. Precisely how man's ideas came to be symbolic of the reality he experienced only directly and irrationally was to be worked out and modified in the years from *The Life of Reason* to *The Realms of Being,* but as early as 1887 he was convinced that "we do not act on the ideas we previously have, but we acquire ideas as the consequence of action and experience" (*Letters,* p. 19).

Nevertheless, it was on the ideas so acquired, not the action and experience themselves, that he focused this early in his career, and they caused him to fix on his Platonizing sonnets as an adequate vehicle for his metanoia, since they, too, moved from experience to the meaning of experience. Therefore he sees no contradiction in the fact that, as he explains in answer to inquiries about the identity of the lady of the sonnets, there was no lady:

> ... they were a perfectly sincere *conviction,* but they were not an actual experience ... The Lady of the sonnets ... is a myth, a symbol: certainly she stands for Somebody, not always the same Somebody, and generally for a hint or suggestion drawn from reason rather than for any specific passion: but the enthusiasm is speculative, not erotic .... (*Letters,* p. 208)

Similarly, he was amused at George Howgate's effort to interpret the poems biographically, positing the existence of two ladies, the one whom he loved successfully but with some absolute fulfillment escaping him and the one who frustrated him. The actual origin of these phantom mistresses seems to have been the idea Santayana had about Guido's attitude toward Giovanna and the change of Dante's love for Beatrice from profane to spiritual.

There are two other paths to the emotional sources of the sonnets that should be followed: one because it is central; the other because, although it is peripheral, it is sure to arise in people's minds. The peripheral first.

Is the absence of an actual lady in the sonnets a result of the fact that the poems were inspired by a homosexual love? Michelangelo, one of the poets Santayana considers in his essays, who also mentions no specific lady, was reputedly homosexual. On this subject Santayana says, "They tell no story; there seems to have been no story to tell. There is something impersonal and elusive about the subject and the occasion of these poems." He dismisses the "attempts ... to attribute them to discreditable passions" and concludes, "It is not necessary to find vulgar causes for the extraordinary feelings of an extraordinary man. It suffices that life wore this aspect to him; that the great demands of his spirit so expressed themselves in the presence of his world" (*Interpretations of Poetry and Religion,* p. 133).

At the same time, Santayana remarked to Daniel Cory, the intimate companion of his last years, that it was obvious from Housman's poems that Housman was homosexual and that he thinks he must have been that way himself in his Harvard years, "although unconscious of it." He thought it accounted for the feeling he had, incomprehensible at the time, that people thought him odd. He had found it very difficult to bear and had almost brought himself to ask William James about it. It contributed to his desire to leave Harvard (Cory, *Santayana*, p. 40). This seems at first like a very considerable confession, but the phrase "unconscious of it" makes it more difficult to evaluate the behavior or state of being he is trying to characterize. If he had had what is ordinarily thought of as a homosexual experience, he would have known it. Nor would he have been dependent on social ostracism to indicate that it was socially unacceptable in late nineteenth-century Boston. What seems more likely, is not that Santayana was saying he was a homosexual in this sense, which is the only real sense, since latent homosexuality is a very slippery concept indeed, considering its universality, but that he was simply trying to characterize an emotional life in which he was cut off from intimate relations with women and relied for affection and close relationship on his men friends.

In the sense that it tells us about his feelings of incapacity in respect to women, it is illuminating for the sonnets and leads us back to the more central consideration mentioned earlier. Again in his old age, and to Daniel Cory, he wrote in answer to the continuing questions about the lady of the sonnets:

. . . you have an intuitive mind, that easily conceives possibilities that may be latent and may never have come to the surface. There is my sister, for instance, certainly the most important influence in my life, psychologically my mother, and one might almost say, my wife. Not that an incestuous idea ever entered my mind or hers; but Freud might have discovered things unsuspected by ourselves. (*Santayana*, p. 210)

We are led back, then, by these considerations to the core emotions of separation and loss for which he enjoyed brief consolation in the love of his sister, only to have the original feelings reawakened after her marriage. He was thus only partly right when he spoke of speculative rather than erotic enthusiasm generating the poetry and was closer to the truth when he spoke of the carnal flame whose fuel was turned to light.

Therefore the key line, "A perfect love is nourished by despair," has implications beyond the ones he pointed out himself. First, the most interesting poems are embodiments of the despair, whether bitter or resigned, rather than the love. Furthermore, the experience of sexual love does not itself seem to yield the despair, because of its fleetingness, its fickleness, or its likelihood of frustration. The experience is rather approached not only with that fear but also with that expectation and even with that desire. It is in this sense that the poems are "an evasion" of experience. The movement of many sonnets is towards death as a symbol of the denial of instinctual needs and of the retreat from the natural sphere of action, where change is a radical feature, to contemplation, where it has no place.

The opening sonnet of the sequence is an ambivalent questioning of his own felt reaching out for love:

> Among the myriad voices of the Spring
> What were the voice of my supreme desire,
> What were my cry amid the vernal choir,
> Or my complaint before the gods that sing?
> O too late love, O flight on wounded wing,
> Infinite hope my lips should not suspire,
> Why, when the world is thine, my grief require,
> Or mock my dear-bought patience with thy sting?
> Though I be mute, the birds will in the boughs
> Sing as in every April they have sung,
> And, though I die, the incense of heart-vows
> Will float to heaven, as when I was young.
> But, O ye beauties I must never see,
> How great a lover have you lost in me! (p. 25)

The season of the sonnet is spring, but the poet is no longer young. He possesses a "dear-bought patience" which need not be disturbed for the sake of nature, since love will live on in the world without him. In the first quatrain, the whole world sings with love. In the second, the poet is patient, wishing apparently to be left in peace. In the third, he is mute and even anticipates his death, reiterating that nature will continue as well without him. Then, in the couplet, all is overturned. The great capacity he feels for love bursts out and affirms itself in an exact reversal of what he has been saying all along. His voice is worth something, after all, in the "myriad voices of spring." But here is established the paramount feature of love to be explored in the sequence, in fact the theme of it: the relationship of beauty and love, even those beauties that are not part of the charms of the beloved. That is why the last two lines have a somewhat detached air. The poem has been talking about love in the world but not in the poet; suddenly there is love in the poet, but is it the same love whose "heart-vows . . . float to heaven"?

Very quickly the next two sonnets establish the spiritual nature of this love. Sonnet XXII speaks of the Platonic conception of love "that moveth the celestial spheres / In endless yearning for the Changeless One" (p. 26). Sonnet XXIII takes us a long way from the simple awakening of desire in the spring right to the carnal flame transformed:

> But is this love, that in my hollow breast
> Gnaws like a silent poison, till I faint?
> Is this the vision that the haggard saint
> Fed with his vigils, till he found his rest?
> Is this the hope that piloted thy quest,
> Knight of the Grail, and kept thy heart from taint?
> Is this the heaven, poets, that ye paint?
> Oh, then, how like damnation to be blest!
> This is not love: it is that worser thing —
> Hunger for love, while love is yet to learn.
> Thy peace is gone, my soul; thou long must yearn.
> Long is thy winter's pilgrimage, till spring
> And late home-coming; long ere thou return
> To where the seraphs covet not, and burn. (p. 27)

The poem begins with that tendency to swooning away that was a feature of the Italian love poems. But no lady appears to be importuned or celebrated. The source of the poet's emotion is not spiritual love, which he conceives of as the only real love, characterizing the yearning that he feels as mere hunger for love. When spring comes in this poem, it will not be in a country where the young are in one another's arms. That is a kind of damnation even as it was to Yeats. The pilgrimage culminates in one of the finest lines of the sequence, reminding us of the Byzantium where the sages stand "in God's holy fire / As in the gold mosaic of a wall." Like Yeats, Santayana wishes to be gathered into the "artifice of eternity."[15]

In "Although I decked a chamber for my bride," true fulfillment is absent even from a happy love affair. The ultimate frustration comes not from the lady but from within the love. Directly after this, the poet's dissatisfaction ranges more widely still in one of the strongest poems of the sequence:

> As in the midst of battle there is room
> For thoughts of love, and in foul sin for mirth;
> As gossips whisper of a trinket's worth
> Spied by the death-bed's flickering candle-gloom;
> As in the crevices of Caesar's tomb
> The sweet herbs flourish on a little earth;
> So in this great disaster of our birth
> We can be happy, and forget our doom.

For morning, with a ray of tenderest joy
Gilding the iron heaven, hides the truth,
And evening gently woos us to employ
Our grief in idle catches. Such is youth;
Till from that summer's trance we wake, to find
Despair before us, vanity behind. (p. 29)

Here frustration has swollen into despair, but controlled with a voice fluent and masterful. It finds easily for the octave the concrete images that encompass the most valued experiences of mankind, ordered in such a way as to indicate their vanity and the marginality of happiness, while the sestet reveals the illusion and vanity even of the consolation we promise ourselves, ending in the vacant landscape of the last line. Its power comes from the fact that it is uncompromising without being painful and unspoiled by any note of personal complaint.

But this is a way station on the pilgrimage. Santayana cannot rest there in that emptiness. He begins to see the way more clearly in sonnet XXVIII:

Out of the dust the queen of roses springs;
The brackish depths of the blown waters bear
Blossoms of foam; the common mist and air
Weave Vesper's holy, pity-laden wings.
So from sad, mortal, and unhallowed things
Bud stars that in their crowns the angels wear;
And worship of the infinitely fair
Flows from thine eyes, as wise Petrarca sings:
"Hence comes the understanding of love's scope,
That, seeking thee, to perfect good aspires,
Accounting little what all flesh desires;
And hence the spirit's happy pinions ope
In flight impetuous to the heaven's choirs:
Wherefore I walk already proud in hope." (p. 32)

Santayana has taken particular trouble with those first five lines; they have a more complicated music than he usually achieves. And well he might, for they are what this sequence is all about, the first version of his continuing concern with the source of the ideal in every form. Compare these lines with those of the last sonnet in the first sequence—"The Soul is not on earth an alien thing / That hath life's rich sources otherwhere: / She is parcel of the sacred air" (p. 22). There is a shift of emphasis in a view sharing many elements. Earlier the problem was to affirm the naturalness of the ideal. Spirit was produced by nature, which itself was seen as sacred. The later poem also shows the ideal arising from nature, but this is not the nature of the early Greeks, marvelously fertile, alive with divinities. This is a poor, broken nature, suitable for a literary tradition that fed on medieval Christianity: the earth is dust, the water brackish, the air common. This nature is unhallowed. This is the source of the bridegroom's unease in "Although I decked a chamber for my bride." But now Petrarch promises the spirit shall ascend beyond the desires of the flesh. In this metaphor the spirit is the rose, the flesh is dust: the source is mean and in itself to be despised. The fertility of nature is submerged in the vision of its movement toward death.

When in another sonnet, "Sleep hath composed the anguish of my brain," Santayana comforts his despairing consciousness with an image of how the "April buds are growing / In the chill core of twigs all leafless now" and writes of how "Each buried seed lacks light as much as thou. / Wait for the spring, brave heart; there is no knowing," it is not an expression of trust in nature. The image of birth in his mind, as we have seen, was darkened by the early still-birth he had seen. There was no spring that could bring to birth a perfectly shaped and beautiful humanity. Humanity was "sad, mortal and unhallowed." Because it was born it would die. Because he could hold it in his arms, it would desert him. The still-born child was perfect and beautiful, and it was dead. So it is that he begs his mistress to surrender to his passion in sonnet XXX at the very moment that he puts her away from him:

> Let my lips touch thy lips, and my desire
> Contagious fever be, to set a-glow
> The blood beneath thy whiter breast than snow —
> Wonderful snow, that so can kindle fire!
> Abandon to what gods in us conspire
> Thy little wisdom, sweetest; for they know.
> Is it not something that I love thee so?
> Take that from life, ere death thine all require.
> But no! Then would a mortal warmth disperse
> That beauteous snow to water-drops, which, turned
> To marble, had escaped the primal curse.
> Be still a goddess, till my heart have burned
> Its sacrifice before thee, and my verse
> Told this late world the love that I have learned. (p. 34)

Yielding to passion is yielding to death. It becomes not a consolation for mortality but an affirmation of it. The images of blood and snow, flesh and marble, love and art are transformations of the basic pair of life and eternity. For it is neither life nor death which brings fulfillment; one is vanity, the other despair—the two sides of the natural process. But marble and verse transcend that process. They are the "artifice of eternity." The desire of the first line is the fever that consumes the heart in the sacrificial fire of the last lines, yielding an ideal love and an art to embody it. And in sonnet XLIX, enveloped in his vision of ideal love that can never forsake him, he feels it can even bear him to "eternal rest." The destruction of the world itself is not a threat for he has transcended it:

> Heaven it is to be at peace with things;
> Come chaos now, and in a whirlwind's rings
> Engulf the planets. I have seen the best. (p. 53)

The vision of ideal love is not always apocalyptic. The spiritual experience does not help Santayana merely to transcend his mortality—it returns him to it with a fresh perspective. "A perfect love is nourished by despair" unites the ideal world with the real.

> A perfect love is nourished by despair.
> I am thy pupil in the school of pain;
> Mine eyes will not reproach thee for disdain,
> But thank thy rich disdain for being fair.
> Aye! the proud sorrow, the eternal prayer
> Thy beauty taught, what shall unteach again?
> Hid from my sight, thou livest in my brain;
> Fled from my bosom, thou abidest there.
> And though they buried thee, and called thee dead,
> And told me I should never see thee more,
> The violets that grew above thy head
> Would waft thy breath and tell thy sweetness o'er,
> And every rose thy scattered ashes bred
> Would to my sense thy loveliness restore. (p. 37)

In the octave the poet affirms again the ultimate gift of love, the ideal form of it that lives in his heart and brain without sensuous qualities. But the sestet returns love to the senses, transformed into the beauties of the natural world, not of the mistress herself but all nature. In this way despair, which threatens to separate man from life, forces him to those ideal creations of beauty and art which ultimately restore him to it.

Whether Santayana invokes transcendence or transformation, it is this despair over gratification that leads him to renounce the life of action in favor of the life of art. Only there will possession preclude loss and the self be restored to freedom and potency. For Santayana's sense of freedom and of potency at this period was great indeed: he was teaching and traveling as well as writing his lyric poetry, the verse drama, *Lucifer*, *The Sense of Beauty*, and *Interpretations of Poetry and Religion*, all in the 1890s.

The surrender of a wide range of possibilities in life, dramatized in his poetry, was accompanied by a rising awareness of intellectual power and creative energy. The spiritual crisis was truly what Saint Paul meant by a metanoia, a dying into life, the culmination of a process of sublimation begun many years before and a dramatic symbol for the conscious results of that process.

NOTES

1. *The Letters of George Santayana*, ed. Daniel Cory (New York: Scribners, 1955), p. 236.

2. Ralph Barton Perry, *The Thought and Character of William James* (Boston: Little, Brown, 1936), II, p. 402.

3. George Santayana, "Apologia Pro Mente Sua," *The Philosophy of George Santayana*, ed. Paul A. Schilpp (1940; reprinted New York: Tudor, 1951), p. 588.

4. George Santayana, *Poems*, selected by the author and revised (New York: Scribners, 1928), p. 5.

5. "Bibliography of the Writings of George Santayana (1880–1951)," compiled by Shohig Terzian, *The Philosophy of George Santayana*, ed. Schilpp, pp. 666 ff.

6. Santayana, "A General Confession," Schilpp, p. 7.

7. George Santayana, *Persons and Places: The Background of My Life* (New York: Scribners, 1944), p. 85.

8. "A General Confession," p. 7.

9. *Ibid.*, p. 8.

10. "Apologia," p. 602.

11. George Santayana, *My Host the World: Persons and Places*, III (New York: Scribners, 1953), p. 9.

12. Daniel Cory, *Santayana, the Later Years: A Portrait with Letters* (New York: Braziller, 1963), p. 210.

13. This is another interesting mistake in memory; the line is really, "A perfect love is nourished by despair."

14. George Santayana, *Interpretations of Poetry and Religion*, Harper Torchbooks, The Cloister Library (1900; reprinted New York: Harper and Row, 1957), p. 144.

15. William Butler Yeats, "Sailing to Byzantium," *The Collected Poems* (New York: Macmillan, 1952), p. 191.

Lucifer: The Limits of Scepticism

The connections between spiritual love, beauty, and natural passions play an important part in Santayana's poetic drama, *Lucifer: a Theological Tragedy.* In this enormously interesting and complex work, touching at points a genre that includes Arnold's *Empedocles on Etna,* Shelley's *Prometheus Unbound* and Byron's *Manfred,* but surpassing them in richness of conception, the more romantic attitudes of the odes appear to dominate. Closer analysis, however, reveals the extent to which the play celebrates the death of romantic ideals. Entombed with them is Santayana's will to dominate the world of experience.

The poem was not published until 1899, but Santayana was putting the finishing touches to it in 1897, according to his letters (p. 57), and the conception of it went back to his undergraduate days and was related in his mind to his reaction to Josiah Royce and the kind of idealism he represented. Santayana disapproved strongly of what he saw as a justification of evil in Royce's philosophy. He sympathized with the romantic view of life he saw in Royce, with its elements of pessimism, stoic courage, pantheistic piety, and conformity with fate. But he saw there, as well as in Hegel, Browning, and Nietzsche, a "moral equivocation" by which the world, perceived in all its cruelty and wrongs, was nevertheless made a standard for morality. Santayana believed, rather, that the moralist's function was to mark out that part of reality, however small, which alone should be loved. This was the belief that lay at the root of his critique of romanticism. We are in the area here of a major philosophic dilemma over how much of experience, irretrievably irrational in many of its aspects, must be sacrificed in the effort to understand it through philosophic concepts and art forms. Santayana's solution is always in the direction of understanding at the expense of fullness, a solution encouraged by the lessons he drew from that disordered household of his Spanish childhood. His early family experience was always to make him choose knowledge over action. Intellectually this resulted in his dedication to significance and value as those parts of experience deserving his loyalty, although, as he was aware, they might be a small part of experience as a whole. In this perspective, therefore, the indiscriminate affirmation of the adventure of experience without regard to its meaning or the possibilities of perfection was the preaching of barbarism. It went beyond the intelligent submission to necessity, as he called it, to the enslavement of the soul by the "random labours of the contemporary world" (Schilpp, p. 12).

The contemporary world, as such, does not appear in *Lucifer*, but the tragedy of its hero is the tragedy of reason for whom the truth of things alone is barren because it does not encompass a submission to the natural order which underlies it, nor does it recognize the independence from itself of other spiritual forms which might reconcile it fruitfully to that natural order. The meaning of experience and the possibilities of perfection lie forever beyond Lucifer in his exclusive and fruitless attachment to the affirmation of his freedom of action. In the preface to a later edition of *Lucifer*, Santayana reminds us that his "philosophy is conveyed in an image. It is not identical with the sentiments of any one of the characters but lies implicit in their tragic juxtaposition. All spirits are dependent on a latent power, but independent of one another."[1] By 1924, when he wrote this, Santayana was definitely a philosopher who had written poetry and felt it necessary to explain the mechanism of poetic expression. In the nineties, according to Wallace Stevens, as well as by the evidence of his own work, "he was . . . still definitely a poet."[2] So we must look in the play not only for the spirit of revelation, the spirit of nature, and the spirit of abstract doubt—which he told his audience through an anonymous review of his own play published in the *Harvard Monthly* he had put there—but also for the meaning inherent in the plot, which he followed Aristotle in thinking the most important element of drama, and for the significance of the "persuasive sadness of the verses . . . instinct with too much piety and with too positive an appreciation of the beautiful to be called pessimism," which he also points to.[3]

Briefly, the main action of the play consists of the temptation of Lucifer, through the agency of his love for Hermes, to return to his place in Heaven. The secondary action concerns the fears of Zeus over his replacement by the Christian God. In the first act, Hermes meets Lucifer in the barren retreat that shelters him after his exile from Heaven. Hermes has been sent by Zeus to sound the depths of his danger from Christianity, but he does not know where to look. Lucifer's account of his fall opens a new world to him, and he asks Lucifer to be his guide to it, showing him first the abandoned souls in Hell. Lucifer, his emotions stirred for the first time since his fall, agrees. In Act II, Mephistopheles, Lucifer's regent in Hell, meets Hermes and Lucifer in the Garden of the Hesperides, mocks Lucifer's love for Hermes, and reveals his envy of Lucifer. Nevertheless, he is chosen to accompany Hermes to Heaven to speak with God, which Lucifer is understandably loath to do. Act III is the scene of a proposed banquet in Hell for Lucifer and Hermes, but Mephistopheles foments a revolt against Lucifer, who is in turn overcome by disgust with the damned and their incapacity for independence, and leaves Hell permanently. In Act IV, Lucifer joins Hermes at the gates of Heaven and, despite Saint Peter's efforts to keep them out, goes in with him to confront the Risen Christ for the first time since his fall. Here Christ claims to be tempting Lucifer through his love of Hermes to return to Heaven. Lucifer agrees to return if Hermes will acknowledge Christ his Lord. Act V shows the confrontation in which Christ attempts to persuade Zeus of his loving supremacy and to reconcile the Olympians to the rule of Christianity. They refuse, and Hermes, alone drawn to Christ, must remain with the Olympians. In the last scene, Lucifer is again in his mountainous exile, with foreknowledge of the inevitable death of the Olympians and Hermes with them, which he will do nothing to forestall. At the last he is alone, contemplating an icy eternity.

There is both an historical and a philosophic perspective in the play. Historically, the dramatic movement mirrors the development of monotheism, the decline of the Greek religion, the Christian revelation, the revolt of reason against Christianity, its inability to draw sustenance from either Christianity or paganism, and its consequent isolation and sterility in the modern world. Historical perspective is a favored principle of organization for Santayana. It underlies *Interpretations of Poetry and Religion* as well as *The Life of Reason*, where it merges with a sense of the evolution of human capacities and social forms on a biological model. However, the sense of evolution and the historical perspective are often at odds, for while the one is associated with the generation of new and more complex forms of life, the other is associated, as it is here in *Lucifer* as well as in *Interpretations of Poetry and Religion*, with a sense of loss. This is another example of the fertile confluence of the interests of late nineteenth-century intellectual life and Santayana's private constellation of time, deprivation, and natural hopes aborted.

The play abounds in the sense of change and decay; time harasses the protagonists and hurries them to dissolution. After Lucifer's rebellion, those who still served the old God are seen by Lucifer as alienated from nature, floating on "the current of a dream,"[4] while those who left Heaven with him became depraved victims of physical lust. None, either victors or defeated, remained themselves; all were diminished. The initiation of the action of the play depends on Zeus's consciousness of a decline in potency, of forsaken altars and empty shrines. Lucifer finally leaves Hell, unable to bear the sight of how far its inhabitants have fallen from his ideal of freedom and truth for which they revolted. In Heaven, Lucifer finds Michael changed. And the old God is no longer King; the rulers of Heaven are described by Lucifer in these terms:

> . . . a man the Romans slew
> For working wonders to the gaping mob.
> And who is Queen? The daughter of a Jew,
> And Heaven trembles at a girlish sob. (p. 117)

Of course, this is the attitude of doubting reason, but the significant thing here is the sense of change involved. When Lucifer sees the Risen Christ he says, "What, so? No more?" and then:

> . . . What? So shorn
> Of all his glory? A Man? O pitiful thing!
> Why did I tremble? I come to Triumph here
> And find my conqueror more lost than I. (p. 121)

The last act particularly emphasizes the theme of time and change through Zeus's preoccupation with his overthrow of Cronos. There is a charming exchange in which Zeus misunderstands Christ and his mission in terms of his own obsession. The dialogue is a witty summing up of one of the major aspects of the play. It profits from the best characterization, that of Zeus, an aging ruler, jealous of his authority, having forebodings of death, enjoying his political power, remembering and regretting the treason which brought him to the throne. The resolution of the play depends on Zeus's response to Christ. Hermes, who, in this search for Christ at his father's request, brings a reawakening of love and a sense of beauty to Lucifer, is claimed by Christ to be his temptation of Lucifer. Hermes's ultimate refusal to follow Christ is clear evidence that Christ has not the power he claims, that he cannot bring about events, that, just as Lucifer has claimed, he is dependent, as they all are, on circumstance: events are the accidents of nature in whose sphere spirit is impotent. In Hermes's failure to act as Christ's plan requires lies the affirmation of the independence of all spirits from each other that Santayana spoke of in his preface. In the change of the embodiment of God from the Old King to the Risen Christ and in the decay of the Olympians lies the affirmation of that process of change, which only Zeus as the spirit of nature can wholly perceive and accept and which is the result of "an unfathomable power, presupposed and unexplored" (p. xv), that sustains all events and all spirit. When Christ comes to Zeus, Zeus mistakes him for Cronos returned to overthrow him. And Christ *will* triumph, although Zeus cannot see that it is eternity, not time, standing before him. For Christ has come to offer eternal life to Zeus, which Zeus must reject. What has nature to do with eternity? As Athena says, when Christ tells them his name is Victory:

> That is a thought thou tak'st the title of
> And not a thing of life. To be "the Truth"
> Is to be bright in every spirit's love,
> Being nothing in oneself. (p. 168)

Aphrodite, Ares, and Athena also feel the incompatibility of eternal truth with their being, which is in nature. Truth for them would be death, even if Christ calls it eternal life.

> . . . What calls itself the Truth
> Wraps in an evil dream the things we see,
> And henceforth naught is pleasant, fair, or free
> In all the world, till in her ecstasy
> The soul, bereft of light, her heavenly food,
> Deems her last agony, her perfect good. (p. 172)

Only Hermes, the inventor of the lyre and an embodiment of love and beauty, would follow Christ if he had the choice, but he feels he has not, for his life is "knit for better or for worse" (p. 174) with his father and his brothers. He is after all a creature from the world of the first sonnet sequence; he says to Lucifer in the first act, "with no leaf unfurled / Dies the imprisoned deity within" (p.7). Spirit lives only as a manifestation of the flesh. It is ideal, the meaning of things, but as Athena says, "nothing in itself," only as it signifies. It is a *carnal* fire that is transmuted into light. The last word in this confrontation between Christianity and naturalism belongs to Zeus. In his final speech he regains the calm and wisdom of the rightful ruler:

> If I must die,
> Today at least I sit upon my throne;
> And not in fief I hold it. 'Tis mine own.
> The earth my temple stands. (p. 177)

Of Christ, whose immortality he doubts, he says:

> Some comfort it will be when we abide
> In that unbodied realm, to see this ghost,

Ill-boding spirit of impalpable pride,
Enter oblivion, and hearing still his boast,
Feel o'er our face the shade of laughter glide.
We also thought we should not taste of death,
But it is fated. Fleeting is the breath
That saith: I am eternal! We were born
And we must therefore die. Such is the wage
Of being. (pp. 177-78)

In the last scene of the play, Lucifer reveals that the Olympians have died. Hermes, alone surviving, seeks Lucifer but will not find him, by Lucifer's own decision, and therefore, says Lucifer, it is he himself who has killed Hermes, just as he has denied Christ. He entombs himself eternally in the truth, giving up the realm of time "in scorn to all that live / Through hope and anguish and insensate wars" (p. 187). This frozen, impotent, fruitless reason alienated from all forms of art, beauty, and religion is all that is left to the modern world.

Although the working out of Lucifer's doom is the central action of the play, the confrontation between Christ and the Olympians constitutes an important secondary theme, connected to the primary action through the shared motif of freedom. It is a confrontation not only between Christianity and paganism, religion and naturalism, but ultimately between value and experience. Much as Santayana clearly admires Zeus, and attractive as he makes his position, in the final vision of the play the Olympians, too, are dead. As we shall see in the following chapter, Santayana unhesitatingly rooted all value in experience, but with equal steadfastness he maintained the position he took in the essay on the Italian love poets: it was the significance of experience, not merely its extension, that produced value, which alone was eternal. Early in the play, to a Hermes who knows all potency is in nature, Lucifer speaks of his belief in his freedom and so foretells the final tragedy. Lucifer believes himself to be free in several ways in which he is mistaken; he is not free from desire, nor is he autonomous. His quarrel with God is over nature's resistance to God's will. Lucifer presses God to admit that he doesn't know "why the winds are docile to thy voice / And why the will to make us was in thee" (p. 11), and that He, like every other being, was Himself born subject to the obscure movements of nature. When God refuses, Lucifer rebels and is forced into exile. Now, in his rebellion against a god whom he believed subject to nature's circumstances and accidents, he suffers from the same illusion he taxed God with. He is not subject to any of the other spiritual forces in the universe, but he is powerless to work out his will or to know the sources of his desire; he cannot be autonomous. For one brief moment, out of love for Hermes and out of despair over his own barren life, he is seduced by the Risen

Christ's claim of power: not in the sense that he believes Christ's claim of
having brought about his love for Hermes and his disgust and consequent
flight from Hell, however, for his answer to these claims is crucial to the
justness of his rebellion. Christ says:

> I showed thee hell and its unrighteousness,
> And tempted thee to cast thy kingdom off
> For a just life; and in that trial's stress
> A second time I vanquished. (p. 135)

And Lucifer answers:

> I might scoff
> But that which vanquished was a holy thing
> And even thou if thou usurp its name
> Shall find me patient. (p. 136)

Lucifer here is denying that Christ exercises any power over him, but
he is not denying his submission to some "holy thing," the force which
truly holds sway in the universe, although the Old King and the Risen
Christ both deny it. This is essentially the same position Zeus expounds in
his final speech, although from a somewhat different point of view, for
Zeus is a more historical figure than Lucifer. Insofar as he is *Greek* naturalism, he can die in a way that Lucifer cannot. But they are both affirming
their independence from Christ and the dependence of all three on a further, unfathomable power.

In what way, then, is Lucifer tempted by Christ? Although he calls it
"vain" to ask if he will follow Hermes into allegiance with Christ, for the
Olympians "never can submit" (p. 136), yet he is so far drawn by the
vision of a restoration of harmony through his love for Hermes that he
kneels, if only for a moment, and recognizes a kind of victory for Christ,
although in equivocal terms:

> It ne'er can come again,
> That ancient life, nor can my faithful pain
> Be swallowed up in empty mockery.
> Yet I confess to thee thy victory,
> If such it be.
>
> XXX
>
> If he believe and enter through the gate
> His faith has opened, I will follow him,
> Resume my throne and wear my old estate,
> Making thy glory bright, which shows so dim,
> For I have wholly understood my fate,

And know there is not in this scheme of things
Room for my soul. (p. 137)

Here Lucifer is in part the romantic hero who will later answer Christ's plea to yield his misery and wrath up to Christ with the lines, "That cannot yield which is invincible. / This wrath is I; I am this pain and hell" (p. 139). This is the temper of the early sonnet, "Wretched the mortal, pondering his mood, / And doomed to know his aching heart alone." Lucifer here is the defiant rebel, alone against the universe with a depth of disillusion and despair that makes Shelley's Prometheus seem fatuous in comparison. He does not hope for peace, or reconciliation, or victory; he exults in his pain insofar as it defines his distance from his old, unenlightened life in Heaven and is therefore the very essence of his being. In *The Sense of Beauty*, Santayana wrote about a sense in which reason is a consequence of the ill-adaptation of instincts, for if an instinct were perfectly adapted to the environment so that its activity resulted directly in satisfaction, it would be unconscious, like the instincts in animals. In such a paradise, an unconscious harmony of need and gratification, there is no place for Lucifer, nor anywhere else in the universe. He expects "Nor truth, nor hope, nor certainty, nor rest / But only laughter in my hollow breast, / Laughter and in the night a gust of tears" (p. 141). Here is an echo of "Dover Beach," and in the entire speech a hint of Arnold's Empedocles as well. Like "Dover Beach," this speech reflects the modern inability already discernible in Arnold, either to believe in the myths that had sustained its values in the past or to place those values on a basis acceptable to reason. What, after all, men increasingly asked in those decades on either side of the turn of the century, was the place of reason in a naturalistic scheme of things? The resemblance to Empedocles is somewhat less direct, for Empedocles saw the cause of his despair less in the world and more in himself. He speaks of that "something that has impair'd his spirit's strength, / And dried its self-sufficing fount of joy."[5] He has no Hermes to tempt him to choose life, but, like Lucifer, he prides himself on being a witness to truth:

That I have loved no darkness,
Sophisticated no truth,
Nursed no delusion,
Allowed no fear! (p. 174)

Thus far we can see the lines of tradition in Lucifer's position and the restatement of positions Santayana has taken earlier, but, before this speech is over, he has stated a new possibility which was to become a major theme in subsequent work and a fundamental element in Santayana's theory of the imagination:

LUCIFER: THE LIMITS OF SCEPTICISM

All things are parts of me, and I the whole;
And if entangled in the web I weave
To stars or gods or men I yield control
Over my heart, and bowing down believe,
Me headlong in their dance of death they roll
And with perpetual mockeries deceive.
Steadfast I therefore stand, enwrapped about
As with this mantle in my large despair
As with this lance by piercing doubt
I scorn the gathering armies of the air. (p. 142)

These few lines radiate meaning in several directions. First of all, it appears that Lucifer's position here is essentially the solipsism that Santayana found inescapable in romantic idealism, a position he was simultaneously drawn to and critical of. Lucifer himself projects the world and is the world. Santayana was drawn to it because he believed with the romantics that human reason constructs the world man moves in, providing form and meaning, value and event, out of a flux of experience, which without consciousness would remain what it is in his own view at bottom: unfathomable, irrational, and innocent of value. Lest this broadening of Lucifer's attitudes appear to endanger the balance and intended meaning of the play, we should remember that Santayana, unlike Lucifer and the romantics, believed that conceiving of the forms of reality as dependent on the workings of our own minds did not give us any added power over them. What, he asked in *Interpretations of Poetry and Religion*, was less amenable to us than the workings of our own minds?

Lucifer speaks here from the world of the early sonnet that asked what was dreaming, what was waking. The threat in the sonnet was that truth might be a dream. For Lucifer it is, and he will believe nothing of the world his dreaming makes. By the time the idea of the constructive imagination appears in Santayana's criticism, as it does in the first essay in *Interpretations of Poetry and Religion*, it has been liberated from the threat of solipsism by making the dream symbolic of reality, verifiable as such through tradition, community, and science. But Lucifer also embodies an aspect of Santayana expressed in the sonnets he wrote before his metanoia. The metanoia, as we saw, entailed the surrender of power and freedom of action in return for spiritual freedom. Lucifer here identifies his being with autonomy and freedom from belief. For him deception is the same as death, and his only protection is his own despair and doubt. This is the rational side of the sensibility obsessed with the evanescence of love. Just as the heart that loves must be disappointed, so the mind that believes will be deceived.

The revolution in feeling that allowed Santayana to overcome that despair and to possess the whole world in idea appears here in the form of Christ's temptation of Lucifer, which, of course, is unsuccessful. On a symbolic level, its meaning is that Lucifer may possess beauty and love only by renouncing his freedom. On the historical plane, the tragedy lies in Lucifer's incapacity for faith in the Christian revelation. He has seen through its myth; it is too late for a reconciliation. This is a dramatization of the crisis in belief Santayana discusses in *Interpretations of Poetry and Religion*; there he will explore the way reason and beauty may come together in another sort of heaven, a new synthesis in which the method and function of religion are transferred to art. Underlying Santayana's concern with this crisis and dictating the form of its dramatization, of course, is the problem involving impulse gratification which lay at the heart of the metanoia as well. On every level, freedom, gratification, and value are removed from the real world of action to the symbolic world of art.

But in the play, Lucifer will not renounce his freedom or his will. If he could do so, he would not be left alone at the end, contemplating the icy eternity of truth. He would be immersed in the various and everlasting forms of the imagination. He cannot. He is Lucifer; he can only doubt. He is not an artist. The concept of reason constructing the world out of flux, left in his hands, remains unproductive. Like the romanticism of which he is representative, he can only clear the ground of convention and outmoded beliefs; he cannot build. As Santayana points out in his preface, Lucifer's is only one of the points of view represented in the play, whose meaning does not rest on him alone but on his relationship with the other two embodiments of spirit.

When Lucifer tells Christ to take Hermes from him, Christ, not perceiving the bitterness of the reply, thinks his plan is succeeding, that the desire to save love from death prompts the speech. But that would be for Lucifer to enter the world of the Platonizing sonnets. His unyielding exit line is, "the death of gods is mine immortality" (p. 142). That is, the doubting reason thrives on exploded myths. But the angels sing two short songs after he leaves to foretell the emptiness of the immortality Lucifer prides himself on. These songs close the scene on a different note. They share Christ's perspective, the perspective of spiritual love, not of reason. In it concepts of divinity are not merely sophisticated make-believe figures but embodiments of truths about experience which it is perilous to ignore. That is the perspective in which art and religion will come together in *Interpretations of Poetry and Religion.*

The conception of the inevitably tragic fate of the claims of reason in the realm of action should be recognized as an intellectual form of the prior surrender of the demand for direct emotional gratification that we have traced in the lyrics. It is grounded, like Santayana's dramatic representation of his mother's rejection of him, in a vision of the unalterable nature of things. The source of its strength lies in its necessity, which is also the source of its superiority as a tragic conception over the death of Arnold's Empedocles or Byron's Manfred, both of which stem from choices dictated by personal divisions and sufferings and which leave one with a sense of waste and interrupted action. In *Lucifer,* an action is clearly worked out to its inevitable conclusion. Lucifer's fate reveals again the psychic mechanism through which Santayana was able to come to terms with his frustrations, and, even more important, it reveals how productive that mechanism was. For this dramatization of the ultimate sterility of sceptical reason is intimately connected with the growth of Santayana's concept of a realm of art where fulfillment is possible, where what has been renounced may be repossessed.

The sense of necessity vital to the poem and to Santayana's emerging literary theory is significant in other writers of his period. It is one of the fundamental sources of the tragic and noble strains in both Conrad and Yeats, for example. It is the ground bass on which each works out beautiful, self-sustaining, and futile arabesques of the spirit. It is easy to see how Conrad's heroes, even at the height of their splendid self-assertion, are bowing to the necessity of things, but a little reflection shows as clearly that Yeats reaches Byzantium only by an equally complete surrender of claims on the natural and social order. The central position of necessary frustration and defeat distinguishes emerging modernism both from the romantic from which it developed and the absurd to which it gave birth. In the earlier period the hero may very well be defeated, but he blames himself, and, whatever our admiration, we do too; in the later, there is no victory, no defeat, and no one to blame. Only in modernism is our attention directed from the beginning to that necessity in the order of things which defeats humanity when it tries to transcend nature; everything follows from that first great fact. Biology was the terrible revelation of nineteenth-century thought. It so dominated social theory and history and so infected those two modes of organizing and controlling human life with a sense of natural evolution, growth and decay—all outside human agency or domination—was it any wonder that, for men, only art escaped the plague? When Yeats sailed to Byzantium with so many of his younger contemporaries, he turned his back, not only on biology but on social organization and history as well, all the modes of reality that seemed so intransigent to human control.

Lucifer in his most admirable aspect, then, is doomed by necessity. But his character also contains other elements which are destructive in themselves but which ultimately become vantage points for the creation of

45

the realm of art that would transcend necessity. Lucifer is Santayana's version of the romantic hero he was to write about in *Three Philosophical Poets*, who wishes to possess experience directly, undeterred by conceptualizations that seem to him to falsify it. He resembles Byron's Manfred in several interesting ways. Like him he denies supremacy over himself to any of the spirits he traffics with; he submits only to the natural order. Both believe that only their own minds may punish them for their sins and that their spirits are the equal of any others in the universe. Manfred, like Lucifer, is intensely concerned with his freedom, which extends also to freedom from deception or temptation by what is external to him. He says to the spirits of Hell very much what Lucifer says in the moment of his defeat:

> *Thou* didst not tempt me, and thou couldst not tempt me;
> I have not been thy dupe, nor am thy prey—
> But was my own destroyer, and will be
> My own hereafter.[6]

For, as he has already said:

> The mind which is immortal makes itself
> Requital for its good or evil thought, —
> Is its own origin of ill and end—
> Is its own place and time . . . . (II. 129-32)

Manfred's sin, never made quite explicit in the play, is incest. We have seen that Santayana was aware of the enormous role his sister, Susana, played in his life—my mother, almost my wife—these were the terms in which he described his sense of their relationship. He used these words in an attempt to explain the emotional sources of the second sonnet sequence, especially to identify the lady of those sonnets, an attempt in which it is also necessary to weigh the feelings he experienced toward his students and younger male contemporaries who were his closest friends during his Harvard years. Those feelings, which he looked back on as having been homosexual, certainly stand behind the figure of Hermes here in *Lucifer*. The passionate quality of Lucifer's relationship with Hermes is commented on sarcastically in the play by the unpleasant Mephistopheles, and Santayana is evidently ambivalent about it.

These are all indications that the cluster of feelings of frustration and abandonment that gave rise to his metanoia and much of his lyric poetry are involved here in Lucifer's tragic end as well. The Heaven of gratification, no matter what the temptation of Hermes's beauty and Christ's promise, is denied him. It is revealing to ask, how, in the movement of the plot, it is denied. It depends on Zeus and the Olympians being unable to recognize Christ's spiritual dominance. God himself, the Old King as he is called, does not appear in the play except in Lucifer's account of him. Christ appears in the form of a mere man, as Lucifer wonderingly puts it. Whatever claim he exerts is on behalf of God, not for himself. The only king who appears is Zeus. At first, when the relationship between Hermes and Lucifer seems most promising and re-entry into Heaven most possible, he is in eclipse, frightened, unsure of his power, on the verge of being supplanted by Christ. In fact, only if he is supplanted can Lucifer re-enter Heaven. Lucifer is frustrated by Zeus's victory over his own fear, his resumption of his own rightful powers.

On the psychological level, it is the strong older male who comes between desire and fulfillment. We should remember Santayana's resentment and ridicule of Susana's husband, as well as the fact that he was left with his father when his mother returned to America, for it was that original abandonment and desolation that Susana's marriage reawakened. It is no coincidence that he conceives of Susana's marriage, like that of his own parents, to be lacking passionate motivation. Furthermore, there was a much older half-brother for whose sake his mother went off to America, and it was a promise to another older male, her first husband, which she fulfilled by that journey. How many were the males who stood between him and primary gratification of his need for closeness to his mother, not to mention the infant Pepin, who was the only child to enjoy her love and in whose early grave Santayana imagined her capacity to love to be interred! Fortunately for Santayana, his feelings toward his father were strongly positive as well as critical, as we shall see in the following chapter, and what is crucial for the play, as well as for his continuing creativity, is his psychological acceptance and admiration of Zeus's resumption of power.

For there is also a great gulf between Manfred and Lucifer. Almost a full century looms between them. Byron's hero denies with the full assent of his creator. And what he denies is the force and power of the external world in his life. The pathos that underlies his defiance comes from his inability, in spite of himself, to affirm the impulses of his own nature, although he acts upon them. He considers his incest sinful and seeks forgetfulness. Yet there is a bafflement at the heart of the romantic hero which stems from a failure to account, in his assumption of absolute spiritual independence, for his sense of sin.

In contrast, one of the main themes of *Lucifer* is the affirmation of the force and power of the external universe over any of the different manifestations of spirit within it, of which Lucifer is only one. In one sense it is the re-establishment of the natural physical universe which the romantic movement called into question in its passionate attachment to absolute mind. It is the reintroduction of necessity into the unlimited plasticity of the romantic world. The ultimate source of this necessity is the same psychic mechanism by which Santayana came to terms with his feelings over separation from his mother and through which he converted his instinctual energies, the carnal flame as he called it, into the light of creative effort. While the conflicts of the piece unquestionably mirror the intellectual questions of the late nineteenth century, on a psychological level the entire machinery of Lucifer, the Risen Christ, the Olympians, Heaven and Hell, time and eternity, are all brought into play to affirm again the impossibility of impulse gratification. Santayana writes that impossibility into the foundation of the universe.

Unlike Byron, Santayana does not identify completely with his hero. One of the things *Manfred* is implicitly about, as is much of romantic literature, is the failure of impulse gratification to gratify. One of the great differences between Lucifer and Manfred and between the intellectual periods they represent is that Manfred trusted his mind and impulses, trusted them only. At the end of the century, Lucifer is aware of the disguises and deceit implicit in his own impulses and concepts of reality. Like the dreams of a person undergoing psychoanalysis, they become only more devious as they are subjected to more sophisticated scrutiny. One of the major efforts of this phase of Santayana's career is to discover how, without direct impulse gratification, he could be gratified. His journey's end is that realm he first projected in the first sonnet sequence, "High above the battlements of heaven," the realm of art where symbolic action brought symbolic gratification. There delight would rest on knowing, not on having, and the risks of commitment would be banished from a world of significant pretense.

At the same time Lucifer's desire to maintain his freedom from belief in the web he weaves allows us to see the bridge in Santayana's mind between the renunciation of the world and the symbolic repossession of it. At the end of the play Lucifer stands on the barren frontier of scepticism. But Santayana is not Lucifer. His metanoia returned the world to him in the sense that, leading him to regard the world without expectations, it permitted him to discover the idea of essence. For despite the many confusing and foolish things that have been said about essences, they are simply images of sense or imagination, or concepts, whatever we may sense or imagine or think, without regard to their existence or their truth. Having no existence themselves, being merely formal, they may become the medium for man's knowledge of reality, in itself unfathomable but symbolized for him by all those essences inexplicably accompanying the interaction of his organism and the environment that both supports and threatens it. But the first use Santayana put this notion to was in his theory of poetry. For isn't that what the poet did— used images of sense or imagination or concepts without regard to their existence or their truth? The crucial difference was that the world he constructed could have the actions he wanted it to have and the meanings he gave it.

The Risen Christ, serenely confident in his prophecies of reconciliation, so unafraid of deception, unconscious even of its possibility, overcomes for one moment Lucifer's pride and brings him to his knees. His notion of his own hegemony in the world of spirit and his ability to bring things about is quite mistaken. He exists on equal terms with the others, like them thrown up by the accidental, blind movements of that substance alone potent that Santayana called matter. This truth, however, is a tragedy solely for Lucifer, for only his being depends on his freedom; only to him is submission painful and destructive. This analysis of reason's dilemma is part of a naturalistic dissolution of the concept of reason as a force informed by human will. The concept of reason that emerged in *The Life of Reason* six years later was that it was a process in which harmony was maintained among the many conflicting impulses in the organism rather than a question of conscious will and judgment. This concept of reason is not so likely to make for heroes of tragedies.

For the Risen Christ there is no tragedy. For him, as for Zeus, the movement of the play is more that of a divine comedy. The essence of Christ in the play is submission to God the Father; spiritual love, not reason, is the core of his being, and without awareness of error there can be no tragedy. When his actions prove that his assumptions were mistaken his essential being is undisturbed; he can, with a blandness that must infuriate Lucifer, merely affirm the necessity of his failure, for he is not attached to any particular forms and can identify his will with the course of events without realizing his own impotence.

Similarly, the outcome is not tragic for Zeus. The last view we have of him is accepting and dignified. His fear has been that another power would take his throne before his time was rightfully over. To the will of nature itself he opposes no stubborn insistence on the order of things as he has known them. He is content to pass away as the forms in which he has manifested himself are themselves dissolved. Until then he is free; after that freedom is irrelevant. To any existence apart from existence in natural forms he is indifferent, just as Aphrodite is uninterested in the kind of love Christ talks about.

Christ and Zeus have in common, then, the ability on some level to affirm their own ultimate impotence. Similarly, Christianity and naturalism, the two great views of life Santayana admired in spite of their apparent antagonisms, both conceive of wisdom, as Conrad, whose heroes suffer from illusions of self-determination, puts it, as willing what the gods will. That the point at which those disparate ways of organizing experience come together is their affirmation of man's powerlessness as an autonomous being shows us that what has appeared to many as a discontinuity in Santayana's intellectual life originates in the continuity of his emotional needs. The sacrifice of direct gratification in social and emotional spheres is projected here in the form of the sacrifice of the will, seen in any case as illusory, not a real loss. This is precisely the way he dealt with his emotions of loss when abandoned by his mother. That was not a real loss either. Particular loves for particular people could not in their nature be lasting. At the same time we can see clearly in *Lucifer* the liberating effects of this sacrifice of will. Zeus and the Risen Christ, like the snowflake in the storm of the first sonnet sequence, enjoy serenity and enjoy without anguish the experience proper to their natures.

Only Lucifer has both the insight and the need for freedom that renders his loss of love and sense of his own impotence tragic. His final refuge will be truth, but to find refuge in eternal truth is to be removed from all the possibilities of existence, an icy quasi-death, since he cannot really die. It is an imaginative equivalent for the volcano into which Arnold's Empedocles threw himself. Arnold was also concerned with the limits of reason. He was acutely aware of the ways in which we are the "prisoners of our consciousness"—the ways our minds and thoughts "never let us clasp and feel the All / But through their forms, and modes, and stifling veils" (p. 172).

This was a form of the problem on which Santayana was to spend a great deal of energy. It was a major aim of his to deny the possibility or the need for this direct apprehension of experience and to affirm the necessity of those forms and modes for the very existence of knowledge, as indicated briefly above. But he worked his way to that position through the despair of his early manhood. He had experienced acutely the sense of alienation from reality that Arnold struggled with, and behind Lucifer undoubtedly echoed the "maze" Empedocles feared, that was "forged by the imperious lonely thinking-power" (p. 173). Furthermore, just as Empedocles looks to a fidelity to some deep-buried self as the source of reconciliation with the world, so Santayana was always to evoke individual instincts and capacities as the only sanction of value. The buried life of physical impulses was also for him the point of juncture with external physical reality. However, whereas difficulties for Arnold seemed to arise simply from being cut off from this buried life, itself conceived in a simple unitary fashion, in Santayana's view human society and art were expressive, willy-nilly, so to speak, of this buried life. The difficulty for the civilized man lay in the complexity and conflict within that instinctual life at least as much as in its differentiation from civilized life.

We have passed repeatedly, in our discussion of the play, from the historical perspective to the philosophic or psychological one. For its characters are not merely movements in history but capacities of the human mind and even different emphases coexisting in any human being. Insofar as the Risen Christ represents Christianity, the Olympians, Greek religion, and Lucifer, modern scepticism, we are in the realm of historical accident and Zeus's judgment is correct. There all is born and all dies. But insofar as Christ represents the poetic truth of religion, the Olympians, naturalism, and Lucifer, reason, then we are in a realm of eternal confrontation. It is a coexistence analogous to Santayana's notions of the coexistence of two kinds of morality: rational and post-rational. Rational morality denotes the harmonizing function of the human mind, not any single set of precepts, but the ongoing attempt to bring the claims of the self and society into a satisfying relationship. Post-rational morality, as in Christianity, for example, involves the surrender of worldly claims of all kinds based on a sense of the vanity of all attempts at satisfaction. In *Reason in Science,* a developmental approach prevails. There post-rational morality is seen as arising in a period where rational ethics begin to be seen as inadequate for human needs. Post-rational morality, then, emerges from the ensuing despair. The effort of bringing all human needs into a satisfying relationship gives way to the renunciation of the majority of these needs and the emphasis of one of them in pursuit of redemption. The treatment is critical in tone of post-rational morality; it is seen as a falling away from a more fully human endeavor. It is also conceived of as lacking in insight into its own sources and as deluded in the sectarian structures it erects later in its development. Santayana finds in it an unacceptable pretension that it has reached a point of view from which *all* impulse may be criticized and finds a moral value in it only insofar as it restores in some way all "the natural virtues and hopes"[7] it had renounced. The aim of the discussion is to criticize post-rational morality from the point of view of the origin of all value in natural human impulse.

Here we can see the themes of the poetry emerging in the philosophy of the next decade with a very different emphasis. It is as if he is criticizing his own metanoia, which he describes in his autobiography as having changed his thinking so decisively ten years before. But the conflict over impulse gratification was never resolved with finality. For that very reason his account of it is so artful and moving. The force of it is present throughout his life—to his creative gain. In *Reason in Science*, he supports the Greek naturalistic position over the Christian tradition which succeeded it. Like the psychological acceptance of Zeus rather than Lucifer that emerges in the play, it was part of the dynamic movement which reconciled him to his sense of powerlessness. For, as we have seen, both Zeus and Christ signify the surrender of will. We ought not to be misled by the word reason; even in *The Life of Reason*, it is essentially a process dominated by the unconscious.

When he was in his seventies, after he had written *Realms of Being*, in answer to criticism that he had changed positions, in fact deserted rational ethics and gone over to the enemy, Santayana put the matter in a different perspective. He regretted the historical approach in *Reason in Science* and preferred to see both a continuity and a coexistence of all kinds of morality, including what he called pre-rational morality:

We begin with the instinct of animals, sometimes ferocious, sometimes placid, sometimes industrious, always self-justified and self-repeating; we proceed to a certain teachableness by experience, to a certain tradition and progress in the arts; we proceed further to general reflection, to tragic discoveries, to transformed interests. For instance, poets begin to be elegaic and to insist that everything is transitory; all is vanity; even our virtues and our prayers, before God, are impertinent. (Schilpp, p. 564)

That was the way he conceived of the continuity; he saw the coexistence in this way:

To draw the sum total of our account, and ask what do we gain, what do we lose, is possible at any moment of reflection, whatever the wealth or paucity of our experience. But it is the impulse to reflect, not the impulse to acquire or to venture, that is here at work . . . . (Schilpp, pp. 564-65)

This brief glimpse into Santayana's later attempts to clarify his state of mind around the turn of the century should lead us to see even more clearly that the impulses to acquire or to venture insofar as they are associated with Lucifer and his will are being sacrificed. However, insofar as these impulses are associated with the Olympians, that is, with "a certain teachableness by experience, . . . a certain tradition and progress in the arts" (p. 564), for that was what Greek civilization meant for Santayana, they may be retained. This is the importance of the classic tradition in the disposition of Santayana's creative energies and in his poetic theory. It permits him to restore, as he says in *Reason in Science* post-rational systems must, the "natural virtues and hopes" that he himself has renounced during the reflection on the vanity of all things that he called his metanoia. When we come to discuss the internalization of value that takes place in *The Sense of Beauty*, in which all value is seen to depend on these very impulses which are so problematic for Santayana, we will see further the vital importance of classicism, along with social community and science, as restraints on individual drives, restraints calculated to prevent the romantic tragedies of a Lucifer or a Manfred.

NOTES

1. Santayana, *Lucifer* (Cambridge: Dunster House, 1924), p. xiii.
2. *Letters of Wallace Stevens*, selected and edited by Holly Stevens (New York: Knopf, 1966), p. 481.
3. Santayana, review of *Lucifer* published anonymously in the *Harvard Monthly*, quoted in George Howgate, *George Santayana* (reprinted Cranberry, New Jersey: Barnes, 1938), p. 76.
4. Santayana, *Lucifer: A Theological Tragedy* (Chicago and New York: Herbert S. Stone, 1899), p. 13.
5. Matthew Arnold, "Empedocles on Etna," *Poems*, III (London: Macmillan, 1894), p. 157.
6. *The Works of Lord Byron, Poetry*, IV, ed. E. H. Coleridge (London: Murray, 1922) p. 135.
7. Santayana, *Reason in Science, The Life of Reason*, V (1906; reprinted New York: Collier, 1962) p. 208.

The Sense of Beauty

From 1892 to 1895 Santayana gave a course in the theory and history of esthetics from which *The Sense of Beauty* emerged in 1896. It is an effort to understand the experience of beauty in terms of its psychological origin and the significance of our judgments of value, moral as well as esthetic, in terms of the part they play in individual psychology. It extends from the most general considerations of the meaning of the ideal through the structure of particular art forms to the elements of those art forms. It is concerned with ridding the subject of the obfuscating effects of the Platonists and other idealists, with combatting those elements of moralism he detested in Royce and the tendency to find in experience only preparation for more experience that he disapproved of in James and in romanticism. His naturalism here is allied with his classicism and leads him to see and emphasize those elements in psychology that lead to community, continuity, and tradition. At the same time there arise implications that do not support the rationality that in general he is aiming to define. He does not avoid them, but they do not weigh heavily enough for him to modify his overall view; they are not what he chooses to underline at this point in his career.

He distinguishes his psychological method not only from the didactic but also from the historical, by claiming that it should yield an understanding of why we think anything beautiful and also "enable us to distinguish transitory preference and ideals, which rest on peculiar conditions, from those which, springing from those elements of mind which all men share, are comparatively permanent and universal."[1] The commitment here is not to an individual psychology envisioning a unique combination of historic and genetic factors, not to a particular human being embedded in a web of family, civic, and professional relations, but to the universal. Psychology led Santayana, as it led Jung, away from the adventitious, the historical, those disorderly events that distinguish one man from another, to the beautiful patterns of the archetype, repetitious, unchanging, transhistorical.

At the same time, Santayana saw these values, "comparatively" permanent and universal as they might be, as inseparable from immediate emotional responses to life. Esthetic judgments, like moral judgments, differed in this way from intellectual judgments, which were of fact. Any value judgment depended on human preference; a mechanical world, or one in which the human organism was entirely adapted to its environment, or in which minds were capable of intellection only, but not of emotion, would be a world without value. It was from what Santayana called "vital impulse"—irrational, inexplicable, immediate—that value sprang. Aside from instinctive reaction there could be only verbal form or appeal to usage. Rationality itself, then, in this view, is as dependent on human need, as ultimately irrational and arbitrary in its worth. Those critics of Santayana who made so much of his late disloyalty to rationality might have found in this early work clear enough warning of his deepest allegiances, if they had cared to see it. He writes here of rationality, "Only as ultimately securing tranquility of mind, which the philosopher instinctively pursues, has it for him any necessity" (p. 17).

As Santayana saw, this position has important practical results: it directs the critic's attention to the work itself and away from its historical and technical classification. It also opens the way to the destruction of realism as an esthetic standard for it regards the demand for representational correctness in art as a species of substitution of facts for value, that is, of intellectual for esthetic judgment. Santayana could not consider fidelity to nature as a prerequisite for all beauty but only one element or effect that could be a factor in pleasure and on that ground had worth.

What we are witness to here is the way in which realism in art, like every other movement, contained the seeds of its own destruction. The conventions of realism gave way to the techniques of abstraction that increasingly dominated modernism, at least in part as a result of its own commitment to the way things really are. Fidelity to the way things look at particular moments led to the disintegration of the objects themselves in impressionist painting. Fidelity to the way people really feel and act led to the disintegration of the individual as an agent, judging and choosing among the solid objects of his existent world, and the appearance in his place of a shimmering, unstable mass of myth, impulse, dream, and complex, occupying an imagined space outside of space and time.

Santayana's analysis of value continues by distinguishing between esthetic and moral judgment for, in his view, esthetic judgment involved the perception of good to which utility was irrelevant, while moral judgment was chiefly of evil and, even when positive, was based on the awareness of benefits. Morality is seen as chiefly concerned not with pleasure but with the avoidance of suffering, as a means, not an end. Santayana contrasts it with esthetics, as work contrasts with play: that work which is "done unwillingly and by the spur of necessity" and that play which is "done spontaneously and for its own sake, whether it have or not an ulterior utility" (p. 23). This distinction appears again in *Reason in Art* in the development of the terms "servile art" and "fine art." It is from this position that he can criticize those philosophers who paradoxically conclude that good cannot be conceived without evil, for that conclusion arises from the assumption that "moral values are intrinsic and supreme" and yet "would not arise but for the existence or imminence of physical evils" (p.24). But if morality is a means, not an end, then the conclusion may be quite different: "Remove danger, remove pain, remove the occasion of pity and the need for morality is gone. To say 'thou shalt not' would be an impertinence" (p. 25). In the ideal world that remains, Santayana discerns the elements of positive happiness: nature, art, and other people.

Perceptions of value which are positive and immediate are not all perceptions of beauty. Santayana makes a further distinction between the pleasure essential to the perception of beauty and physical pleasures. All pleasure depends on physical organs, but Santayana thinks of the organs of esthetic pleasure being in a sense transparent, not focusing our attention on our bodies but directing it to the object perceived. Physical pleasure makes us more aware of our own bodies and the organ in which the pleasure originated.

Santayana's rejection of the two qualities commonly held to distinguish the beautiful from the pleasurable inevitably follows from the foundation he has laid for the origin of value in instinctive human preference. On the one hand, esthetic pleasure is no more disinterested than any other pleasure; it is merely, like any real pleasure, unmixed with "the satisfactions of vanity and proprietorship"; on the other hand, it must stem from the interests of a particular person. The disinterested quality Schopenhauer speaks of comes from the fact that as a "primitive and intuitive" satisfaction, esthetic pleasure is not "conditioned by a reference to an artificial general concept like that of the self, all the potency of which must itself be derived from the independent energy of its component elements" (p. 32).

Similarly, esthetic pleasures cannot be said to be universal if they depend on individual preference, except insofar as men share the same needs. Beyond basic similarities, variations in senses, associations, dispositions and circumstances must affect what will be beautiful. It is in this connection that Santayana gives his first indication of how one judges a work of art. This is quite a different thing from experiencing beauty, in which we have not yet had any hint of hierarchical organization among the atomistic preferences that nourish our sense of beauty. He tells us that "nothing has less to do with the merit of a work of the imagination than the capacity of all men to appreciate it; the true test is the degree and kind of satisfaction it can give to him who appreciates it most" (p. 34). But upon examination this statement yields only the form of a test, not its content. "Degree," "kind" and "most" are blanks which have to be filled in before it has any real meaning.

However, the claim to universality in esthetic judgments is an expression of our belief that qualities we identify as beautiful in an object are qualities of the object. We believe our judgment to be the "discovery of an external existence, of the real excellence that is without" (p. 35) and therefore to be seen by any observer. Santayana regards this as the survival of the once universal tendency to suppose every effect of a thing part of that thing. With this observation on the conversion of the subjective to the objective, he felt its definition was complete: " . . . value positive, intrinsic and objectified. Or in less technical language, Beauty is pleasure regarded as the quality of a thing" (pp. 38-39).

In a characteristic movement of his mind, Santayana here developed a definition of beauty that enabled him to separate the emotional experience from the self and place it at a distance where it might be safely regarded. At the same time, it can be seen as another form of what he called his "vital philosophy," that earliest rationalization of his emotional conflicts which saw everything good in the world put there by the human imagination.

In later years, after he had worked out the concept of essence, he was somewhat dissatisfied with the presentation of his idea of beauty here. In "The Mutability of Aesthetic Categories," he explained that he did not intend the term "objectified pleasure" as a definition of beauty, because pleasure did not have to be objectified "in order to be fused into an image felt to be beautiful."[2] What he was after in the early concept was the unitary quality of the experience involving a subject and an object, which he might later have expressed by saying that beauty was a "vital harmony felt and fused into an image" (p. 44). The second definition is not actually new; it appears at the end of *The Sense of Beauty* in the discussion of the quality of expression, where he points out the unity of consciousness in which the esthetic "object is not really independent but is in constant relation to the rest of the mind, in the midst of which it swims like a bubble on a dark surface of water." It further identifies as an essential quality just that vital harmony which the later essay stresses: "Now, it is the essential privilege of beauty so to synthesize and bring to a focus the various impulses of the self, so to suspend them to a single image, that a great peace falls upon that perturbed kingdom" (p. 177).

The second definition of beauty is a kind of mirror image of the first. The effort of both is to unite the thing felt to be beautiful and the feeling of beauty in such a way as to protect the self from any destructive consequences following emotional gratification. In the first definition, the emotion is dealt with by thrusting it from the self; in the second, the thing felt to be beautiful is taken into the self, losing its independent existence to become an image in the mind. It is an internalization resulting in enormous gratification, gratification so great as to suspend all the conflicts in the self. It must remind us of the sonnet in the first sequence which describes the realm of spirit and of art in essentially the same imagery:

> Above the battlements of heaven rise
> The glittering domes of the gods' golden dwelling,
> Whence, like a constellation, passion-quelling,
> The truth of all things feeds immortal eyes. (p. 21)

In the poem the truth is seen as a beautiful image, like a constellation, that quiets the passions by feeding. Visual apprehension is clearly here an emotional equivalent of being fed, and further, of being fed by something beautiful but remote, and unreachable by one's own efforts. Through this metaphor we glimpse the never-to-be-gratified young Santayana, estranged from his icy and remote mother, and learning very clearly to take from her through various visual symbolic substitutes the emotional satisfactions she was unable to give him. Not the least of these was the image he built up of her as embodying a noble ideal of renunciation in response to bereavement which served him so well in the resolution of his own crisis. In the passage from *The Sense of Beauty*, too, the esthetic object quells passions by being taken in through the eyes; the visual imagery here lies in the impulses of the self being brought to a focus.

The theme of the visual was also related, as we shall see shortly, to Santayana's feelings about his father, which in turn were a link with the strong force exerted in nineteenth-century literature by the visual mode. Its usefulness to Santayana in his writing was further determined, of course, by its public meanings. Here is a prime example of the enabling effect of a writer's private emotional conflicts on the contribution he is to make to cultural life. The conceptions of beauty as objectified pleasure and the sense of beauty as an internal harmony "felt and fused into an image" were developed under the pressure of Santayana's drive for compensatory gratification; the energy and purpose with which he focused on the terms of the concept came from the emotional symbolism with which he had invested them. But the terms had a public existence as well, and the concepts embodying them came to be dominant in twentieth-century critical investigations.

The passage in *The Sense of Beauty* which defined beauty as a vital harmony bringing peace to the perturbed kingdom of the self is marked by a use of imagery that is characteristic of Santayana's style, in which concepts are frequently explained in metaphors and poetic images. An exception is *The Life of Reason*: there that feature is suppressed in favor of a more technical and academic temper that Santayana later expressed great distaste for; he declared it unreadable. The adherence to the later embodiment of the idea of beauty rather than to the definition given first in the book is expressive of the move away from physiological psychology as an adequate source for philosophic discourse, toward what he later called literary psychology. It also reflects the way in which a poetic imagination asserted itself stylistically, just as the idea of the creative imagination became a ruling concept philosophically.

Although both a scientific and a literary approach to beauty are in *The Sense of Beauty,* the domination of psychological method was brought about by a combination of factors. In part it was the continued working out of the possibilities of naturalism, the exploration of the real as opposed to the mythic basis of beauty that began in the first sonnet sequence. The Platonizing sonnets were testimony to his ability to deal in myths but, as we have seen, all that was natural to him, a way of thinking that he was aware of even in childhood but that never deceived him. Now his energies were focused on the origins, not the meanings, of ideals. Another factor was the vacuousness of the current approaches to esthetics, characterized by George Boas as "Hegelian dealers in edifying abstractions who valued a work of art because of the spirit which infused it and psychologists who held up pieces of paper divided in two and asked their students whether the division was beautiful or not" (Schilpp, p. 260). The third element was social. Santayana was finally in the process of making a career for himself. The dominating figure in his early career seems to have been William James. It is to him that Santayana wrote letters from Germany justifying his activities before his return to Harvard. It was with him that he argued over the meaning of his books and the significance of his irritation with Harvard. And he wrote of the William James who had been his master:

. . . not this William James of the later years, whose pragmatism and pure empiricism and romantic metaphysics have made such a stir in the world. It was rather the brilliant but puzzled doctor, impatient of metaphysics whom I had known in my undergraduate days . . . or it was the genial author of *The Principles of Psychology*, chapters of which he read from the manuscript and discussed with a small class of us in 1889. (Schilpp, p. 15)

He felt that he had learned from James a sense for the immediate: "for the unadulterated, unexplained, instant fact of experience," its existence "momentary and self-warranted" (p. 15).

It is this James who is an ally against Royce, the Hegelian enemy, and it is this James who became identified for Santayana with the confrontation between reason and the flux of experience, which was Santayana's existential situation, so to speak, at this time. His career depended on his domination of his environment as nothing previously in his life had. Even the writing of *The Sense of Beauty* depended on this, for he explained its origins in the fact that "they" had let him know through "the ladies" that if he wanted to stay on at Harvard he would have to produce.[3] Up until this time his survival depended in a sense on understanding only, on the extraction of ultimate values as the only gain from situations in which he remained essentially passive, if not always victimized. But now he was pressed to consider instrumental values. It is this combination of factors that disposed him to consider in psychological terms not only beauty itself but the materials and forms of beauty. Important as ideals were to him, they were not self-generating; their deepest source was the psyche, which in his understanding was part of man's physical constitution. His own gratification now depended on producing. Naturally enough, his own concerns influenced the terms in which he conceived his work. In the section on expression, where questions of value and human implications are most important, psychology is by no means abandoned, but it is broadened and deepened by the reintroduction of questions of significance which had originally been banished along with Platonic theory as useless for an explanation of beauty.

Proceeding from a concept in which beauty is dependent on the observer, the second part of the book considers the materials of beauty from the point of view of the human organism and its functions; that critical philosophy for which "visible objects are . . . nothing but possibilities of sensation" (p. 54) is never absent from his mind. Once his epistemology has removed sensory qualities from the object, he is not about to put them back for purposes of esthetic analysis. In fact, it is this very dissolution of the object that permits him to carry on his naturalistic explanations. It is because it is a constant element in the discussion that he is able to bring esthetics up to date, so to speak, into the circle of modern critical thought.

For the various elements of consciousness themselves are materials of beauty which, in association with the operations of the mind, produce the sense of beauty. In the metaphor he used again in *Lucifer*, Santayana writes, ". . . whenever the golden thread of pleasure enters that web of things which our intelligence is always busily spinning, it lends to the visible world that mysterious and subtle charm which we call beauty" (p. 42).

He is not concerned only with the senses, the imagination, and the memory, which he calls "more or less external divisions" of consciousness, but with "less obvious processes" and "deeper roots" as well (p. 43). He stresses the importance of the basic vital functions, like blood circulation and tissue changes, as productive of "great and painful changes in consciousness" and therefore important for the value of experience. This is the first appearance of his continued conviction that the balance and health of the entire organism was the necessary condition for the growth of art and rational experience. A vital function may also have a more specific effect, as in the relationship between the pleasure of breathing and our ideals, the associations between breathlessness and awe, for example, depending on actual sensations in the throat and lungs.

The most interesting of the considerations here is the influence of the sexual instinct. (The nineties were also the years of Freud's collaboration with Breuer on the function of sex in the etiology of hysteria and the writing of *The Interpretation of Dreams*.) Again it is the fruitfulness of ill-adapted instinct that strikes Santayana here, reminding us of his concern with the technique of compensation in human behavior. He sees our emotional life as dominated, not so much by what sex we have, but by our having sex at all, for he sees sexual organization as fundamentally similar in men and women and therefore would not expect any difference in their esthetic interests.

Santayana conceives of the effects of sexual instinct on esthetic sensibility as stemming from the incomplete "differentiation of the instincts in respect to sex, age, and species," which leads to "a great deal of groping and waste," itself the reservoir of warmth and tenderness toward objects. "The capacity to love gives our contemplation that glow without which it might often fail to manifest beauty; and the whole sentimental side of our aesthetic sensibility—without which it would be perceptive and mathematical rather than aesthetic—is due to our sexual organization remotely stirred" (p. 46). Furthermore, in those circumstances when a specific love object is not found, or when sexual passion is sacrificed to another interest, there is a more generalized sexual reaction in other areas: religion, philanthropy, pet animals, as well as nature and art. This generalization will take place even when passion itself is fulfilled: "For the same nervous organization which sex involves, with its necessarily wide branchings and associations in the brain, must be partially stimulated by other objects than its specific or ultimate one, especially in man, who unlike some of the lower animals, has not his instincts clearly distinct and intermittent, but

61

always partially active, and never active in isolation" (p. 48).

In contrast to sexual instincts, Santayana did not conceive of an important role for the social instincts in the development of the sense of beauty. To a degree he is forced to that position by a definition of beauty in which objectification is the key. Social objects like friendship, wealth, reputation, power, and family life are not composed of definite images. As he says, "They are diffuse and abstract, and verbal rather than sensuous in their materials" (p. 50). At the same time he recognizes the criticism that must immediately spring to mind and states at the outset that "Indirectly they are of vast importance and play a great role in arts like poetry, where the effect depends on what is signified more than on what is offered to sense" (p. 49). He promises to deal with the question again when he considers that aspect of beauty which has to do with associations and significations—expression. So in a sense this is merely a problem of the organization of the book, but beyond that he seems not to have fully thought through the implications of his theory, for he still insists after these concessions that the social impulses support beauty least. His attachment to this judgment comes in large part from his emphasis at this time on the sensuous element of art. His model for the art object is indeed an object, one available to sense and especially to the eye.

Furthermore, the visual, the pictorial, were of central importance to major nineteenth-century figures with whom Santayana is related through influence and interest. Emerson's theory of imagination, whose transcendental aspects Santayana rejected but with which his own is intimately connected, is based on a multiple understanding of the poet as "seer," and the epitome of his spiritual experience was that moment in *Nature* when he became an eye himself. This spiritual dimension of the act of seeing, through which one might pass into a mystic enlightenment, was one which disturbed Santayana throughout his career. The psychological aspects of it were more agreeable to him, and they certainly played a part in his concept of the sublime. But since such a transcendent state was an experience which negated discrimination, he fought against any view which exalted it above sensuous and moral experience. It was not until the 1920s, when he began work on *Realms of Being*, that he was able to see it as anything but destructive of values.

In a second generation variant of the Emersonian vision, Henry James built his art around the moral consequences of "seeing," while technically the major novels often turn on scenes offered to the hero who is made to "see" both immediate and ultimate things, as in the famous scene where Strether sees Chad and Mme. de Vionnet together, or the one where Isabel sees Mme. Merle and Osmond. The technical experiments of *The Awkward Age* smack of the spotlighted picture as well as the stage. Similarly, Joseph Conrad, in his famous preface to *The Nigger of the Narcissus,* put the task of the writer in terms of the effort, above all, to make us *see*. In another area, the Pre-Raphaelites were, of course, primarily painters, and their poetry repeats the carefully observed and elaborate pictorial detail of their painting. Furthermore, Rossetti shared with Santayana an interest in the Italian love sonnet, in which convention prescribed that love should enter in through the eye.

In the examples Richard Le Gallienne uses to characterize the point of view of the decadent artist in the nineties is the significant fact that all refer to the isolation of visual detail: "The picturesque effects of a beggar's rags as Gautier, the colour-scheme of a tippler's nose like M. Huysmans ... the consideration of one's mother merely prismatically, like Mr. Whistler .... [4]

Similarly, Santayana's rejection of the barbarism, as he called it, of Whitman and Browning was the rejection in them of a certain kind of blindness. Whitman self-consciously followed Emerson in the tradition of the poet as seer. In him Santayana felt it led to a preoccupation with particulars in long catalogs which pointed to nothing beyond themselves, while the crucial revelation when it came, as it did in the "kelson of the creation is love" episode of "Song of Myself," was not visionary so much as visceral. To Santayana, this was a mystical disintegration of the forms of reality that was barbaric because it did not lead to a new vision of it, a reintegration. It rested triumphant in sensation. But to remain there, as Browning did in passion, was *not* to see either significance or the world that lies outside one's feelings.

We should recognize that there are several aspects to this preoccupation with sight in the nineteenth century. The image could either involve the dimension of significance and moral value, as in James and Conrad, or it could become in itself the focus of artistic energies as in an impressionist art dedicated to the exploration of visual effects, or it could be used, as in symbolism, as a vehicle for the evocation of the inner world of reverie and emotion. Or the latter aspects might be converted to the uses of the more expansive art of a James or a Conrad, as Santayana would hope it might. Such an art uses impressionist and symbolist techniques in a dramatic framework of essentially realistic dimensions, although in a work like *The Golden Bowl* the realistic intent is considerably crowded by the symbolist techniques. Nevertheless, the technique is in the service of judgments about the nature of experience foreign to the purely symbolist art.

Santayana's childhood interest in architecture, his father's painting, and his own drawing (cartoons were his first contributions to the *Harvard Monthly*) all contributed to his tendency to use visual metaphors when he talked about art and philosophy. His use of them for both categories of experience betrays the single root of these interests as well as their development under the same pressure to manage the threatening world of feeling which resulted in his poetry.

Characteristically, in a letter of 1888 explaining his interest in philosophy, he began by denying that philosophy meant for him, "a personal problem, as a question of what was necessary for salvation. I was simply interested in seeing what pictures of the world and of human nature men had succeeded in sketching: on better acquaintance I see reason to think that they are conventional and hieroglyphic in the extreme. But the interest in these delineations is no more destroyed for me by not trusting their result or their method than the charm of a play is destroyed if it is not historical" (*Letters*, p. 33).

In these lines, philosophy is entirely dominated by art, its traditional pursuit of truth transformed into an artistic effort at symbolic representation. He thinks of it first as a casual, personal "sketch," such as he enjoyed making himself, and then in terms of a highly conventionalized Egyptian-like art, calling to mind the Byzantine image of his sonnet where the saints burn but do not covet. In this vocabulary he turns away from personal emotion in the denial of a search for salvation, first to a subjective sense of imaginative effort and finally to a concept formal and separate from its creator. Through the passage also runs the theme of suspension of belief, which turns philosophy, as it was to turn religion, into a species of poetry.

When Santayana was a child living on Beacon Street in Boston, he liked to sit reading and drawing close to a window that afforded the family "the feminine Spanish entertainment of looking out of the window and watching, a little below our own level, the stray passers-by" (*Persons and Places*, p. 144). Another favorite pastime was reading the *Encyclopedia Britannica:*

The article in our Encyclopedia on architecture, which I studied persistently, was an excellent corrective to Ruskin, to Ferguson's *History of Architecture*, and to the taste of my time. The illustrations were all plans, elevations, and sections; and the only styles treated were the classic and the "Italian." There were no perspective views. I was thus introduced to the art professionally; and the structural interest became as great for me as the picturesque. Yet I was never to build anything except in fancy, and even if I had become an architect could never have built great English country seats like those depicted in my text; I turned all these technicalities to imaginative uses. Here were the magnificent houses in which the English nobility lived; I had only to supply the landscape, the costumes, and the characters—and vivid representations of all these were accessible to me—in order to complete the picture, and bring it to life. (p. 146)

Even at the very beginning of the influence of visual art on his imagination, we find him making use of it in a characteristically dramatic way. These English houses become the basis, he tells us, of a view of history in which English life appeared on a par "with ancient and Catholic life as one of the high-lights of history" (p. 147). When we recall that this reading and watching were the primary recreational activities of the young boy, it reinforces our sense of all the ordinary social and physical activities of life that imagination became a substitute for. It further suggests the emotional gratification involved in a concept of imagination that stressed its activity rather than its passivity.

His interest in architecture continued; when he finished his graduate work in philosophy, he thought of going to architectural school in the event that he could not get a job teaching. That in his old age he wrote to a friend about his philosophy in architectural imagery seems further to verify the extent to which it was gratifying to think of himself as a "maker" rather than a "thinker."

I may be wrong, but I find great comfort in Nietzsche. He is not explicit, he is romantic, but he *implies* my world of two or more storeys, if he does not draw its plan and elevation, as my architectural propensities lead me to do—without, I admit, any technical accuracy; because I am really a self-indulgent impressionist, like Nietzsche himself, and wish to sketch my buildings in perspective. (*Letters*, p. 342)

Santayana's opposition here is between the subjective, impressionistic, and the explicit, formal, both of which he felt in himself. These conflicting impulses were implicated in his feelings about his father's painting, still another great factor in Santayana's absorption in the visual. His references to his father's work reveal the extent to which his feelings toward him as well as toward his mother affect his critical categories and judgments.

When he first speaks of his father's painting in the autobiography, he contrasts it with the taste of the 1880s in English-speaking circles: "As to painting all in England was a matter of culture, of the pathos of distance, of sentimental religiosity, pre-Raphaelitism, and supercilious pose. Even the learned and gifted that I saw in Oxford were saturated with affectations" (*Persons and Places*, p. 14).

His father's attitude was quite different:

... my father's ideas were absolutely those of the craftsman, the artisan, following his trade conscientiously with no thought or respect for the profane crowd of rich people, who might be babbling about art in their ignorance. This jealous professionalism did not exclude speculation and criticism; but they were the speculation and criticism of the specialist, scientific and materialist. (p. 15)

There is admiration here and, to the young child who observed the painting itself, "his easel, his colors, ground by himself with a glass pestle and carefully mixed with the oil, his palette and his brushes were objects of wonder . . . ." In addition, there is an indication of an emotional source for the identification of science and art which was to be a central feature of his criticism of romanticism.

He wondered afterward, when drawing became a pastime for him as it remained throughout his life, whether his father's example and lessons would have helped him in draftsmanship where he was weak. He was separated from his father in those early years of drawing; when he was with him, he was too young to learn; when he began to see him again regularly, he was in his late adolescence, not a propitious time for lessons from one's father. Since he could not have his father's help, he concluded characteristically that it would have been no use to him: "because composition and ideal charm which are everything to me in all the arts seemed to be nothing to my father. I might have acquired a little more manual skill, corrected a few bad mannerisms; but I should soon have broken away and turned to courses he could not approve" (p. 16).

He associates his father's failure as a painter with a lack of "ideal inspiration." His father claimed to have no ideal, to know only what he didn't want. From all his father's expressed dislikes, Santayana inferred that he loved "the garden of Epicurus, with simple natural pleasures, quietness, and a bitter-sweet understanding of everything. This garden of Epicurus, though my father would have denied it, was really a vegetable garden, a convent garden; and it seemed strange to me that a man who had been so much at sea, and seen many remote countries, should take such a narrow and stifled view of human nature" (p. 17). He concludes, "I am afraid my father, unlike my mother, was not brave."

And to this lack of bravery, so different from his mother's ability to live an ideal with which Santayana, as we have seen, identified, Santayana ascribes in the long run his father's artistic failure:

My father's style in painting . . . inclined to clear shadows, pure outlines, and fidelity to the model, with little thought of picturesque backgrounds or decorative patterns. Had he had greater decision and dared to follow the ideal he possessed; had he simplified his surfaces boldly and emphasized characteristic features and attitudes without exaggerating them, he would have painted like Manet. But perhaps when he was at work on a canvas that promised well, he would visit the Prado, and some lurid figures by Ribera would catch his eye, or the magic lights in darkness of Rembrandt, and he would come home and spoil his picture by incongruously deepening the shadows. (pp. 18-19)

He is pointing out here his father's inability to affirm the ideal growing naturally out of himself, the ideal by which one excludes, ruthlessly separating what one is from what one is not, that he returns to again and again as the foundation of art. As he wrote to Thomas Munro:

. . . you . . . seem to me to confuse the liberty and variability of human nature, which the naturalist must allow, with the absence of integration in each man or age or society; for if you felt the need of integration, you would understand that fidelity to the good or the beautiful is like health, not a regimen to be imposed, by the same masters, upon men of different constitutions, but a perfection to be jealously guarded at home, and in one's own arts; and you will never have any arts that are not pitiful until you have an integrated and exclusive life. (*Letters*, p. 239)

Amid a mass of criticism of his father's attitudes and sensibility is a re-vealing comment on his father's scepticism, which he points out is a restatement of Hobbes's "No discourse whatever can end in absolute knowledge of fact." This is a position Santayana elsewhere ascribed to himself; as he said, he "made the *authority of things*, as against the pre-sumption of words or ideas, a principle of" his philosophy (p. 18). But it is used here to criticize his father's incapacity to go behind fact, to use analogy, to admit responsibility for anything "a bit paradoxical." "My father feared to be cheated" is the way he puts it. And behind this phrase echoes the significance of his father's life—a minor colonial servant in his prime coming home to a meager Spain and a late marriage, to be deserted by his wife, abandoned by and in turn abandoning his family, a frustrated amateur painter with a sterile technique, unable to complete his pictures. Behind Santayana's idea of his father's fear lurks also his own pervasive sense of loss, Lucifer's urgent need not to be deceived, which ultimately yielded the philosophic synthesis of his later years. The rejec-tion of the fear was not productive in itself; it had to be fructified by the significance he saw in his mother's life. It is interesting how much harsher his treatment of his father is. Even those elements in his father that Santa-yana clearly admired and were part of his own life, like the scepticism and the pursuit of art without thought of a career, which was his own ideal of the philosophic life, are presented from a negative point of view. Yet his mother's icy exclusion from life is surrounded with the attributes of no-bility, courage, and spiritual resource. Still the memories of his father are filled with intimate personal detail, and there is nothing in his account of his mother to approach the warmth of the story of how his father, having been on a strict diet for his digestion which excluded chicken, a favorite dish, felt himself to be dying, and supposing he could no longer do him-self harm, called loudly for extreme unction and a chicken.

67

However more loving, we cannot say stronger, the tie was with his father, he clearly saw his father's life as a failure. His father seemed to him submerged by experience, unable to find in professional technique or scepticism a means of transcending the sensuous level of his life, itself meager and desperate. He had failed to achieve any vision of purpose or significance which alone would have justified it in his son's eyes. This was the life to which his mother had abandoned him when he was five. It was his father's pathetic end he imagined for himself in that crucial period around his thirtieth year when he sought urgently for a means of dominating his own experience.

It is through Santayana's complicated feelings toward his father, then, that the nineteenth-century emphasis on the visual and his own talents and interests in drawing and architecture, fed no doubt by the extent to which he was, as a child, an observer of adult tragedy in those early Spanish years and of adult trivia through that window and those books of his American boyhood, all came together to be invested with the energy and drive which enabled him to structure experience in terms that remind him of his father and yet transcend his father's failure. At the same time the cluster of emotions around the theme of the visual image, whether in painting or poetry, led him to exploit in it the possibilities of distance and conceived meanings so that seeing could become at times distinguished from and opposed to feeling, in the way that, in his essay on the Platonic poets, the contemplation of experience was opposed to the continuation of it. When he comes to define imagination in *Reason in Art,* he does it in terms of that opposition:

Between sensation and abstract discourse lies a region of deployed sensibility or synthetic representation, a region where more is *seen* at arm's length than in any one moment could be felt at close quarters, and yet where the remote parts of experience, which discourse reaches only through symbols, are recovered and recomposed in something like their native colours and experienced relations.[5]

The region of the imagination, then, is one where things are seen. Seen is used here with the Jamesian sense of "realization" and "understanding." What is seen is at a distance, whereas what is felt is close. What is seen is superior to what is felt because it gives us more of the experience. So to begin with, Santayana is saying, we get more experience at the same time that we thrust it from us. Seeing is somehow a more ample mode of experience than feeling. At the same time, "the remote parts of experience"—that which we thrust from us by our intellectual apprehension of it, by our discourse which touches the experience only through symbols—these parts may be recovered in something like their original guise.

Santayana is defining the imagination here so that it does the two things most necessary to his psychic life. It reduces the immediacy of the experience so that the self is not overwhelmed by the disorder of feeling, and it promises fuller enjoyment of the experience. The sacrifice of feeling and actuality is compensated for by the recovery of the color and form of the experience. Santayana ascribes to the imagination, then, the same function he ascribed to his metanoia. It enables him to take possession of the world again, quite safely, in idea, once he has given up actual claims to it.

Once we realize the service such a definition of imagination performs, we ought not to wonder at the elevation of this imagination by a culture that shared with Santayana his broad sense of the disorder and powerlessness of personal life. T. S. Eliot was a student at Harvard and an assistant in the philosophy department just after Santayana articulated his ideas about the imagination. Eliot spoke forcefully for the escape from personality, yet behind his renunciation of personality lies the same need to grasp the world. Once he has purged himself of his will, he will not only be vouchsafed his vision of eternity—the still point of the turning world—but he will, through his poetry, retain the experience in his temporal state. The burden that poetry is asked to bear by the modernist poet is staggering, nothing less than the integration of time and eternity. The psychological reward made possible by such a notion of imagination and such a submission of the will is enormous. The cost to society, of course, is commensurately large. For the withdrawal of energy from ordinary social life that we have seen in Santayana is prophetic and representative of the withdrawal the modernist writer made. One of the implications here is that we might want to revise our notions of the relationship of social failure and decay and the modernist writer for whom it was such an important subject. The social decay was, at least in part, a function of the withdrawal of energy—itself caused not by the vision of decay but by the experience of powerlessness. The pervasive cultural sense of powerlessness, in turn, springs again, at least in part, from the inevitable disappointment attendant on the claims made by earlier romantic writers like Byron and Emerson on behalf of the self. At the same time that Santayana recognizes the fantasy in Emerson's expectation of the infinite plasticity of the world, he does not surrender his own wish to possess but merely transfers it to the world of the imagination. The inhumanity of modernist literature is perhaps inseparable from the elevated position that was pressed on it by modernist culture. We are just now coming to realize that neither attribute is inherent in the nature of art. But how easy it is to come to the conclusion that art is the highest experience of life if what it gives us symbolically is the whole world.

The effect on society and its members, however, may be dangerously close to what Montaigne warns us about at the close of his essay, "Experience." He is afraid of transcendental humors, of the men who leave their bodies to live in the mind. He tells us the story of Aesop and his transcendental master. "Aesop, that great man, saw his master pissing as he walked. 'What next?' he said. 'Shall we have to shit as we run?'"

This discussion began with an account of Santayana's difficulty in *The Sense of Beauty* in reconciling the concept of objectification, dominated as it was by visual connotations, and social instincts whose satisfactions tend to be verbal rather than sensuous. There were implications in the theory that would permit the integration of social associations so important in the verbal arts. A few years later, Santayana wrote of the way the meaning of a poem should emerge through the development of the form and the working out of the central metaphors so that the structure and meaning *are* the poem. Here was a sense in which the form of a poem might be conceived of as an object also. It was a line developed in works like Cleanth Brooks's *The Well Wrought Urn* and an attitude common to those poets who saw themselves as "makers" and their poems as artifacts rather than statements, all those who agreed that a poem should not mean but be. It was a line of thought contributing to Suzanne Langer's development in *Feeling and Form* of the concept of virtual worlds created by art, concepts objectified, discourse converted into symbol, autonomous but significant. In this view, then, all art accomplished what Schopenhauer claimed for music, a claim to which Santayana referred in *The Sense of Beauty*. It repeated the world of sense, making a parallel expression of the underlying substance.

In considering the nature and function of poetry, Santayana will develop further the possibilities of the notion of objectification in *Interpretations of Poetry and Religion*, as we shall see. There art as an art object gives way to art as a theater of emotions, and drama replaces painting as the representative art. This was a direction to be followed by R. P. Blackmur (language as gesture is a phrase of Santayana's) as well as Kenneth Burke in the kind of criticism exemplified by his well-known analysis of Keats's ode.

In spite of the fact that Santayana's notion of the imagination turns the artist away from social activity, he was himself to prove an acute social critic. In *The Sense of Beauty*, he expresses the conviction that "man is preeminently a political animal, and social needs are almost as fundamental in him as vital functions" (*Sense of Beauty*, p. 50). Nevertheless, when he talks about the place of art in society, his highest ideal seems curiously like the transformation of social experience into esthetic experience. It is a concept of life itself as art. Activity is pursued for its own sake, its original instrumentality absorbed and transmuted by the gratification inherent in the act so that concern for reward is replaced by concern for the perfection of the act itself. In this way the qualities of immediacy, intrinsicness, and, even in a sense, objectification, can be seen as qualities of acts as well as things. All those aspects of life which he had originally distinguished from fine art and labeled servile, like industry, science, business, and morality, all those activities which might be described as preparing the raw materials of life for the artist, may in themselves become art.

. . . fit form turns anything into an agreeable object; its beauty runs as deep as its fitness . . . . (*Reason in Art*, p. 64)

Literature in particular (which is involved with history, politics, science, affairs) might be throughout a work of art. It would become so not by being ornate, but by being appropriate, and the sense of a great precision and justness would come over us as we read or wrote . . . . It would delight us; it would make us see how beautiful, how satisfying, is the art of being observant, economical and sincere.[6]

Furthermore, as the conditions of life were modified in the direction of art, the inner life would expand and become richer. Using the notions of work and play, as he did in *The Sense of Beauty*, he wrote:

Life has a margin of play which might grow broader, if the sustaining nucleus were more firmly established in the world. To the art of working well a civilized race would add the art of playing well. To play with nature and make it decorative, to play with the overtones of life and make them delightful, is a sort of art. It is the ultimate, the most artistic sort of art. (*Three Philosophical Poets*, p. 214)

When fit form turns life into an agreeable object, when nature is made decorative, what begins as an attempt to abolish the superiority of art as separate from life, to denigrate the notion of "fine" art, is subverted. Instead, what happens, under the pressure of his profound conviction of the inevitable failure of action to achieve its ends and the ultimate uselessness of instrumentality, is the abolition of instruments, the conversion of means to ends and life into art. We are witness to the triumph of the imagination enacted yet again in Santayana's intellectual life.

The definition of the imagination we have been following thus far in *The Sense of Beauty* emerges through Santayana's discussion of the materials of beauty, consisting, as we have seen, in large part, of human functions: sensation, cognition, emotion, physical process. The sensuous components of the art object itself are also, of course, part of the materials of beauty, according to Santayana's model. We should not be surprised, however, to find that they are not, in his view, very important elements. They might be indispensable, both logically, for "form cannot be the form of nothing" (p. 60) and as a source for the enhancement of the finished work. Nevertheless, the most important effects of a work of art stemmed from the arrangement of the significant relations of the materials, not the materials themselves.

In turning to the exploration of the idea of form, the most abstract, apparently least human, aspect of beauty, Santayana's perspective remains that of the attentive human organism. Form is conceived of as a synthesis of elements by an active mind. The unity of that synthesis cannot be absolute, or it would be a sensation, not a form. The mind maintains both the sense of separate elements and their relation to each other. "It differs," he writes, "from sensation in the consciousness of the synthesis, and from expression in the homogeneity of the elements, and in their common presence to sense" (p. 74). (That is, memory plays no role here as it will in expression.)

As part of his continuing effort to ground the experience of beauty in the entire human experience, rather than in the topmost levels of consciousness, he has an interesting discussion of the physiology of the perception of form in which retinal tensions and eye movements are the basis of our sense of space as well as our delight in perception of simple geometric forms. Complete with diagrams of the way the eye works and references to a parallel explanation of the way the ear works, not to be attempted because of its technical difficulties, it was a method to gladden the heart of I. A. Richards.

In the discussion of form, Santayana discriminates three varieties, a division whose suggestion he credits to Fechner's *Vorschule der Aesthetick*. One type of form organizes elements that are all alike, although many. Another is an organization of differing elements that does not prescribe one particular way of ordering them. The third organizes differing elements in a specific way, the way being clearly determined in the object itself. It is apparent that the role of the mind in the experience of these forms varies, and especially in the second and third types, the difference in what the mind brings to the perception and what it takes from it is sure to be a source of Santayana's ultimate judgment of the value of the forms. The more the form imposes its organization upon the experiencing mind, the more value it has for him. We shall see why shortly.

The infinity of stars is an example of the first kind of form, which moves us by a "sense of multiplicity in uniformity" (p.74), and he ascribes the ultimate feelings aroused in him by them as "sensations of physical tension" (p. 80). In the idea of democracy itself, political and moral though its basis might be, he saw an illustration of this esthetic form, as were the poems of Walt Whitman:

Never, perhaps, has the charm of uniformity in multiplicity been felt so completely and so exclusively. Everywhere it greets us with a passionate preference; not flowers but leaves of grass, not music but drumtaps, not composition but aggregation, not the hero but the vulgarest moment; and by this resolute marshalling of nullities, by this effort to show us everything as a momentary pulsation of a liquid and structureless whole, he profoundly stirs the imagination. (p. 87)

It is in dealing with the second kind of form, in which the object contains different elements that the observer may order differently, that Santayana has the opportunity to continue with the analysis of the relationship of the imagination, experience, and the ideal. Platonic ideas are the starting point here as they were in the essay on Platonic love poetry and the second sonnet sequence, with the same intent to explain the mythic elements in terms of their naturalistic meanings. He sees eternal types as the "instruments of aesthetic life." They are eternal only in the sense that they are treated as absolute standards, but when they are studied, they are "seen to be a product of human nature, a symbol of experience, and an instrument of thought" (p. 86).

He spends some time in analyzing the development of the ideal type, indicating the way it is a "residuum of experience" (p. 89), how it is affected by our expectations and bias. However, what he really cares about is its meaning, that is, significance and use, drawing out the implications of this origin in experience.

The first implication is that when we say something is ideal we are really naming what pleases us in reality. We ought not, therefore, to allow any notion of an ideal to prohibit us from appreciating new qualities not included in it which may nevertheless please us, for if we do "we are simply substituting words for feelings . . . . Ideals have their uses, but their authority is wholly representative. They stand for specific satisfactions, or else they stand for nothing at all" (p. 95). Santayana returns to this touchstone throughout the book; it is a major theme throughout this period of his career and crucial in the change in intellectual perspectives going on at the turn of the century. Ideals, he went on, like "the whole machinery of our intelligence, our general ideas and laws, fixed and eternal objects, principles, persons and gods, are so many symbolic, algebraic expressions. They stand for experience; experience which we are incapable of retaining and surveying in its multitudinous immediacy" (p. 95).

Santayana is not disturbed by this, of course. This is the natural function of human intelligence. The subjectivity of its products is not problematic for him in itself, only insofar as our attachment to them may interfere with our experience, instead of facilitating it as they are meant to. We are reminded, however, that in *Lucifer,* the subjective nature of our apperceptive forms was an occasion for greater anguish, for a radical doubt that does not find expression here.

Santayana commented in a letter to Thomas Munro on the difference in attitude toward art in the late twenties from what it was when he wrote *The Sense of Beauty:*

You must remember that we were not very much later than Ruskin, Pater, Swinburne, and Matthew Arnold: our atmosphere was that of poets and persons touched with religious enthusiasm or religious sadness. Beauty (which mustn't be mentioned now) was then a living presence, or an aching absence, day and night; history was always singing in our ears; and not even psychology or the analysis of works of art could take away from art its human implications. It was the great memorial to us, the great revelation, of what the soul had lived on, and had lived with, in her better days. But now analysis and psychology seem to stand alone: there is no spiritual interest, no spiritual need. The mind, in this direction, has been *desiccated*: art has become an abstract object in itself, to be studied scientifically as a *caput mortuum*; and the living side of the subject—the tabulation of people's feelings and comments—is no less dead. (*Letters,* pp. 238-39)

This is a masterly and moving summation of the change in the meaning and importance of art from the last quarter of the nineteenth century to the second quarter of the twentieth. Santayana mourns the change, yet he does not comment on the extent to which the self-consciousness of his generation in respect to the religion of beauty, their sense of it as a "memorial" was already an expression of the loss of it as a living force. He sees only the difference between his period and that of the late twenties, not the continuity. Yet his own analysis and psychology were part of the disintegration of the sense of beauty as a religion, as the consolation it was to the mid-Victorians, the form in which human aspirations could still be honored. What is extraordinary in his own work is the ability to retain the sense of wonder and beauty in the product of the human imagination while maintaining a working model of the complicated neural conditions in which it probably originated. For Santayana, ideals never became an occasion for psychological reductionism. That was why he commented late in life on his lack of interest in the unconscious mind. What investigation turned up there, he thought, was either dreadful, which was not so surprising to him, or what was worse, trivial. At the time he wrote *The Sense of Beauty*, it was much more important in a public sense to tie down the ideal to the specific experience without which it was nothing at all. For all the dandyism which proclaimed Santayana's involvement in social estheticism at Harvard in this period, [7] *The Sense of Beauty* was a profoundly anti-esthetic book, dedicated to the destruction of the artificial isolation around art, insisting here on that element in Ruskin which was overlooked in the nineties but which was a link to the twentieth century—the functionalism of art. Santayana's feeling for the roots of art in specific experience combines with his awareness of the wide social context of art in the continuing effort of his criticism to maintain the world of significant character and dramatic event as opposed, on the one hand, to the vapid idealism of polite art and, on the other, to the symbolist removal of art utterly to an interior private world. This effort anchors his work at one point in realism, a precarious balance, upset time and again by the fertility of romantic, impressionist, and symbolist strains in his thinking.

Another implication of the origin of ideals in human experience is a necessary uncertainty in the scale of esthetic values and a concomitant reliance for anything like a standard on a conservative notion of tradition in order to avoid an anarchy of judgments. Any idea of "real and objective beauty in contrast to a vagary of individuals, means only an affinity to a more general and fundamental demand" (*Sense of Beauty*, p. 99). This, of course, he wrote, must be the other side to the emphasis on fidelity to what actually pleases a particular human being. Every activity that demands community agreement finds its basis for that agreement ultimately in those physical and social needs that continual interaction of the species and its environment reproduces in each member as an aspect of what we call human nature. The common organization of our nervous system and the anxiety over physical survival fixes our attention on the flux of experience with the shared intent to endure and to avoid pain, which permits agreement on values in the human community, just as it is the individual variation in these things which permits personal preference. Santayana tried to compensate for the scant measure of restraint on individual impulse provided by the natural environment with a due respect for society, which he also saw on a biological model as an evolving form and which ought not to be tampered with by what a later generation might call sociologists or technocrats. Further restraint might be found in science and history, which were ways in which society remembered the fruits of its earlier experience.

The formation of an ideal is a way of giving meaning and value, then, to experience, thereby dominating it. Santayana points out that our love of landscape is the same kind of activity—giving form and significance to indeterminate visual material. In fact, all organized knowledge—history, philosophy, science, religion—all are the same kind of enterprise:

All theory is a subjective form given to an indeterminate material. The material is experience, and although each part of experience is, of course, perfectly definite in itself, and just that experience which it is, yet the recollection and relating together of the successive experiences is a function of our imagination. Theory can therefore never have the kind of truth which belongs to experience; as Hobbes has it, no discourse whatever can end in absolute knowledge of fact. (p. 105)

In this quotation from Hobbes, connected as it is with his feelings toward his father, there is a glimpse of the emotional bridge which helped him to connect the origin of ideal types in esthetic experience with a concept of all theory as the idealization, so to speak, of the baffling flux of experience, that is, as the imaginative creation of significance not inherent in immediacy.

He did not hesitate to draw the conclusion that two different theories might therefore be equally true, in the sense that they would be

equally complete schemes for the relation and prediction of the realities they deal with. The choice between them would be an arbitrary one, determined by personal bias, for the object being indeterminate, its elements can be apperceived as forming all kinds of unities . . . . Although our first concern is naturally the adequacy of our instrument of comprehension, we are also influenced, more than we think, by the ease and pleasure with which we think in its terms, that is, by its beauty. (p. 106)

What has happened here is that while "art for art's sake" has been banished by the importance in art of function, an estheticism even more far reaching has come in as a measure and sanction of meaning itself. That beauty is, as Santayana saw, an underlying factor in scientific research is revealed in the willingness of scientists to speak of the elegance of an hypothesis, and a further example of it appears in James Watson's account in *The Double Helix* of the beauty of the structure of DNA as it began to become clear to him, before its formulae were actually worked out. Santayana viewed science and philosophy, then, like mythology and theology, as imaginative constructs which could be justified only by their congruence with human experience. But no matter how suitable it was, on the one hand, to the mind that used it, and, on the other, to the experience it surveyed, any of these remained theories, "forever utterly heterogeneous from fact . . . ." (p. 107).

Is this, then, a curious version of the Wilde life-for-art's sake paradox, written surprisingly by a man who was at pains to deny any possible separation of esthetic experience from other areas of human life? In his effort to keep esthetic experience in its place with all experience, had he allowed it to swallow up all the areas about it like some imperial power sucking up raw material in exchange for values? Was life, after all, given significance by the effort that Wilde was reputed to have made, to live up to one's blue china?[8]

In a sense, yes, that is what happened. Or rather the Wilde paradox and posturing were trivializations of the common effort of the late nineteenth-century mind to discover meaningful sanctions for value outside of the rapidly failing structure of authoritarian church and state. It would be more illuminating to say that Santayana's analysis here, which reveals all human effort to impose form on the indeterminate matter of experience to be analogous to the esthetic imposition of form on material, is the real significance of the Wilde quip. In insisting that the value of a theory lies in its suitability to the mind as well as to the material it organizes, Santayana is emphasizing that the essence of a theory is formal and, as such, quite other from the facts it gives form to. It is only because it is different that it can give us knowledge of our experience, which directly apprehended is incomprehensible, for only if it is something different can it work as a symbol. And it is Santayana's concern with this function that separates his analysis from the attitude of the esthetes. He has already demonstrated the development of the ideal type out of the mind's experience of its environment, and, every step of the way, in developing the analogy to history, science, and philosophy, he has insisted on the experience the theory stands for. To say the theory is heterogeneous from the fact is only another way of saying the ideal is not the same as the real. By keeping in mind the reality that the ideal has grown out of and symbolizes, he avoids, as the esthetes do not, that idolatry he speaks of which is taking words for things.

Santayana's analysis of indeterminate form had definite implications for his literary theory. Since by its nature indeterminate form is ambiguous, its effect is uncertain, and it fails to communicate meaning unequivocally. In landscape and architecture, where meaning is not to be conveyed, he does not find it objectionable. Where there are sensuous and associative values, especially in music, he thought there could be beauty without clear form. But in literature he considered it fatal to beauty and, in its extreme, to expressiveness. He saw two stages in the absence of form: one, as in Emerson, where there was sense enough in the individual sentences and paragraphs, but no unified thought emerging from them. The second stage he saw in the symbolists, who kept back meaning in the individual word or even in the syllables. This absence of form, he saw, focuses the attention on the materials and accents the "beauty of sound and verbal suggestion" (p. 110). He could never concur in such an effort truly subversive of the values he is analyzing, for he correctly understood it as a "tendency to surrender the use of language as an instrument of thought."

Feeling and sensuous beauty alone cannot generate values; without reason there is only the anarchy of individual impulse. It is a logical esthetic corollary to a view of art that separated the esthetic product from the human process which brought it into being. What he is not interested in here is that other aspect of the symbolist enterprise, the attempt to exploit possibilities in language for nondiscursive symbols that would involve the expressive rather than the formal qualities of poetry. He is alert to the very real dangers in symbolist poetry: first, the easy descent into meaninglessness and second, the poem's conversion into a vague stimulus to the mind, calling up memories and associations, and its dependence on the furnishings of that mind rather than its own structure for the kind and quality of its effect. For indeterminate form brings little that is new: "We can respond only with those forms of apperception which we are already accustomed to. A formless object cannot *inform* the mind, cannot mold it to a new habit. That happens only when the data, by their clear determination, compel the eye and imagination to follow new paths and see new relation. Then we are introduced to a new beauty, and enriched to that extent" (p. 110).

The highest fruits, then, of indeterminate organization issue from its stimulation of the imagination to create apperceptive forms, as in religion and science. Beyond that, an object which stimulates the observer in this way may come to have a special value that Santayana calls the "illusion of infinite perfection." It encourages in the observer a state of mind full of yearnings and an inexpressible desire and seems to promise some exalted satisfaction that it never defines. But it is an abortive promise of expression, an illusion of significance, for the emotion remains unembodied in the object and "what we have is merely a sentiment, a consciousness that values are or might be there, but a failure to extricate those values, or to make them explicit and recognizable in an appropriate object" (p. 114). He was to return to this question in a later essay, and T. S. Eliot came to analyze Hamlet essentially in terms of this esthetic requirement and Shakespeare's failure to meet it. It is a criticism as well of an incapacity common to romantic art. Santayana could value indeterminate form only as a potentiality of imagination, while he identified the highest esthetic good rather as the "greatest number and variety of finite perfections . . . . Progress lies in the direction of discrimination and precision, not in that of formless emotion and reverie" (p. 115).

Interestingly enough, when Santayana turns his attention to determinate form, in spite of the heavy emphasis, as we have seen throughout his discourse, on the art object as an object, his chief concern becomes literary. It is the experience of the Platonic love poet repeated; the eye is the focus of attention because love enters there; it is the sensuous source of the ideal.

But once the material is collected, Santayana cares chiefly for the imaginative use of it, and it is the poetic imagination which yields him the kind of significance he is looking for. Discussion of the poetic mind is likely to turn into discussion of the mind itself, while the function of the mind is seen in the image of the poet.

In *Reason in Art*, for example, on page 91 he is discussing the nature of poetry, characteristically enough through the critical analysis of one of Plato's myths—that of the inspiration of divine madness:

A poet is inspired because what occurs in his brain is a true experiment in creation. His apprehension plays with words and their meanings as nature, in any spontaneous variation plays with her own structure . . . . This inspiration, moreover, is mad, being wholly ignorant of its own issue; and though it has a confused fund of experience and verbal habit on which to draw, it draws on this fund blindly and quite at random . . . . (*Reason in Art*, p. 91)

By page 98 he is characterizing the difference between poetry and prose in terms of the way they render experience. By page 105 he is concerned with the cognitive value of poetry, calling it " a makeshift," and "in this respect, what myth is to science." But by page 106 he concludes, as he does in *The Sense of Beauty*, that since apperception is itself an art, that is, we perceive reality in forms which we impose on it, ideas are by no means obliged to conform with cognitive function. This continues into a consideration of the nature of discourse in general and moves finally by page 110 into the area of cognitive theory itself: "We should not wish to know things in themselves even if we were able. What it concerns us to know about them is merely the service or injury they are able to do us, and in what fashion they can affect our lives. To know this would be, in so far, truly to know them; but it would be to know them through our own faculties and through their supposed effects; it would be to know them by their appearance." He may also follow the train of thought between knowledge and poetry from the other direction. In *Scepticism and Animal Faith*, for example, he begins with the indirect nature of knowledge and ends with the characterization of the mind as a poet: "It does not seem to me ignominious to be a poet, if nature has made one a poet unexpectedly. Unexpectedly nature lent us existence, and if she made it a condition that we should be poets, she has not forbidden us to enjoy that art, or even to be proud of it."[9]

So, although he begins in a critical spirit, judging poetry to be deficient by the standard of cognitive value, he mitigates this judgment by the discovery that none of our ideas are essentially any less makeshift in this regard and concludes finally by finding severe limits to the whole idea of cognition. We never know things in themselves and, in fact, should not wish to know them.

However, an important difference in the first two quotations reveals a serious question implicit in the third. In the first passage, he speaks of the poet as drawing on his experience "blindly and quite at random." In the second, we know things through their effects on our lives. If, then, nature, as he says in the second passage, has made us poets, how responsible is our poetry, that is, our ideas, to the reality it enables us to know? In the second passage, it is entirely so: as clearly as to Emerson, appearances body forth the invisible, or, in any case, that part of the invisible that matters to us. But, in the first passage, the ideas, our poetry, are not at all responsible. This ambivalence is an important element in modernist literary culture and has important consequences. It underlies both the extravagant claims made for art by writers from James to Stevens and theoreticians from Suzanne Langer to Blackmur and Burke as a way of knowing and dominating reality, and the great weakening of writers' commitments to experience that proves, in fact, to be outside individual understanding or control. The social self, with all its political and familial ties, is sharply diminished. At the same time, the notion that ideas are not responsible to reality, that psychic accident may rule them, not external necessity, further confines the artist to the circle of his own mind.

Santayana's ambivalence toward the irresponsibility and isolation of the poet combines with other observations on literary form to throw light on his own practice and on his later abandonment of poetry. They reflect, like all of his work, his primary moral as well as artistic aim, the domination of experience. So, for example, the most highly inflected languages seem to him to have a source of unity unmatched by the modern languages. He considers rhyme most valuable as a substitute for the interpenetration of words possible in Latin verse due to its inflection. It gives them artificial cohesion without which the phrases "would run away from one another in a rapid and irrevocable flux" (p. 131). The sonnet, therefore, was the most classic of modern forms through its power to synthesize and make the unexpected seem inevitable. He did not believe modern languages were capable of much formal beauty, and they could equal the classics only in suggestion and feeling. It is interesting to see his emotional concern over the transience of experience translated here, without much change in language, to concern over the "rapid and irrevocable flux" of uncohesive poetry. Rhyme dominates his own poetry where he is most driven by his central concern to convert his sense of loss into some permanent gain. In the sonnets and *Lucifer* he aspires most clearly to what he conceived of as classic.

He wrote late in life that he had come to feel, "as so many recent poets have felt—that what I had to say could be said better without the traditional poetic form, that is, in prose; because the invention of typographical devices for turning prose into poetry did not occur to me" (Schilpp, p. 598). As so many of Santayana's explanations of his motives have been, this is insightful as far as it goes. It is certainly true to a great extent of one line of development in modern poetry, and he ascribes his feeling of alienation to other factors as well: language difficulties, the disparity between what he thought of as his southern temperament with its respect for " the great world, for fate, for history, for matter" and the language he was compelled to use, which was sympathetic to the "northern respect for the inner man." But there was another development in poetry that this explanation scants. His own distinction between northern and southern is part of it, as was his criticism of the symbolist poets. For poetry was fast ceasing to be an effort to dominate experience, to impose form and create significance. The scope of modern poetry was fast shrinking: the gaze was turning inward. By the time of *The Waste Land*, even for a poet with a comparable drive for order, only a few fragments could be shored against the general ruin.

What Santayana saw in *Reason in Art* as characteristic of "irrational" poets was becoming increasingly true of all poetry: "To dwell, as irrational poets do, on some private experience, on some emotion without representative or ulterior value, then seems a waste of time. Fiction becomes less interesting than affairs, and poetry turns into a sort of incompetent whimper, a childish fore-shortening of the outspread world" (*Reason in Art*, p. 102).

The internal, largely subconscious world did not seem to him a likely place to find order and stability, or even significance. As we have seen, he believed its revelations to be either dreadful or trivial. Under the influence, then, of his own drives and what he saw in poetry before World War I, he began to see the difference between poetry and prose in terms likely to facilitate a shift in allegiance from one to the other. In *Reason in Art*, which, with the other volumes that make up *The Life of Reason*, dominates the first decade of his career not productive poetically, he speaks of the "descent" of poetry into prose, but quickly modifies it into a kind of progress. In it language becomes transparent and instrumental. Without it experience remains "a constantly renovated dream" as poetry conspires to keep it. He differentiates them further in this way:

In poetry feeling is transferred by contagion; in prose it is communicated by bending the attention upon determinate objects; the one stimulates and the other informs. Under the influence of poetry various minds radiate from a somewhat similar core of sensation, from the same vital mood, into the most diverse and incommunicable images. (p. 98)

The key opposition here is between "determinate" and "diverse and incommunicable." It is reminiscent of Santayana's distinction between determinate and indeterminate form, of which he also said "the one stimulates and the other informs." What has happened clearly enough is that he has come to see poetry chiefly in terms of indeterminate form with all its drawbacks; determinate form, the vehicle of the highest beauty and, even more important, significance, no longer seems a possibility in it, with the implication that the ideal, Santayana's primary concern, can no longer be realized by it. To this is added an outright identification of prose with maturity; he sees poetry as an indulgence for youth and aspiration, while a "mature and masterful mind will often despise it, and prefer to express itself laconically in prose" (p. 101). Similarly, maturity, greater service to the ideal and to the universal rather than the personal, all become associated with prose rather than with poetry in *Reason in Art*.

This shift of allegiance, however, appears conclusively only after the turn of the century. Santayana's interest in and commitment to poetry continue throughout the nineties, and, of course, he never gave up the image of the poet as the controlling metaphor for the mind. It was the transparency and functionalism of prose that became necessary for his purposes, but the poetic imagination was still the paradigm of man thinking. His notion of the creation of character in literature claims true creation, yet identifies it with a dream, in the way that Lucifer, reason itself, creates the web of the world that cannot be depended on not to deceive him. We are still in the world of the sonnet that asked which was dreaming, which waking.

The implications of this theory for art are again antirealist: "Imaginary forms then differ in dignity and beauty not according to their closeness to fact or type in nature, but according to the ease with which the normal imagination reproduces the synthesis they contain" (p. 138). And it can be invoked to sustain both a continuous revolution in taste, or, in less extreme terms, continuing gradual change as new forms provide minds with new ideas of beauty; and an appeal to tradition as well, in that the normal imagination is broadly based in fundamental human needs that change within narrow limits and is unlikely therefore to respond to the merely idiosyncratic or pointlessly iconoclastic. Here we see again the burden that devolves on normal human experience by placing the ultimate validation of values within the individual. If tradition and community fail, values are in danger from what Santayana called barbarism. He was aware, as we shall see in the essay on Browning, of the extent to which tradition and community, that is, shared concepts of value, are all that stand between normality and pathology, once the internalization of values takes place. At the same time this view contributes toward turning the artist's eye inward, for it affirms the underlying solidarity between his own ideals and other people's. Through self-dramatization he enacts the tendencies of other men.

The greatest of the imagination's creations was for Santayana the religious, taking place over a long period and modified and added to by many individuals. But it appears in *The Sense of Beauty* briefly and as a subdivision of literary creation. He ends his discussion of form with an ambiguous plea for contentment with our religious syntheses on the original grounds that they have as much veracity as any of our intellectual activities and that however our ideals may change in response to changes in our experience or our capacities, "the chief intellectual and aesthetic value of our ideas will always come from the creative imagination" (p. 144).

In the last section of *The Sense of Beauty*, Santayana considers the value beyond that of form and materials that a beautiful object may possess. It is a value that originates in the fluidity of human consciousness. There ideas emerge only to be changed or lost, fixed for a time by our construction of unities and types but never losing altogether the sense of association with other ideas arising with them in experience. This value, then, which an object has by virtue of its meaning and associations, Santayana calls expression, and finds it to consist of two terms and a necessary relation between them: the first is the object presented, a word, an image, an object—the expressive thing. The second is the object suggested, a thought, an emotion, an image—the thing expressed. The value of the thing expressed must be experienced as in the expressive object; like the value of material and form, it must be objectified to be experienced as beauty.

The possible values of the second term are many and varied. They may be esthetic themselves, such as the beauty of the characters and physical settings in Homer; or utilitarian, such as the satisfaction of curiosity by a map beautifully drawn; or functional, as in any of the circumstances of human life which may be the subject of art.

Now, since evil may be one of the values of the second term, the question arises as to the relationship of evil and beauty. Here Santayana analyzes that function that has always been vividly apparent to him and that has already served as a subject of his poetry: the capacity of art to make the painful aspects of life tolerable. This is linked in his mind with his distaste for the moral position which sees good and evil inevitably interdependent, for he is anxious to sever any dependency of beauty on evil; we are pleased, he insists, in spite of the suggestion of evil, not by it. The experience of tragic emotion consists of both the feeling of pain and the balancing of it by pleasure and in a consequent "conflict and rending of our will, this fascination by what is intrinsically terrible or sad, that gives turbid feelings their depth and pungency" (p. 170).

The beauty of the first term, which might consist of the charm or nobility of the language or behavior of the characters in a tragedy, is one of the possible elements in the "compound nature" of tragic effects. Or other expressions may be mingled with that of pain, such as a glorification of the life led by the characters. But higher than all is the compensation provided by the truth of the tragedy. At the same time Santayana finds in this compensation a danger for the esthetic experience. For as well as reconciling us to pain, truth may be used as an excuse for ugliness. In contemporary life he sees this leading to the production and admiration of work having only this justification and no intrinsic value. For expressiveness is not in itself an esthetic value; it is merely the power to call up other associations. It becomes an esthetic value, that is, expression, when the values are incorporated in the present object, which itself has material and formal values. It seemed to him that the use of the arts to record "scientific ideas and personal confessions" (p. 175) was doomed to failure. He went on to say:

But the sudden inundation of science and sentiment which has made the mind of the nineteenth century so confused by overloading us with materials and breaking up our habits of apperception and our ideals, has led to an exclusive sense of the value of expressiveness, until this has been almost identified with beauty. This exaggeration can best prove how the expression of truth may enter into the play of aesthetic forces and give a value to representations which but for it, would be repulsive. (pp. 175-76)

Nevertheless, Santayana felt that the balance of positive and negative was sufficient to explain the "wholeness . . . strength, and rapture" (p. 176) of the most profound tragedy. He found the explanation of tragedy's impact in the heroic "attitude of the will, by which the voices of the outer world are silenced, and a moral energy, flowing from within, is made to triumph over them," by which he meant the quality of feeling called sublime, an experience of liberation in the observer, not a quality of the work. In this analysis the sublime is not seen in opposition to the beautiful, as frequently occurs, but as a kind of beauty itself. Nevertheless, the presentation suffers from a lack of ultimate clarity; while what Santayana says of each, the beautiful and the sublime, seems clear, accurate, and revealing, their internal relations remain somewhat obscure.

He begins with an evocation of the conflict and chaos in the idea of the self, a state it is the "essential privilege of beauty" (p. 177) to synthesize in harmony. This is, of course, the image referred to earlier in the discussion on the definitions of beauty to be found in the book. There are two methods for achieving this harmony: one, to unify all the given elements, results in the beautiful; the other, to reject all recalcitrant elements, results in the sublime. The sublime, achieved by "exclusion, opposition and isolation," is a "cold, imperious" pleasure that raises us above the world while the beautiful is "warm, passive and pervasive" (p. 177) and identifies us with it.

Santayana doesn't clarify this double use of beauty or the simultaneous identification of the sublime with beauty and its contrast to it. His attention is really directed toward the relationship of the sublime to the evil which is the occasion of it. He conceives of the sublime as a reaction to evil, an assertion of our unity and transcendence in the face of a fate that would break and submerge us. Only an identification of the self with that idea of the self as whole and inviolable can survive the actual ruin of our lives. Again, he contrasts the sublime with the beautiful:"What we objectify in beauty is a sensation. What we objectify in the sublime is an act." He glosses Aristotle's concept of tragedy in this way: "Our pity and terror are indeed purged; we go away knowing that, however tangled the net may be in which we feel ourselves caught, there is liberation beyond, and an ultimate peace" (p. 180).

The sublime, then, is an emotion of detachment and liberation often occasioned by the expression of evil but not dependent on it. The immense is also sublime, as is the simultaneous view of many things, and he identifies an Epicurean sublime born of broad perspective that contrasts with the Stoic sublime bred by terror. It may also be a growth of wide experience and long life, in which a man who has loved many things no longer loves any of them exclusively.

Again, in conclusion, he contrasts the sublime with the beautiful, finding it superior. This conclusion is somewhat at odds in spirit, it seems to me, with most of the book, insistent as that is on the perfection of finite form and on the value of discrimination. Now, however, we are in the atmosphere of Santayana's metanoia, that whole complex of desire and loss which ended in his being able to lay claim to the whole world by giving up every particular thing in it. Here he writes:

For while in the beautiful we find the perfection of life by sinking into the object, in the sublime we find a purer and more inalienable perfection by defying the object altogether. The surprised enlargement of the vision, the sudden escape from our ordinary interests and the identification of ourselves with something permanent and superhuman, something much more abstract and inalienable than our changing personality, all this carries us away from the blurred objects before us, and raises us into a sort of ecstasy. (pp. 183-84)

Santayana's interest in the sublime and his conception of its importance as an esthetic effect were shared by important contemporaries. Heroic spiritual action with its effect of sublimity is the aim of the last great works of Henry James, as Joseph Conrad in his famous essay concludes, and Conrad paid tribute in James to those qualities and effects that he sought himself. Both of these writers shared with Santayana that passionate concern with "seeing," that identification, as Conrad expresses it, of the power of art to make us see with the power of moral revelation. For in all three men it is significance, the unity of the ideal, that is to carry the revelation, not the particularity of the actual physical world, with a resulting diminution, in differing degrees, of course, of the contribution the concrete might make to their work. When Santayana says of the sublime, "It is the pleasure of contemplation reaching such an intensity that it begins to lose its objectivity, and to declare itself, what it always fundamentally was, an inward passion of the soul" (p. 183), it is in a voice that might have whispered in the ear of the creator of Strether or Lord Jim.

Between Santayana and Henry James, a spiritual consanguinity is especially apparent, for some voice said to Santayana as clearly as James's father said to him, "Convert, convert," that is, frustration into spiritual gain. James's increasing allegiance to the sublime in his later work suggests a concerted effort somehow to possess a world in which he was an expatriate and which increasingly denied him, as he grew older, the public success he hoped for.

Santayana's observations on the comic, wit, humor, and the grotesque are miscellaneous and not particularly illuminating, except where they confirm further his conviction that "no esthetic value is really founded on the experience or the suggestion of evil" (p. 183). What appeals to us as beauty is intrinsically good, no matter how mixed with the expression of evil. Otherwise, any expression is justifiable whereas Santayana wishes to maintain that the essence of beauty is delight, not expression, and certainly not expression in the sense of artistic self-expression, an increasingly popular notion which appalled him. His emphasis on the beauty of the effect as a criterion for art is opposed to any affirmation of the world as it is, whether it was made in the spirit of optimism with Royce, or the spirit of despair. He ascribes, as Arnold did, the failure of just artistic discrimination and creation to the unpropitious times in which "the soul is subdued to what it works in, and loses its power of idealization and hope" (p. 194). It is this power that Santayana must at all costs support for it is essentially the basis of all value in his world. If man loses his power of idealization, he is at the mercy of the meaningless succession of moments as sensations in an accidental universe. The greater the deterioration of this power, the closer civilized man comes to barbarism. Whatever glimpses of perfection man has in a moment of love or contemplation, when he can use all his faculties freely and gratify all his desires, these glimpses are the origin of art which, in turn, serves to recreate them.

The conclusion of the book, then, re-emphasizes the unity of the esthetic experience, the division into material, form, and expression having been only a tool for analysis. Beauty itself is seen as indescribable and self-justifying. Our sense of it is the momentary harmony between the world and our desires, that brief peace in the "perturbed kingdom" of the self. That harmony is, after all, the image of good as well for Santayana, and it is no surprise that as the pursuit of beauty in the Platonizing sonnets ended in moral vision, so this exploration, overwhelmingly psychological and esthetic, ends in moral affirmation. His concluding sentence is "Beauty is a pledge of the possible conformity between the soul and nature, and consequently a ground of faith in the supremacy of the good" (p. 203).

By consistent emphasis on the source of all value in human preference and the origin of the pleasurable in the natural, the continuity of esthetic experience with all human experience that he insisted on at the start is maintained, and the danger of esthetic imperialism narrowly aborted. For the sense of beauty is seen to be one mode of apprehending the possible harmonies between man and his experience. The affirmation, nevertheless, is a limited one; it leaves us merely with faith in the supremacy of the good. The heart and mind are not as educable as the eye and cannot adapt themselves as easily to reality, he tells us. Just so, mind is conceived of as a poet between whose conception of the world and the world itself there is only the bridge of necessity informed by faith. Beauty is not only an earnest of good but of meaning too. Just as each individual esthetic object is a symbol, so the sense of beauty is a symbol of ultimate harmony and therefore a promise of significance, for discontinuity precludes significance. The way is open at this cultural moment, on the one hand, for a further development of art as symbolic action and, on the other, for a further integration of art into life in the pursuit of rational goals.

But this second alternative was just the road not taken. Once beauty is seen to hold out the profound gratifications of harmony and significance and the mind is seen as a poet, what need to turn back to frustrating social reality? The vision of beauty here is that of the realm evoked in the sonnet where "like a constellation, passion-quelling, / The truth of all things feeds immortal eyes." Once a writer sees how to live "amid angelic powers," what will return him to men and women?

NOTES

1. Santayana, *The Sense of Beauty: Being the Outline of Aesthetic Theory* (1896; reprinted New York: Scribners, 1936), p. 6.
2. Quoted in Irving Singer, *Santayana's Aesthetics: A Critical Introduction* (Cambridge: Harvard, 1957), p. 44.
3. An account of a conversation between Santayana and Professor Arthur Danto of Columbia University after World War II in Rome.
4. *Aesthetes and Decadents of the 1890's*, ed. Karl Beckson, Vintage original (New York: Random House, 1966), pp. 134-35.
5. Santayana, *Reason in Art, The Life of Reason*, IV (1906; reprinted New York: Scribners, 1937), p. 15.
6. Santayana, *Three Philosophical Poets*, Harvard Studies in Comparative Literature, Volume I (Cambridge: Harvard, 1910), p. 213.
7. See especially the account of estheticism at Harvard in M. F. Brown, "Santayana's American Roots," *New England Quarterly*, XXXIII (June, 1960), 435-51.
8. Frances Winwar, *Oscar Wilde and the Yellow Nineties* (New York: Harper's, 1940), pp. 29-30.
9. Santayana, *Scepticism and Animal Faith: Introduction to a System of Philosophy* (1923; reprinted New York: Dover, 1955), p. 100.

The Primacy of the Imagination

Interpretations of Poetry and Religion is a collection of essays written at various times in the nineties but with three exceptions appearing before the public for the first time in 1900. Santayana emphasized in his preface that underlying the apparent diversity of subject is a single aim that he states in two different ways. He wants to show, he writes in the first paragraph, the essential identity of religion and poetry, or, as he puts it in the last paragraph, that imagination has a moral function and religion, a poetic form, which is not to say the same thing. This discrepancy in the statement of his aim leaves room for yet another version, for the real aim of this collection of essays is the assertion of the primacy of the imagination in human life. Published in that year when the century turned, tempting the mind to see culminations and inaugurations, it calls up in its individual parts and in its shape as a whole one of the major conflicts of the Victorian age, its increasingly unavoidable resolution, and the possibilities bequeathed in that settlement to the new century.

In 1838 Emerson said at the Harvard Divinity School in the last address he was invited to make at Harvard for thirty years, "And thus, by his holy thoughts, Jesus serves us, and thus only." Somewhat later, in "The Study of Poetry," Arnold encouraged his countrymen to turn with him to poetry "to interpret life for us, to console us, to sustain us" and later still, in 1873, in *Literature and Dogma* he sought to apply literary criticism to the Bible as appropriate to its "approximative language thrown out at certain great objects of consciousness which it does not pretend to define fully." Finally, Santayana meditated at the end of the century on the poetry of Christian dogma. Through each of these the strands of religion, morality, and the imagination had been invariably intermingled in the attempt to rescue human values from the increasing defeat religion was sustaining from scientific attitude, dogmatic theologists, and revisionists.

Santayana's *Interpretations* includes both an attack on and a restatement of essentially romantic positions, and in this respect the work is an indication of the breakdown in the categories of classic and romantic as we approach modernist literature. They particularly lose their usefulness in labeling a complex figure like Santayana, who inherited and transcended both traditions as they manifested themselves in the nineteenth century.

The purpose of the book becomes apparent in an examination of the arrangement of its contents. The structure is essentially chronological except for the opening essay, which seeks to define the source and scope of human capacity in the realm of values, and the closing essay, which examines the nature and function of poetry, the instrument of the imagination, in that realm. The essays between trace the development and dissolution of particular mythic concepts in the history of western civilization, not through an account of their history or philosophy but through a close reading, so to speak, of the literary forms in which they were embodied. The second essay considers the pagan myths alive in the Homeric hymns. The third essay follows the dissolution of that paganism, the reduction of those myths in the Greek philosophers to conscious fables, and the rise through them of more austere symbols for organizing the cosmos, symbols which failed to meet the religious needs of the people. The fourth essay is an explication of the central symbolism of Christianity, not attempting to show, as Arnold did in his analysis of Jesus's language, that Jesus himself, at least, did not mean his parables literally, but insisting on the literal belief the early Christians had in the symbolism of their religion. By the fifth essay Santayana has arrived at the Renaissance in the first of the post-Christian essays, for he finds there the beginning of the failure of Christian symbolism except on a literary level. The spiritual aspirations and transcendental strivings have passed for a second time, in his view, from social action, from community religion to private experience and to literary rather than religious myths.

In the sixth essay, "The Absence of Religion in Shakespeare," Arnold's sea of faith has receded sufficiently from western life to leave a literature which did not any longer aspire, in Santayana's view, to myth and which no longer sought for significant organization of the world beyond social forms. In the famous seventh essay on "The Poetry of Barbarism," we are in the modern world where even those social forms have lost their significance in poetry and where the scope of usable private experience itself has been narrowed to feeling and sense. The proper uses of the imagination have been largely forgotten. But not entirely. The eighth essay is on Emerson and not on those aspects only which Santayana might very well at another time or for another purpose criticize harshly. It includes, importantly for its place in this collection, a celebration of Emerson as the type of the poet, as he might have said himself, Man Imagining. The forms rise and dissolve; the man remains unattached to any one of them, but utterly loyal to the process that produced them and to the meaning they body forth. Similarly, in the ninth essay, the Frenchman, Jean Lahor, now forgotten, stands as an exemplar for modern life. His religion of disillusion is an attempt, in Santayana's view, to create a cosmos founded on what we really know and can really do. It is a sign that man's urge to build a civilization is not dead. The final essay, then, is, as we have said, outside the chronological order, for it says finally: here, this is the way it works. All the myths that live and die, this is where they came from and how they are made. But in another sense it remains part of the chronology, for it announces one of the great themes of modern poetry, the source of its own being, the myth-making imagination itself. The closest analysis of religion yields a meaning inseparable from its form; in its greatest significance it is swallowed up by poetry.

This is the shape of the book, then, a kind of explication of the dominant myths of the western world with a view to salvaging their life-giving technique for the health of civilization. The tone is never destructive. The essays are dominated by admiration for what past societies were able to do, while his own thrashed about apparently impotent. It is an enormously valuable moment in that search for a usable past, both cultural and psychic, which came to dominate modernist intellectual life. It was inspired by Matthew Arnold, no doubt, but differed from him, as we shall see. It differed also from later Freudian analysis of similar subjects in its concern for ends rather than origins and in the fact that Freudian analysis tended to be reductionist and demolitionist, even if that was not the initial intent. Religion and myth were placed in the vise of the "nothing but." They became in dream and in literature an occasion for the achievement of personal psychic freedom, a new state in which the functions of the imagination remained obscure.

The spirit of the book is very close in an essential way to Emerson. While the value Santayana places on tradition seems at first quite in opposition to Emerson, on reflection it is clear that he does not urge a building on that tradition in the conventional classic manner. He, too, urges us, in Emerson's famous phrase from *Nature,* to "enjoy an original relation to the universe"; on that his hope for a new synthesis rests.

The first essay, "Understanding, Imagination and Mysticism," seeks to understand the basic features of the matrix from which human values emerge. One of the initial steps in this effort is to deny the romantic distinction between the understanding and the imagination. In Santayana's view, concepts arise in the mind spontaneously bred from the interaction of our perceptions and our nervous systems. Some prove useful in our life in the world and are called ideas of the understanding; the others remain products of the imagination: " . . . we discriminate various functions in a life that is dynamically one."[1] Darwinian biology dominates this view of the origin of thought. It is an accident, useful in adaptation, and thus comes to be dominant in the species. In *Reason in Common Sense*, Santayana amplifies the way concepts come into being, but the notion of spontaneity never disappears and becomes especially prominent in the development of his idea of essence. Essence also emerges from analysis of rational function, and it, too, is free, undetermined by the external physical universe for which it comes to serve as symbol in the life of the mind.

Those concepts that can be validated by action and sense, the argument of *Interpretations* continues, compose a poor stock for the understanding trying to deal with the mysteries of existence. The imagination must then be invoked. "Thus the stone which the builder, understanding, rejected, becomes the chief stone of the corner; the intuitions which science could not use remain the inspiration of poetry and religion" (pp. 6-7). But then, Santayana points out, his contemporaries have customarily called it revelation or higher reason. This bit of analysis is imbued with the same spirit Arnold brought to the analysis of New Testament language. In *Literature and Dogma*, Arnold repeatedly attacked misguided attempts to validate religion on pseudo-scientific grounds but appealed to our own emotional experience of the truth of Jesus's words as we act on them. This is the same validation that Santayana invokes when he explains:

Faith and the higher reason of the metaphysicians are therefore forms of imagination believed to be avenues to truth, as dreams or oracles may sometimes be truthful, not because their necessary correspondence to truth can be demonstrated, for then they would be portions of science, but because a man dwelling on those intuitions is conscious of a certain moral transformation, of a certain warmth and energy of life. This emotion, heightening his ideas and giving them power over his will, he calls faith or high philosophy, and under its dominion he is able to face his destiny with enthusiasm, or at least with composure. (p. 8)

Santayana goes beyond Arnold in realizing that once these forms are subjected to defense and analysis, whether friendly or hostile, it is a sign that they have lost that capacity to transform our lives. Arnold's emphasis on that ability as the true function of the Bible is what Kenneth Burke might call rhetorical compensation for that loss. Having once isolated the secret and method of Jesus, as he called them, and their role in helping men to concentrate their energies on their moral conduct, that area composing three-quarters of their lives which eluded their wills, Arnold stopped. He did not see the difficulties in substituting the esoteric religious ideas of Christianity for its exoteric ones. Did he think they would be easier to live by in an acquisitive, materialist society than the founders of Christianity did in their simpler agricultural world? In spite of his references to the *Zeitgeist*, Arnold seems not wholly to have accepted the organic unity of religious ideas and their forms. He could no longer take seriously the social manifestations of Christianity, but he could not envision, as Santayana could, any other foundation for moral values. His primary concern in religion is its connection with conduct, as he prefers to call it. Arnold seems to suffer from a loss of faith in the creative capacity of man that causes him to be deeply attached to a form he no longer believes in for the sake of its significance, which remained vital for him. He could not envision a new form of that perennial secret and method which would be adequate and meaningful for his contemporaries in the way he was futilely striving to make Christianity. There is a temptation to see in this a reflection of a sense of loss of his own creativity, revealed in his decision to stop writing poetry. Is it a coincidence that poets like Arnold and Eliot write literary criticism in their prime and take religious tradition for a subject when the large body of their verse is behind them? Poetry is conceived of by Arnold as a criticism of life, not as Santayana saw it, another life in itself, sensuous as real life is, but free. In this Santayana followed Emerson, who said of poets that they were free and made free. Arnold is attached to the past in a way that Santayana is not, because revelation took place there. Santayana is critical of the barbarism of modern life in the way that Arnold is, and he sees the failure of contemporary poetry, but, like Emerson, he believes in a continuing revelation. He looks at Christianity in the same perspective as pagan religion. Neither is a contemporary form of the imagination, but he does not hold on to them for fear new forms will not arise. Those who see him only as an advocate of classical culture misinterpret the significance of his admiration of tradition, just as they underestimate the complexity of his relations to it. Arnold concerns himself with the moral fabric of society as if great art could grow only out of particular moral contexts. To a certain extent Santayana shares this view; that is, he believes certain social views are more productive of art than others, but a sense of morality itself, discrimination of values, is what he believed to be essential for art; particular moral choices were private and depended everywhere on internal harmonies not to be dictated by convention. To the extent that Santayana did not require, as Arnold did, a determining social situation, he resembles Emerson and Henry James, who also believed there was a moral tradition available to the individual, transcending any continuing social tradition. If men rise at all above feelings and sense to concepts of value, then art can grow. Santayana is willing to trust the continuation of human nature to produce ideals and pursues his task of showing how those ideals and the realities of life together produced art. That the ideals might be quite different, even conflicting, did not disturb him. He expected it. *Three Philosophic Poets* and "The Poetry of Barbarism" are testaments to his ability to understand radically different achievements in poetry, to make the difficult discrimination, not between good and bad poetry, which is not so hard to do, but between good and better, and to document that discrimination with detail and analysis.

However, the emphasis on a morality that transcends society, the trust in individuals apart from their social roles that he shared with James and Emerson, was precisely one of the forces which weakened modernist literature's ties with actual social relations and encouraged the view of literature as a closed, self-sufficient world.

Santayana was also able to perceive a greater threat to the strivings of the imagination than the convention or scepticism that so occupied Arnold. He recognized that once the forms of religion and science were seen to originate in the human mind, many, perhaps the most thoughtful, would be appalled at the relativity of all values so derived and would mistakenly embark on a search for some value, some knowledge not so derived. In *The Sense of Beauty*, Santayana had demonstrated his own ability to maintain a delicately balanced view of values in which their roots lay in individual experience as did their sanction, while they were valid for the community to the degree that that experience was shared by the species, but valid for the individual no matter what their communal fate— absolute for him as every preference is, but in no other sense. He was satisfied that there could be no other kind of absolute value. The search for it could only lead varying distances along the road to the disintegration of human powers he called mysticism, of which the essence was the "surrender of a category of thought on account of the discovery of its relativity" (*Interpretations*, p. 14). In an analysis similar to the one he subjected post-rational religion to in *Reason in Science*, the search for an absolute uninfected by humanity is, in fact, revealed to be a surrender of all human ideals and passions in favor of one human ideal and passion: absolute truth. Furthermore, to "aspire to see, reason and judge in no specific or finite manner" was "not to see, reason or judge at all." It was an abdication of humanity supposedly made in favor of the superhuman but actually on behalf of the subhuman.

Yet, Santayana points out, it is a movement of the imagination which so carries the mystic away from the ideal of human reason. It is as legitimate in its origin as any imaginative act. The human mind is drawn naturally to abstractions; they are a promise of perfection and of harmony. But, although Santayana does not discuss this aspect, to the poet they are fatal. He speaks of the "better side of mysticism" being "an aesthetic interest in large unities and cosmic laws" (p. 19). Esthetic attitudes are, of course, self-validating and individual. Santayana's preference at this point is not esthetic, that is, from the perspective of the sense of beauty, but instrumental, that is, from the point of view of the poet, whose medium is the concrete sensuous detail of the world and whose forms depend on discrimination and preference. Santayana, we are reminded, had given up hope of possessing the world personally, but symbolically he meant to have it all, and only an imagination committed both to the concrete and to the values that come out of it was capable of that creative feat.

If the imagination merely alienates us from reality, without giving us either a model for its correction or a glimpse into its structure, it becomes the refuge of poetical selfishness. Such selfishness is barren, and the fancy feeding only on itself, grows leaner every day. (p. 20)

In view of this attack on the tendency Santayana calls mysticism, which encompassed most of the forms of idealism current in the nineteenth century, it is interesting to puzzle over one of William James's reactions to *Interpretations of Poetry and Religion*:

... how fantastic a philosophy!—as if the "world of values" *were* independent of existence. It is only as *being*, that one thing is better than another. The idea of darkness is as good as that of light, as ideas. There is more value in light's *being*. And the exquisite consolation, when you have ascertained the badness of all fact, in knowing that badness is inferior to goodness, to the end—it only rubs the pessimism in. A man whose egg at breakfast turns out always bad says to himself, "Well, bad and good are not the same, anyhow." That is just the trouble! Moreover, when you come down to the facts, what do your harmonious and integral ideal systems prove to be? in the concrete? Always things burst by the growing content of experience. Dramatic unities; laws of versification; ecclesiastical systems; scholastic doctrines. Bah! Give me Walt Whitman and Browning ten times over, much as the perverse ugliness of the latter at times irritates me, and intensely as I have enjoyed Santayana's attack. The barbarians are in the line of mental growth, and those who do insist that the ideal and the real are dynamically continuous are those by whom the world is to be saved. But I'm nevertheless delighted that the other view, always existing in the world, should at last have found so splendidly impertinent an expression among ourselves.[2]

Something keeps William James from seeing that it is precisely the dynamic continuity of the real and the ideal that Santayana's work is all about. To him the various cultural forms of the imagination Santayana traces loom threateningly between him and the experience he sought alternatively to open himself to in its most primitive form and to dominate by effort of will. Although James speaks of the ideal, his reaction to form here is so gross and so determined by what he imagines Santayana's position to be, in terms of conventional classic positions, that one wonders if he could really conceive of any ideal, so uncongenial is its necessary formal aspect to him. Perhaps the same mechanism operates in this almost willful misunderstanding as in his inability to read his brother's novels. Perhaps the world of feelings and immediate personal reactions was so problematic that any strategy for dealing with it other than direct physical confrontation was an overwhelming hindrance.

Santayana, attacking just that kind of philosophic justification of the status quo that enraged James in his zeal for active intervention in life, must have been taken aback at James's reaction. He wrote to assure James:

> . . . apart from temperament, I am nearer to you than you now believe. What you say, for instance, about the value of the good lying in its existence and about the continuity of the world of values with that of fact, is not different from what I should admit. Ideals would be irrelevant if they were not natural entelechies, if they were not called for by something that exists and if, consequently, their realization would not be a present and actual good. And the point in insisting that all the eggs at breakfast are rotten is nothing at all except the consequent possibility and endeavor to find good eggs for the morrow. The only thing I object to and absolutely abhor is the assertion that all the eggs indiscriminately are good because the hen has laid them. (*William James*, II, 320-21)

This last is a rejection of the idea that experience was good in itself.

Late in his life Santayana was in turn to criticize James for the inadequacy of his ideals to his experience, to see him as handicapped in following the true implications of his philosophic explorations, his own inherited system burst by the content of his experience which he nevertheless was unable to throw off completely. He describes him as "worried about what *ought* to be believed and the awful deprivations of disbelieving . . . . and he was bent on finding new and empirical reasons for clinging to free-will, departed spirits, and tutelary gods."[3]

The criticism that James makes of Santayana can itself be criticized not only on the grounds of its inappropriateness but also as revealing a concept of experience in which the synthetic powers of the imagination, rational and creative, are seen as less real than sensuous experience and feeling. Santayana was not guilty of such a simplification. It is in terms of his more complicated notion of reality that the tendency to mysticism, while potentially a great threat to the fullest apprehension of experience, might nevertheless be particularly useful, especially for a poet:

" . . . a partial mysticism often serves to bring out with wonderful intensity those underlying strata of experience which it has not yet decomposed. The razing of the edifice of reason may sometimes discover its foundations" (*Interpretations*, p. 15). In fact, in the last essay of *Interpretations* this will appear as a major aspect of the method and function of poetry, but the purpose of this first essay would be obscured by following up this theme. Here the creative imagination must emerge in unquestioned primacy. For the "truth beyond the conventional truth," the "life behind human existence" which the mystic sought in the wrong place, Santayana looked to the future discoveries of science and history, but without the illusion that James seems to harbor in his letter that science was any less a form of the imagination than those dramatic unities and ecclesiastical systems he so vehemently swept away from between him and experience.

The spectacle which science and history now spread before us is as far beyond the experience of an ephemeral insect as any Absolute can be beyond our own; yet we have put that spectacle together out of just such sensations as the insect may have—out of this sunlight and this buzz and these momentary throbs of existence. The understanding has indeed supervened, but it has supervened not to deny the validity of those sensations, but to combine their messages. We may still continue in the same path, by the indefinite extension of science over a world of experience and of intelligible truth. Is that insufficient for our ambition? With a world so full of stuff before him, I can hardly conceive what morbid instinct can tempt a man to look elsewhere for wider vistas, unless it be unwillingness to endure the sadness and the discipline of the truth. (p. 21)

There begins to emerge from this one reason why—when Santayana's theory of creativity is so grounded in the natural world, his values so sanctioned by experience, his ideas of art so dominated by the visual—the actual physical world should figure so marginally in his writing. Science is also intent on a physical world that hovers in a ghostly fashion behind its analytic or synthetic results. What, after all, did Conrad mean to make us "see"? Not the sunlight, buzz, and throb of existence, but the significance of it. This art is a way of knowing, and a way of knowing what is "out there," what is not the self. Paradoxically, in a poetry that is not concerned with external reality, symbolist poetry, the physical object seems to figure more prominently, but in a special sense, as it figures in a dream, heavier with meaning than existence. Santayana wrote about the symbolists in these terms:

. . . poets who are fascinated by pure sense and seek to write poems about it are called not impressionists, but symbolists; for in trying to render some absolute sensation they render rather the field of association in which the sensation lies, or the emotions and half-thoughts that shoot and play about it in their fancy. They become—against their will, perhaps—psychological poets, ringers of mental chimes, and listeners for the chance overtones of consciousness. Hence we call them symbolists, mixing perhaps some shade of disparagement in the term, as if they were symbolists of an empty, super-subtle, or fatuous sort. For they play with things, luxuriously, making them symbols for their thoughts, instead of mending their thoughts intelligently to render them symbols for things. (*Three Philosophical Poets,* pp. 56-57)

To tell us, in short, about the world, not about the inner man. Santayana's overwhelming experience was that the world was intractable, and since consciousness was not, wisdom consisted, as evolution did, in adaptation. What Santayana is concerned about here is the proper direction of the pointing finger, which, like the Zen Buddhist, he didn't want confused with the moon. The reality to be prized was not the thought, in internal consciousness, but the world out there, the proper object of our attention and our concern, to know it our only salvation. Yet, ironically, his concept of poetry as another life in itself helped to turn the poet away from the intractable world.

For, as he carried on the Emersonian belief in the imagination as revelation, he believed also that ultimately all our knowledge was the knowledge of our own imaginative forms. Still, the temper and intent of the men diverge. When, in *Nature,* Emerson stood on the bare common, glad to the brink of fear, he wrote of the experience:

I become a transparent eyeball; I am nothing; I see all; the currents of the Universal Being circulate through me; I am part or parcel of God. The name of the nearest friend sounds then foreign and accidental: to be brothers, to be acquaintances, master or servant, is then a trifle and a disturbance. I am the lover of uncontained and immortal beauty.

This was the mysticism that, raising one form of the imagination above all others, threatened the proper function of imagination. Other forms of life became foreign and accidental. In identifying himself utterly with that one form, Emerson believed himself identified with divine creativity itself. The uncontained beauty is absence of form, that illusion of infinite perfection Santayana analyzed in *The Sense of Beauty.* The concrete world becomes a trifle and a disturbance. It is this experience that permitted Emerson to entertain the preposterously exalted notion of the potency of the human will. What he seemed to understand at times as an analogy of the creative imagination with actual creation, he confused at others with a real identification of the two. Santayana never forgot it was an analogy. Real creation went on, he remembered, in the world which was not himself. Social relations in themselves might be trifling at times, but the physical and emotional relations that lay beneath were always momentous and always disturbing. He had a respect for the physical world that was missing both in Emerson and in the symbolists, both of whom used it, on a different scale, as a reflection of their own souls. In both there is a passivity in the use, as if the world were an *art trouvé*; while in Santayana there is a sense of confrontation and an urge to dominate that is closer to William James. For this is the double aspect of Santayana's emotional and intellectual strategy. While the world is intractable and the mind adapts, its very adaptation is the mode in which it dominates: knowledge is power.

Nevertheless, the transcendental analysis of knowledge had been made. Since Santayana did not wish to use the common-sense world to symbolize his own thoughts, there was no other way for it to figure prominently in a body of writing dedicated, on the one hand, to understanding how the buzz and sunlight and momentary throb turned into things, ideas about things, and judgments on things, and, on the other, to exploring the method by which that buzz and throb could be retained by removing them altogether from their physical existence. That is why his critical achievement is greater than his poetic work. Although he recognized the need for the concrete world to appear in poetry, his energy is absorbed by demonstration of its proper use, rather than by the actual use itself.

He clearly feels at the end of his essay on understanding, imagination, and mysticism that he has naturalized the imagination in the way he naturalized his religious beliefs in the first sonnet sequence:

If we renounced mysticism altogether and kept imagination in its place, would we not live in a clearer and safer world, as well as in a truer? Nay, are we sure that this gradually unfolding, intelligible, and real world would not turn out to be more congenial and beautiful than any willful fiction, since it would be the product of a universal human labour and the scene of the accumulated sufferings and triumphs of mankind? When we compare the temple which we call Nature, built of sights and sounds by memory and understanding, with all the wonderful worlds evocable by the magician's wand, may we not prefer the humbler and more lasting edifice, not only as a dwelling, but even as a house of prayer? (*Interpretations*, p. 22)

By showing that the understanding and the imagination were two aspects of the same function, he hoped to dispel the mystification with which romanticism had surrounded imagination. He hoped thereby to return it to this world purged of its transcendental humors, even as he had descended from the "piteous height" at which his "sad youth worshipped" in his earliest sonnet. His aim here is that of the first sonnet sequence, to establish the life of the spirit on a naturalistic basis. He calls us in that last sentence, as Stevens was to do in "Sunday Morning," to prefer nature as the most enduring paradise we know and to worship there. He evokes the suffering, striving community of mankind both for sanction and for unction. It is a note struck commonly by writers who share both Santayana's naturalism and his exalted view of creative process, like Conrad and Stephen Crane. It speaks again of Santayana's unwillingness to rest his view of art wholly on such unsafe ground as the individual consciousness. But the appeal to community pales here, as it does in his own work, and that of other writers to follow, beside the image of "memory and understanding" building nature itself, a feat truly surpassing any magician's. The imagination, insofar as it is that function of the mind that produces "willful fiction," is cast down, but its world-building capacity is transferred to the understanding and there enhanced and ennobled to something transcending its original status. This transformation is yet another instance of how the attempt to establish values on a natural foundation leads to the elevation of man as artist, the maker of the world he knows.

Santayana conceived of the development and dissolution of paganism and Christianity as analogous movements in the history of the imagination. No such movements seemed possible in his own times. For the religious imagination differed in one crucial aspect from the poetic: it compelled belief and influenced conduct. He does not make the distinction Arnold makes between religion and Aberglaube in which the latter in some way sets in and corrupts the former. He conceives of the initial religious interpretation, like language and art, as being spontaneous, and becoming superstition rather than poetry because of "the initial incapacity in people to discriminate the objects of imagination from those of the understanding" ("The Poetry of Christian Dogma," *Interpretations*, p. 108). Religious ideas endure if they turn out to have moral significance, that is, if they correspond to natural human demands. "In Darwinian language, moral significance has been a spontaneous variation of superstition, and this variation has insured its survival as a religion."

Compare this with Frazer's attitude in an obituary notice he wrote for the great comparative religionist, Robertson Smith, in 1894:

Regarded thus far, the comparative study of religion possesses a purely historical or antiquarian interest. It explains what the religious beliefs and practices of mankind have been and are, but it supplies no answer to the questions, Are these beliefs true? Are these practices wise? But though it cannot answer these questions directly, it often furnishes us indirectly with at least a probable answer to them; for it proves that many religious doctrines and practices are based on primitive conceptions which most civilized and educated men have long agreed in abandoning as mistaken. From this it is a natural and often a probable inference that doctrines so based are false, and that practices so based are foolish. It should be observed, however, that this inference, though natural and often probable, is never necessary and certain . . . .[4]

It appears that Santayana's perspective was not common to his forward-looking contemporaries. Frazer is as concerned with the blow his research deals to the literal truthfulness of religion as the religious writers of Arnold's generation were. In a fragment of an unpublished essay Santayana remarks that, while Arnold had told the world the Bible was literature, no one had told it that the Bible was legend. Frazer's work certainly threw light on this aspect of religion, but his focus remained on fictional elements of legend rather than on its embodiment of social and moral values. It was left to Santayana as a moral philosopher to judge the religious imagination by its fruits rather than by its origins, the only way the work of researchers like Frazer could be salvaged for constructive purposes in twentieth century literature.

Privately, Santayana agreed completely with Arnold on how to understand Christ: " . . . I take even the eschatology and the coming of the kingdom, in Christ's mouth, to be gently ironical and meant secretly in a spiritual sense. So understood, I accept his doctrine and spirit *in toto*" (*Letters*, p. 237). But he never supposed this could maintain Christianity as a religion. In this he was closer to Newman, writing on another occasion: "In a frank supernaturalism, in a tight clericalism, not in a pleasant secularization, lies . . . the sole hope of the Church."[5] In "The Poetry of Christian Dogma," he disagrees explicitly with that aspect of Arnold's criticism which seems to see the original intent of Christianity as consciously symbolic:

It is one of the greatest possible illusions in these matters to fancy that the meaning which we see in parables and mysteries was the meaning they had in the beginning, but which later misinterpretation had obscured. On the contrary—as a glance at any incipient religious movement now going on will show us—the authors of doctrines, however obvious it may be to everyone else that these doctrines have only a figurative validity, are the first dupes to their own intuitions. (*Interpretations*, p. 107)

He felt the last stage of paganism to be the same as that of Christianity, a natural theology in which the religious reformer retains the habits of "acquiescence and euphemism" which "gives his philosophy some air of being still a religion" (p. 63). He must have had Emerson partly in mind here, the Emerson whom he described as retaining the "spirit of conformity, the unction, the loyalty even unto death inspired by the religion of Jehovah" (*Interpretations*, p. 229). But the generations that are taught by such a reformer will shortly throw off the conformity and unction and come to live out their impulses without fear of divine punishment except for "a few, temperamentally suited for it, who will strive for spiritual independence and knowledge . . . . Thus irreligion for the many and Stoicism for the few is the end of natural religion in the modern world as it was in the ancient" (pp. 63-64).

As to the future of Christianity, Santayana was pessimistic. He spoke of it as a part of history. The most likely and most unfortunate outcome for civilization seemed to be the discrediting of Christianity and the failure of any new religion to develop to take its place. He saw this as the failure of western man, in spite of his domination of mechanical nature, to achieve self-knowledge or a significant view of the universe. It is the world of *The Waste Land* again that he sees.

Nevertheless, as we shall see, Santayana's highest conception of religion is not a myth believed. It is a religion radically different from those he has described, one which Lucifer himself, tempted though he was by Christ, might approve, emptied of its illusions and incapable of deception.

The essay on the absence of religion in Shakespeare is an interesting moment in cultural history. It is an attempt to explain the one thing lacking in a figure usually praised in terms of the fullness of his virtues, and Santayana does not deny Shakespeare any but the highest of accolades; his criticism is really of the moment of civilization which produced him, a civilization whose major elements of classic culture and Christian religion could never, Santayana thought, be perfectly united, so that "where Christianity was strong, the drama whose roots were Greek, either disappeared or became secular" ("The Absence of Religion in Shakespeare," *Interpretations*, p. 159). The serious consequence of this was that a poet of the Renaissance like Shakespeare and poets following him were no longer expected to deal with cosmic themes. Some themes might now be outside the poet's province, which was trivialized by these omissions. This tendency, Santayana felt, was unfortunately enhanced by the growing puritanism of religion in Shakespeare's England so that to choose religion was to choose a narrower life. It is interesting in this connection to reflect that the late romances of Shakespeare came to be understood and appreciated after the period which produced this essay and depended for their appreciation on the discovery of their mythic, essentially religious, dimensions and that they were not Christian but drew on pagan sources still alive in the countryside of sixteenth-century England. These plays were not in Santayana's mind when he wrote the following, but they inevitably come into ours when we read it:

Shakespeare himself, had it not been for the time and place in which he lived, when religion and imagination blocked rather than helped each other, would perhaps have allowed more of a cosmic back-ground to appear behind his crowded scenes. If the Christian in him was not the real man, at least the Pagan would have spoken frankly. The material forces of nature, or their vague embodiment in some northern pantheon, would then have stood behind his heroes. The various movements of events would have appeared as incidents in a larger drama to which they had at least some symbolic relation. (pp. 164-65)

But, for Santayana, Shakespeare marked the beginning of the diminution of poetry in the modern world. He was the prelude to the poetry of barbarism exemplified by Browning and Whitman. The initial strategy of the essay devoted to them is historical. These poets are seen as representative of a cultural crisis, the breakdown of values and beliefs of post-Renaissance civilization. Whereas Shakespeare's view of the world extended to man in society and history, if not beyond, Browning and Whitman were further reduced in their scope: in Browning experience consisted of "passions, characters, persons" and in Whitman of "moods and particular images" ("Poetry of Barbarism," *Interpretations*, p. 175). Santayana sees this not merely as a shift of interests culturally determined but as a disintegration of imaginative function analogous to mysticism. Still, he does not treat it as a decadence but as a new illusion; it is romanticism ultimately that he is engaged with and he recognizes its attractions, its force, and its real achievements. One of the chief merits of the essay is the recognition and appreciation of the successes of the two poets; he knows what they are about and where their genius lies. It is the inevitable ultimate failure of romanticism, as it appears to him, that he is concerned with, the failure that consists in a return to primitive experience in greater and greater degree with no promise, no desire for re-emergence. It is romanticism he is actually characterizing as "a new faith in man's absolute power, a kind of return to the inexperience and self-assurance of youth. . . . The memory of ancient disillusions has faded with time. Ignorance of the past has bred contempt for the lessons which the past might teach. Men prefer to repeat the old experiment without knowing that they repeat it" (p. 170). The use of words like "faith" and "disillusion" indicates very quickly that we are in this matter close to the emotional center of Santayana's life, and that his demonstration of the failure of romanticism and the finding of an alternative come from the same source as his poetry and is as highly invested.

In further characterizing the barbarian, he is also speaking of the romantic as a man "who regards his passions as their own excuse for being . . . who does not know his derivations nor perceive his tendencies, but who merely feels and acts, valuing in his life its force and its filling, but being careless of its purpose and form" (pp. 176-77). In Santayana's brilliant criticism of romanticism, major strands of his intellectual and emotional life come together, and we see it in the language and categories he uses. Romanticism as a breaking up of the hitherto dominant conventions of western culture finds him defending the Greek and Christian contributions he analyzes but venerates. Underneath that opposition is the opposition of art and life, the extension of experience versus the understanding of it. And underneath that, the emotional repossession of experience on an ideal plane by the dispossessed child for whom the obscure, horrible tangle of life, both the external events he witnessed and the feelings of rage and terror which he forever denied he had, could be made to yield a measure of meaning and grace only through some frame of self-discipline and distance. As an adult the horror of experience was submerged, but the obscurity remained, and he wrote in *Three Philosophical Poets*:

To be miscellaneous, to be indefinite, to be unfinished, is essential to the romantic life. May we not say that it is essential to all life, in its immediacy; and that only in reference to what is not life—to objects, ideals, and unanimities that cannot be experienced but may only be conceived—can life become rational and truly progressive? Herein we may see the radical and inalienable excellence of romanticism; its sincerity, freedom, richness, and infinity. Herein, too, we may see its limitations, in that it cannot fix or trust any of its ideals, and blindly believes the universe to be as wayward as itself, so that nature and art are always slipping through its fingers. It is obstinately empirical, and will never learn anything from experience. (p. 178)

The dominating concept here again is learning from experience; knowledge is safety as well as power. What has happened is the identification in Santayana of knowledge with progress and with culture as well as science with art. In contrast, the romantic ideal of the mere repetition of experience is seen as the surrender of the possibility of culture altogether. Behind this concept there is also a controlling figure in this passage, the figure of a child, wayward, full of potential, free, innocent of concepts, incapable of art, frustrated. To be an adult is to be unified, definite, finished: potentiality matures into form; instead of slipping through his fingers, life becomes responsive as material is to an artist. And above all in importance to the man who remembers the bewildered child gazing at his cousin's dead baby, an adult "knows."

He wrote of Faust:

Every romantic ideal, once realized, disenchants. No matter what we attain, our dissatisfaction must be perpetual. Thus the vision of the universe, which Faust now has before him, is, he remembers, only a vision; it is a theory or conception . . . . Experience, as it comes to him who lives and works, is not given by that theoretical vision; in science experience is turned into so many reviewed events, the passage of so much substance through so many forms. But Faust does not want an image or description of reality; he yearns to enact and to become the reality itself. (*Three Philosophical Poets*, p. 141)

But knowledge, as we have seen, is precisely an "image" of reality. Nature made us poets, Santayana thought; it was the very condition of our knowing anything. If we become the reality, we lose even the possibility of becoming aware of achieving our aim. If we are aware, then to that extent we have fallen short. Santayana uses the transformation of science, rather than art, here as the contrast to the romantic yearning for identity with experience. Basically it is the distinction he made in the essay on mysticism, imagination, and the understanding between constructive imagination and mystical disintegration, which operates downward toward the primitive components of experience as well as upwards toward overarching abstractions. It is important to see that it is neither traditional culture, nor religion, nor some kind of art alone that Santayana opposes to the romantic ideal, which might make him seem as he did to William James, merely a "representative of moribund Latinity" beating the drum for dramatic unities or scholastic doctrines; it is the dominating form of the modern imagination, the vanguard of the nineteenth century, science itself, which is opposed to it. In a sense, the success of science was the mainstay of Santayana's faith in the potency of the modern imagination. It is reflected in his enormous admiration for the poetry of Lucretius and in his use of Darwinian terminology and concepts to explain the rise of human arts and the continuities of the human community. He went so far as to write in *Three Philosophical Poets*: "A naturalistic conception of things is a great work of imagination,—greater, I think, than any dramatic or moral mythology; it is a conception fit to inspire great poetry, and in the end, perhaps, it will prove the only conception able to inspire it" p. 27). Similarly, in 1932, he was struck by a change in the modern sensibility in terms of a reaction against science, a change, as he puts it, "from the optimism of our time. It is not our old pessimism either, but a sort of horror of mechanism, which I don't feel, perhaps because I have always believed that the universe is mechanical, and that nevertheless the spirit can be, I won't say at home in it, but supported by it" (*Letters*, p. 269). If we follow the thread of his admiration of science, it will lead us right back to poetry and through poetry to the distance which must exist, despite the romantic's yearning, between experience and knowledge. In *Three Philosophical Poets* he writes of Dante's use of the astronomy of his own day as an effort to "see things as they are" and an example of "imaginative maturity." He strikes the same note there as he does at the beginning of *Interpretations of Poetry and Religion,* where he directs us to seek for the proper field of the imagination in the discoverable and the possible. He also uses it as an occasion to criticize the trivialization of poetry that he described as beginning with the disappearance of religion as a subject of Shakespeare: "It is those of us who are too feeble to conceive and master the real world, or too cowardly to face it, that run away from it to those cheap fictions that alone seem to us fine enough for poetry or for religion. In Dante the fancy is not empty or arbitrary; it is serious, fed on the study of real things" (p. 113).

Science also leads him to a criticism of any estheticism that finds theory to be unpoetical and to a defense of the life of theory as being as human and natural as the life of the senses. Philosophy ought to enter a poet's work, he thought, because it is in his life:

To object to theory in poetry would be like objecting to words there; for words, too, are symbols without the sensuous character of the things they stand for; and yet it is only by the net of new connections which words throw over things, in recalling them, that poetry arises at all. Poetry is an attenuation, a rehandling, an echo of crude experience; it is itself a theoretic vision of things at arm's length. (p. 114)

We have seen that image "at arm's length," before, where more could be seen than felt at close quarters. It is the necessary condition for every sort of imaginative transformation. What William James failed to see in Santayana was that he was urging not *a* system, but *some* system, not *the* tradition, but *a* tradition. What he wants to extract is the form of the imagination itself, not the form the imagination has created. The same fascination with process is here being expressed in literary criticism that appears in his own philosophy and in other forms of pragmatism and later expressions of modernist thought. The same drive toward the making of a tradition, not merely the preserving of it, is manifested as in the twentieth-century cry, "Make it new." What was to be preserved, in Arnold's language, was the secret and method.

Santayana criticizes the poetry of Whitman and Browning largely in terms of the distance they maintain from immediate existence. He finds the essence of Whitman's genius in an ability to respond to and render again the "elementary aspects of things." He sees Whitman's absorption in and surrender to the surface images of life as being without selection or organization. In his poetry, "The world has no inside; it is a phantasmagoria of continuous vision, vivid, impressive, but monotonous and hard to distinguish in memory, like the waves of the sea or the decorations of some barbarous temple, sublime only by the infinite aggregation of parts" (*Interpretations*, p. 180). His social ideal is seen as analogous to his poetry, that of a society still in a primitive, amorphous state. Santayana acutely points out that Whitman's notion of the future of democracy was actually an ideal drawn from a passing pioneer society. The differentiation and organization of actual, evolving society was foreign to his mind, which was both sensual and mystical. But it is the "sensuality . . . touched with mysticism" which constitutes his achievement and his chief appeal is for those moments when "we are weary of conscience and ambition, and would yield ourselves for a while to the dream of sense . . . a means of escape from convention and from that fatigue and despair which lurk not far beneath the surface of conventional life." Nevertheless he is an example of the illusion mysticism furthers, that "we become divine by remaining imperfectly human" (p. 187).

Browning's achievement is conceived by Santayana to be subtler and more complex: the study of individual consciousness, its passions, and its internal movements. What he was incapable of, like Whitman, was the consideration of permanent objects outside the self. Real confrontations between people, and between people and society or some concept of destiny lay outside the limits of soliloquy; all that was available was the hero's view of them and their significance for him. The study of consciousness itself, in this way, without reference to an ideal, was, in Santayana's view, the study of "the pathology of the human mind" (*Interpretations*, p. 214), for the normal without such reference was also pathological. It is interesting to notice that Richard Le Gallienne, just a few years earlier, had characterized decadence in literature in somewhat similar terms:

In all great vital literature, the theme, great or small, is considered in all its relation to the sum-total of things . . . in decadent literature the relations, the due proportions, are ignored. One might say that literary decadence consists in the euphuistic expression of isolated observations.[6]

He further observes that it is not the use of the theme of sickness which makes for decadence, but the use of it without reference to a concept of health.

These observations suggest the literary readiness, so to speak, for the Freudian treatment of the pathology of the mind and help to account for the early acceptance and use of Freudian psychology by writers and people interested in the literary life. One might say about Freud what Santayana says of Browning: "More than any other poet he keeps a kind of speculation alive in the now large body of sentimental, eager-minded people, who no longer can find in a definite religion a form and language for their imaginative life" (*Interpretations*, p. 214).

Another point suggested by Santayana's characterization of Browning's subject as the pathology of the mind is the difficulty Freud had in distinguishing neurosis from normality without a concept of health. On the one hand, lesser eruptions of the unconscious could be termed, as one of his most famous books has it, the psychopathology of everyday life; while, on the other, the universality of unresolved conflicts can be seen as the legitimate factors in character formation.

Santayana's characterization of the study of consciousness without reference to an ideal, Le Gallienne's view of decadence in literature as expression of isolated observations without reference to some idea of the whole, and Freud's view of the eruptions of the unconscious as psychopathology share a characteristic reflective of their period. Each writer, more or less explicitly, expresses an awareness of the dissolution of a commonly held standard of value and a failure of the sense of reality as a comprehensible whole, along with a sense of the consequences of these losses for their own disciplines. Freud's grand mythology of the mind and his aim of replacing id with ego reflect a world-building impulse as great as Santayana's and as vivid a sense of the dependence of the forms of civilization on the human imagination. Nevertheless, Santayana, in his unpublished writings, criticized Freud for what seemed to him a very unsteady sense in his psychology of its own myth-making. Santayana would have liked a less intermittent sense in Freud's description of the psyche of the extent to which it was an explanation of phenomena not scientifically verified, an imaginative projection into the still unknown. Yet it was Freud's very willingness to speak as if his map were true that distinguished him from Santayana, with his insistence that every theory was heterogeneous from fact. After all, only the willingness to act as if a theory is true will bring that theory into salutary collision with things as they are. Santayana's view of theory, sound as it may be logically, and accurate as its judgment of Freud's psychology may be, emphasized a detachment encouraging a sense of the autonomy of the imagination. To be aware always of the imagined quality of theory is to inhibit action on the basis of it. We have seen, of course, that such a removal from action was just what Santayana's experience encouraged.

In a similar way his delineation of the limits of soliloquy and his description of the study of consciousness as the pathology of the mind, acute as they surely are, spring from the same need to transcend the painful contents of his own psyche. "The best things that come into a man's consciousness," in his view, "are the things that take him out of it—the rational things that are independent of his personal perception and of his personal existence" (p. 214). Just so, in his memoirs, as we have seen, his memory of the Santayana full of the pain of his own abandonment by his mother, looking at his cousin's still-born child, is the springboard for an elegant theory of how nature aborts beauty, a theory that wholly denies private, personal suffering. The rational things independent of personal perception and existence were beyond the scope of the poetry of barbarism, as T. S. Eliot was also to conclude. When Santayana describes the gift of Whitman's and Browning's poetry as an illusory consolation that the return of the primitive is progress, we understand how little of a consolation such a return could be to him.

While Whitman's and Browning's satisfaction solely with "energy and actuality" diminished his admiration for their achievement, in Emerson Santayana found a more congenial poet, whose only theme was the imagination. In him the romantic tendency to mysticism served a useful purpose, up to a point. It destroyed the conventional view of the world so that it might be built up again on different lines, with new perspectives and fresh syntheses. But Emerson made no systems. He was "like a young god making experiments in creation; he botched the work, and always began on a new and better plan" (p. 219). He figures for Santayana as his favorite image of the mind as a poet composing and recomposing experience. Yet there was danger in Emerson, in that he seemed to think that the conventions he had upset, even those of common sense, had no truth in them, that his imagination was to supplant the understanding. For Emerson, as for the other romantics, imagination was a higher faculty.

The danger he is so aware of in Emerson, that imagination would supplant the understanding, was a real temptation in his own thinking, and establishing the continuity of imagination and understanding does not eliminate it for, as we have seen, imagination tends to swallow up understanding in the figure of the mind as a poet in the same way that making esthetic experience continuous with moral experience tends to estheticize all judgment. This is the danger against which Santayana must invoke, variously, tradition, science, common sense, and what the psychologists call consensual validation. Yet, in spite of all these defenses, he could not be sure he was safe, as his Lucifer could not, from deception by the workings of his own mind. He was ultimately to fall back for assurance of the reality of his own experience on nonrational aspects of life, just as he anchors esthetic judgment in them. He came at last to invoke his own physical existence and its interaction with other physical existences as the most fundamental community he can invoke. He felt his belief in the independent existence of the world apart from his own thought to be animal in origin, irrational, and its validation by man's interaction with his world to be irrational: "In the act of eating . . . I have my radical assurance of that object bread, know its place, and continue to testify to its identity. The bread, for animal faith, is this thing I am eating, and causing to disappear to my substantial advantage . . . . In seizing and biting it I determine its identity and its place in nature, and in transforming it I prove its existence" (*Scepticism and Animal Faith*, p. 83).

That was in 1923; William James did not live to read it. This was to be in tone and perspective a different moment in his intellectual life, but it was in no way to invalidate his primary concern with rational function. It was prepared for, as we have seen by his early establishment of value in passionate preference, and discontinuity should not be overemphasized. There was rather a shifting of attention to the roots of rational function, which he had always recognized, and a weakening of its claims, which had never impressed him, to efficacy in the real world.

But in the period about 1900, science and tradition remained his chief defense against deception and the guarantee of significance for the constructive imagination. They were the basis as well of his belief that the universe might be partially dominated by human intelligence. That the Kantian revolution had made the world the creature of the mind made it no less intractable or different in any way, it seemed to him:

Because it is a law of our intelligence that two and two make four, and the implications of that law may be traced by abstract thought, the world which is subject to that arithmetical principle is not made more amenable to our higher demands than if it had been arithmetical of its own sweet will. It is not made docile by being called our creature. Indeed, what is less docile to us than ourselves? What less subject to our correction than the foundations of our own being? ... Nay, the conditions of our thought, like the predispositions of our characters, are the most fatal and inexorable of our limitations. (*Interpretations*, p. 249)

He conceived of this recognition as a surrender of illusions for the sake of the realization of social, esthetic, and scientific ideals in a civilization that would carry on the work of the Greeks in the attempt to live rationally. The result would be "a religion of disillusion," its herald, poetry. In his highest function, the poet "either devotes himself, like Homer and Dante, to the loving expression of the religion that exists, or like Lucretius or Wordsworth, to the heralding of one which he believes to be possible" (*Interpretations*, p. 286).

Yet the poet is not only the prophet of a New Jerusalem; in good Emersonian tradition, in naming it, he creates it. "The Elements and Function of Poetry" begins with a meditation on the commonplace definition of poetry as metrical discourse, in which the concept of numbers leads us first to Pythagoras, who saw the essence of things in numbers, then to the Bible, where God creates Nature from the void, and finally, to the human architect who builds with numbered and measured solids like a poet's lines. So the poet is transformed from a counter of syllables to an analogue of the divine.

In Santayana's view, the poet may be said to create in several ways. First, poetry is conceived of as a special kind of discourse, much closer to our actual experience than ordinary discourse, which is characterized in two interesting ways. It is a "bridge of prosaic associations . . .[that] carries us safe and dry to some conventional act" over the "torrent of sensation and imagery" (*Interpretations*, p. 260) that is our actual experience. Or else it is like a map dominating our "experience only as the parallels and meridians make a checkerboard of the sea" (p. 261). Irrationality and dream alternately threatened and tempted the most rational mind. "Sanity is madness put to good uses," he writes. Santayana had gathered from the pre-Freudian psychologists a pretty good idea of the difference between what the Freudians called primary and secondary process.

The poet has the ability to re-enter the underlying chaos of experience, restoring for us in his work the sense of immediate and original perception lost in common discourse. He recovers also the emotional content that is the original foundation for the grouping of data, which grow into objects and concepts in ordinary thought. For this is the feature of dream and primitive thinking, its progress is dictated not by logic, but partly by emotion and desire, and partly by contiguity and similarity. In fact, it is in following the principles of this kind of thinking that the practice of his art largely consists. By the "union of disparate things having a common overtone of feeling, the feeling itself is evoked in all its strength" (p. 263) —for he had not analyzed symbolist verse for nothing—or, in fact, it may be said to be created, arising from the conjunction of elements for the first time.

But that is not the only, perhaps not the major, sense in which a poet may be said to create. "The outer world bathed in the hues of human feeling, the inner world expressed in the forms of things,—that is the primitive condition of both before intelligence and the prosaic classification of objects have abstracted them and assigned them to their respective spheres" (p. 265). This is the condition to which the poet is able to return, in what Ernst Kris called a regression in the service of the ego.[7] He returns in order that he may construct the world again in his art, along lines dictated by his own reason and ideals; he can do in his poetry what Santayana said Emerson futilely tried to do in actuality: disintegrate "normal categories of reason in favour of various imaginative principles, on which the world might have been built, if it had been built differently" (p. 223).

It is in this double creation, first, of another world composed directly out of the sensuous components of the common sense world, and, secondly, of significance out of meaningless accident, that the poet is distinguished from the madman and the themes of art and knowledge come together again in Santayana. The entry into chaos must be only a phase in the artistic process. It is interesting to note the comment of Carl Jung to James Joyce during a conference about the mental illness of Joyce's daughter. Joyce compared her thought processes with his own writing, wondering why they were a sign of madness in her. Jung pointed out that Joyce was diving while his daughter was falling.[8]

If the poet emerges only part way from the chaos, content with " a recovery of sensuous and imaginative freedom, " his poetry remains below its highest potential, remaining on a relatively trivial level and reinforcing the popular notion of "artists and poets as inefficient and brainsick people under whose spell it would be a serious calamity to fall, although they may be called in on feast days as an ornament and luxury together with the cooks, hairdressers, and florists" (*Interpretations*, p. 267).

Rising to his fullest capacity, the poet makes another world, filling it with people, landscape and actions, all of which are, as Santayana puts it, "correlative objects" for his emotions, which refer to the world of nature and history, the original source of those emotions, and whose movements and destinies reveal the significance of the world where our own lives go on, harassed and fortuitous, or desperately conventional. "The highest ideality is the comprehension of the real" (p. 284). At this point creation is revelation, for knowledge does not inhere in experience, only in art, and it is in this sense that poetry and religion may be said to be the same. They are both revelations of the meaning of our experience.

The theory of poetry, then, becomes a guide to the construction of a world he calls "the sphere of significant imagination, of relevant fiction." The moment of sublime detachment and transcendence that climaxed the first sonnet sequence at the beginning of this decade, in which truth fed immortal eyes, the image of beauty as a momentary harmony in the perturbed kingdom of the self a few years later, and now the world remade by the poet who rebuilds "the imagination to make a harmony in that." In this imagined world the disruptions, abortions, and mutilations of real life are raised above accident to the realm of fate. And in this world, life can be "conceived as a destiny, governed by principles, and issuing in the discipline and enlightenment of the will" (*Interpretations*, p. 288). In the art of his autobiography, as well as in his poetry, we have seen this theory at work.

This theory of poetry has its roots in the same need for symbolic gratification that fed his poems and his metanoia, in fact, the whole creative outrush of the decades of which this last essay of *Interpretations* is a summary and climax. While the essay begins with a vision of poetry as an analogue of divine creation, it ends with religion surrendering its illusions and ceasing to "deceive." This last word is one which has echoed through almost two decades and one which reminds us again of the figure of Lucifer, desperate to be free of the deceptive web of his own mind's weaving, doomed to an icy death-in-life. That we remember was the fate of reason without art. But here Santayana takes intellectual possession of the only realm in which the mind can be free of the fear of deception, the realm of art, a world of knowing and significant pretense. To enter instead, as Lucifer did, the realm of truth, was to lose the world utterly, for truth is not a feature of life, but of eternity. In the first sonnet sequence, the truth feeds "immortal eyes." Through poetry we may be fed while we are alive. This is the emotional significance of Santayana's repeated merging of poetry and religion: the poet's act is sacramental and enables us to pass from the human to the transcendent. Santayana uses here in the essay, as he had in the sonnet, an image compounded of eating and seeing. He chooses the doctrine of transubstantiation to illustrate the root identity of poetry and religion. "Under the accidents of bread and wine," he writes, "lies, says the dogma, the substance of Christ's body, blood and divinity. What is that but to treat facts as an appearance, and their ideal import as a reality? And to do this is the very essence of poetry, for which everything visible is a sacrament—an outward sign of that inward grace for which the soul is thirsting" (pp. 285-86).

In three other instances Santayana's argument proceeds by food imagery, in each case mixed with a generative metaphor to demonstrate the sterility of the passions. They can never, he tells us, "breed an idea out of their own energy. This idea must be furnished by the senses, by outward experience, else the hunger of the soul will gnaw its own emptiness for ever" (p. 277). The artist whose mind is not informed by the variety of the world is not only "half-educated" but also "starved"; and those who "have no idea of a cosmic order, of general laws of life, or of an impersonal religion," mistake farce for tragedy and "in the radical disintegration of their spirit, the more they are devoured the more they fancy themselves fed" (p. 283).

But all of this food, all of this breeding is symbolic. Just as the over-arching figure for all food is the eucharist, the highest kind of poetry is religious. Amid all the fatalities and necessities in Santayana's view of life, he rejoices in " how reversible, contingent, and transferable the emotions are in respect to their objects. A doll will be loved instead of a child, a child instead of a lover, God instead of everything" (p. 278). Indeed, were the objects not so reversible, symbolic gratification would be impossible, and the fundamental satisfactions of art for Santayana would disappear. The will, which he sees as "infertile" in itself, yet infinite, can realize itself in the world the poet makes. There the self that experience mutilates will be " expanded into its latent possibilities" (p. 280). For an infinite will, art promises extravagant fulfillments: like Santayana's metanoia, the possession of the whole world in idea. Although the great actions in that imagined world may be tragic, the poet identifies not with the actors but with the power that so ordains such ends. The infertility of the will is exchanged for the creative imagination, which brings together sense and passion in the service of an order and meaning that the power which rules the actual world does not possess, an order and meaning which, but for the poetic mind, would never exist.

This profound sense of power is rationalized and articulated here with a force and elegance never exceeded in the modernist literature also energized by it. In it lies the significance of Santayana's literary career as distinct from his philosophic undertakings. After 1900 he ceased to be a poet who taught philosophy and became a philosopher who wrote poetry. He had mapped a world as a critic that he would not enter as a poet.

Just as his own creativity stemmed from the solution to problems engendered by feelings of loss and impotence, so modernist literature, in a world it depicted as fragmented, meaningless and frustrating, burgeoned with its exhilarated sense of the power of the artist. Action might be doomed, but art was triumphant. The artist became a culture hero, the maker of meanings, descending even into the chaos of prerational experience, as Santayana had envisioned him, to emerge with materials for the revelation which would be his art. Conventional views of reality were to give way, as in Santayana's formulation, before an avante garde whose members disintegrated accepted forms and reconstituted them in ways meant to be more richly true. To the extent that it was able to find overarching significance, create a new myth for its post-Christian audience, or rejuvenate and adapt old myths, it enacted Santayana's hopes. To the extent that the reconstituted world was merely truer to experience, to its sense and energy, not to the significance of it, then it realized his fears of barbarism. Out of his own successful drive to mastery and transcendence came a conception of poetry profoundly gratifying to poets and to a literary culture for which the poet is seen as a representative man. It provides for alienated men a realm in which their imaginations are primary and their egos commensurately authoritative.

THE PRIMACY OF THE IMAGINATION
NOTES

1. *Interpretations of Poetry and Religion*, p. 5.
2. Perry, *William James*, II, 319-20.
3. Santayana, *Character and Opinion in the United States* (New York: Braziller, 1955), p. 9.
4. James George Frazer, "Obituary Notice for Robertson Smith," *Fortnightly Review*, quoted in Stanley Edgar Hyman, *The Tangled Bank: Darwin, Marx, Frazer, and Freud as Imaginative Writers* (New York: Atheneum, 1962), p. 199.
5. Santayana, *Winds of Doctrine* (New York: Scribners, 1926), p. 56.
6. *Aesthetes and Decadents of the 1890's*, p. 134.
7. Ernst Kris, *Psychoanalytic Explorations in Art* (New York: International Universities Press, 1952), pp. 59-61.
8. Richard Ellman, *James Joyce* (New York: Oxford, 1959), p. 692.

Yeats and His Enchanted Stone

Through the vital center of the work of William Butler Yeats, T. S. Eliot, and Wallace Stevens, the major voices of modernist poetry in English, runs the same drive to mastery and transcendence conceived of, like Santayana's, in terms of a realm of the imagination in which the radical fragmentation and imperfection of experience might be completed and made whole. This poetic subject dominates and connects their poetry, so different in other respects, and makes of the period their work spans the distinct and new cultural moment Santayana envisioned and helped bring about. Yeats, of course, is Santayana's contemporary, and his development parallels Santayana's own emerging ideas under the pressure of a good many of the same interests. Santayana was in no sense influential in Yeats's development, but as the question of the evolution of early into mature style in Yeats has been one of the central vehicles for the exploration of the development of modernist poetry, so the analysis of the part in this evolution played by ideas about experience and imagination strikingly like Santayana's sets in sharp relief the way in which Santayana's critical theories were a summation of central changes in literary culture. They explain, as Yeats was never able to, why he stopped writing one kind of poetry in order to write another.

In 1889, only a few years after Santayana wrote in his first sonnet sequence of the sad descent of his soul from the heights of belief and of the disappearance of the Greek gods from nature, Yeats published *Crossways*. Its first poem, "The Song of the Happy Shepherd," begins:

> The woods of Arcady are dead,
> And over is their antique joy;

YEATS AND HIS ENCHANTED STONE

Of old the world on dreaming fed;
Grey Truth is now her painted toy....[1]

In it we read a mood as typical of the eighties and nineties as Santayana's
sonnets. The world of action whirls by, a "dreary dancing . . . / To the
cracked tune that Chronos sings," and "Words alone are certain good"
(p. 7). The young Yeats made the same turn from the world to the word
that Santayana observed and criticized in the French symbolists and to
which he was drawn himself. Eschew action, Yeats writes, even as the
young Santayana admonished himself, standing aside and perplexed as to
the difference between truth and dream. "Nor seek," Yeats adds, "for this
is also sooth, / To hunger fiercely after truth / Lest all thy toiling only
breeds / New dreams, new dreams; there is no truth / Save in thine own
heart." Like the Santayana of the first sonnet sequence, he, too, turns
aside from scientific truth. His comfort is to be the story of the "echo-
harbouring shell" which sings melodiously his own "fretful words" transformed and dying into "a pearly brotherhood." His work as a poet, then,
is to be such a "twisted, echo-harbouring shell," for "words alone are
certain good." The "hapless faun" lies "buried under the sleepy ground,"
just as Santayana's nymphs have vanished from their grove, but Yeats will
"dream he treads the lawn . . . / Pierced by my glad singing through," and
the poem's final truth is the admonition, "Dream, dream."

So many notes struck here are the same as in the Santayana sonnets,
but the shape and weight of the poems are quite different. Yeats surrenders to a world where truth and reality are lost together in a dream,
where words comfort by evoking an indefinite music. The word "fretful"
embodies the diminished, querulous, and soft quality of the emotions of
these early poems, just as the music strives to approximate the "murmur-
ing" ocean, which soothes the dreamer who wishes not to awaken. Santayana, however, as we have seen, though he begins his career in the same
quandary as Yeats and the other poets of the end of the century, unable
to find a solid footing in a world where every material truth dissolved,
every moral certainty evaporated, could not remain in the twilight world
of sensation and indefinite music. Strengthened by his naturalism and by
the Greek tradition that signified the seasons and the life of nature, without the pull of the Celtic Twilight that engulfed Yeats, protected by the
chaste environment of Harvard and Boston against the sensualism of a
Johnson or a Dowson, Santayana fought much earlier than Yeats to remain in a more full-bodied world. He wrote in the 1880s:

'Tis a sad love, like an eternal prayer,
And knows no keen delight, no faint surcease.
Yet from the seasons hath the earth increase,

> And heaven shines as if the gods were there.
> Had Dian passed there could no deeper peace
> Embalm the purple stretches of the air. (p. 18)

The state of longing, dissatisfaction, delight ever-elusive, pathos, the absence of strong emotion, a kind of suspension: these are all here, too. But pushing up through them is emerging a view of something real and definite, sunlit and articulated, the earth: fertile and beautiful, promising fulfillment. No more than Yeats in his early poetry, did Santayana know initially how to release himself from the suspended state of yearning and loss, but he worked through his sonnets and his attempts to define beauty towards an idea of the imagination which would enable him to enjoy the image of the earth that eludes him here. But he begins with a sense of a world of object and event, a promise of the material and the biological which Yeats does not yet entertain. Yeats's early poems are an example of the kind of language, sensibility, and imagination Santayana felt as a threat to poetry's highest function and importance. They suffer from the indeterminacy of form that forces the poem back on the sensuous and associative values Santayana thought brought beauty to music but interfered with the expressiveness of literature. In it attention is focused on the materials, on the sounds and verbal suggestion, which made for one of the lower kinds of poetry and which he saw in *The Sense of Beauty* as a tendency to surrender the use of language as an instrument of thought. To such a poetry, exploiting only indeterminate form, the reader can respond only with "those forms of apperception which we are already accustomed to." We cannot be brought "to follow new paths and see new relations" (p. 110). Such a falling back on the language itself and the formless emotions and states of reverie it summons up seemed to him an esthetic idolatry which took words for things. It promised meaning; it hinted at significance but failed to embody it in "an appropriate object" (p. 114).

There are two weaknesses, then, closely linked in Yeats's early poetry, both from the point of view of Santayana and of the mature Yeats. One is its failure, whether of intent or capacity, to embody some substantial realities of our experience, the actualities of earth and flesh because of and through which our yearnings and strivings arise. The other is the exploitation of the language for its indeterminate effects rather than for its capacity to articulate meaning through definite objects and events.

Richard Ellman, in *The Identity of Yeats*, calls our attention to "The White Birds" in relation to "Sailing to Byzantium" as an example of the thematic continuity of early and mature Yeats. He finds in "both the world of time, while much disparaged, is only partially surrendered."[2] One can see, reading the poems, what Ellman sees and what brings him to this conclusion. In both the poet wishes to be a bird, thus transcending sorrow and loss. From the perspective of the later poem, he finds in the earlier the idea of two realms and sees them used in essentially the same way as in "Sailing to Byzantium." Yet I think the desire to establish continuity misleads him. The most striking aspect of "The White Birds" so juxtaposed, is the quite different use and appearance of the two realms.

The less familiar poem would be useful here:

> I would that we were, my beloved, white birds on the foam
> of the sea!
> We tire of the flame of the meteor, before it can fade and
> flee;
> And the flame of the blue star of twilight, hung low on the
> rim of the sky,
> Has awaked in our hearts, my beloved, a sadness that may
> not die.
>
> A weariness comes from those dreamers, dew-dabbled, the
> lily and rose;
> Ah, dream not of them, my beloved, the flame of the meteor
> that goes,
> Or the flame of the blue star that lingers hung low in the fall
> of the dew:
> For I would we were changed to white birds on the wandering
> foam: I and you!
>
> I am haunted by numberless islands, and many a Danaan
> shore,
> Where Time would surely forget us, and Sorrow come near
> us no more;
> Soon far from the rose and the lily and fret of the flames
> would we be,
> Were we only white birds, my beloved, buoyed out on the
> foam of the sea! (p. 41)

First, while the bird in Byzantium does clearly image a perfection impossible in the natural world, the "white birds on the foam of the sea" do not. The poem seems to promise freedom and escape; as birds the lovers might fly to "numberless islands, and many a Danaan shore, / Where Time would surely forget" them and Sorrow as well. What these islands image is left unclear; the idea of the Greek past is blurred by the idea of the blessed isles. Is it death? Paradise? There is no indication that it is art. Simply somewhere beyond sorrow. Yet the islands and shore are not distinguished in any other way from the realm of the lily, the rose, and the flames, which, like the shepherd's world, are fretful. But the flame of the meteor and the flame of the blue star of twilight have already awaked in the lovers' hearts " a sadness that may not die." There are no indications of why the second world is beyond sorrow. Perhaps we are meant to feel merely that it is outside nature, but the world of the meteor, the blue star, the lily, and the rose hardly seems natural. The clearest distinction of the realms is the weariness of the one and the hinted energy of the other. Were the lovers birds they would be "buoyed out on the foam of the sea" rather than weighed down by their sadness, which we may infer from our own conventional associations to the rose and the lily comes from their own love and their own mortality. So the lightness and infinity of the sea foam, supported by the evoked infinity of "numberless" islands and "many a Danaan shore," carried the poet away from the fatigue and fret of his twilight world. Whether the first realm is only partially surrendered, as Ellman suggests, is in great doubt. It is nowhere clear how the second realm is related to the first. It is "far from." The birds would be sea birds, and the ideas of eternity and death are indistinctly summoned up. If we can make any judgment, it seems to me that the poet is indeed surrendering the world of time, if the world so immaterially imaged may ever be said to have been possessed.

It hardly seems necessary to recall the mastery of concrete imagery in the famous later poem which distinguishes the country the poet leaves for Byzantium. It is not merely the general natural world, it is specifically the world where creatures who die, procreate, and where birds sing of generation. Apart from this is a world of spirit within "the aged man," Byzantium, imperial, holy, hieratic, eternal, its art famed for its lack of naturalism. Here the emotions are all contained in their "appropriate objects," as Santayana would say, and we are able to speak of the meaning of the realms and their relationship. Again, we can see why Ellman concludes that the world of time is only partially surrendered. The bird, he says, while out of generation speaks of generation and is "irrevocably dependent upon the nature which it affects to spurn" (p. xxii). The bird sings "Of what is past, or passing, or to come" (p. 192). He sings, from Ellman's point of view, about time. Yet it seems to me crucial here and for Yeats's career, for the distance traveled from "The White Birds" to "Sailing to Byzantium," to make finer distinctions about the realms than that.

The Byzantium poet, "once out of nature" resolves not to take "bodily form from any natural thing." The artificiality of the bird he will imitate is the subject of the entire stanza. Ought we to see its last line, in which he sings "Of what is past, or passing, or to come," as running counter to the stanza it completes? Is it meant to bring us up short somehow with the undeniable connection of this so unnatural world to nature? I don't think so. Not yet. This is not "The Circus Animals' Desertion." It isn't about ladders. The relation of the world of art and value to the world of generation is undeniably Yeats's central theme, as it is Santayana's, and our analysis of Santayana's development should help us to see Yeats's. The last line of the stanza about the golden bird certainly refers back to the world Yeats leaves in the first stanza; the construction is insistently parallel. The three moments—past, passing, or to come—parallel the three verbs in the first stanza—begotten, born, and dies—just as this bird is set against the dying generations of birds in the first. But something has happened to transform the immediacy and materiality of the first set of three words into the second. The vocabulary of the first is that of generation, biology, mortality. The vocabulary of the second is that of abstraction, prophecy, transcendence. The first words circumscribe human life, which is the realm of time. The birds, mortal, full of their own desire, sing so that they may mate. The golden bird sees all the moments of time at once. To call up the phases of time in that way is not really to speak of time at all but of eternity. The golden bird does not sing his own desire out of his own death as the actual birds do, because in stanza three the poet has given up his own desire. The holy fire of Byzantium has consumed his heart which, "sick with desire," had not known itself. We have a moment here like that in Santayana's "Above the battlements of heaven rise," where Santayana first envisioned the world of the imagination in which "the truth of all things feeds immortal eyes": a place of value and meaning where "we live o'er, amid angelic powers, / Our lives without remorse, as if not ours, / And others' lives with love, as if our own" (p. 21). It, too, is a realm where all of time and experience is laid out before the poet from a height which speaks of his detachment from them, a detachment also achieved through the renunciation of desire. Yeats is working with the same material that engrossed the first decades of Santayana's creative life and comes to the same conclusion. The world of human experience is a world of frustrated desire, imminent loss, mortality; it can never be wholly possessed by anyone in its midst. "Sailing to Byzantium" speaks of the same discovery as Santayana's metanoia. He may possess the entire world in idea once he gives up claim to all the particular things in it. So that in one sense Ellman is mistaken: the world of time *is* entirely surrendered. Yet in another sense he is right. It is taken up again, not, however, partially, but wholly, and not, as Santayana saw was impossible, through experience itself, but through a transcendence of that experience, through the grasp of the significance and value of that experience and the embodiment of that significance in art. Furthermore, although it is a *golden* bird which signifies this new state, it is a golden *bird*; that is, the poet does not turn away as wholly from the natural world as his anger at his aging body and the generating young might suggest. In the very same moment the image of the golden bird insists on the separation of art and experience, on art's alienation from nature, and on the artist's detachment and surrender of desire, it also insists on the transformation of experience into art, on nature subsumed by art, on the artist's total possession of the world through his perspective from that golden bough.

The bird in the later poem, then, does in fact image perfection in the sense in which a perfected object is finished, whole, completely articulated, all potential actualized and known. In that sense the second world is the perfected version of the first. In the earlier poem, however, the bird flies from one undefined state to another, from an unarticulated infinite yearning to an unarticulated infinite escape from yearning. What we can see by this juxtaposition of poems is the relationship between two kinds of solutions Yeats arrived at in his poetry to progress from his early style to his mature style. One is a solution to a thematic problem, the problem of the two worlds, the discovery of the source of his dissatisfaction and fretfulness and how to overcome it. The other is the solution to the problem of form, of finding an appropriate theater for his emotions, as Santayana put it, of embodying his emotions in appropriate objects, of supplanting indeterminate forms with determinate ones. In fact, the solution to the thematic problem could not be found without the solution to the formal problem because the thematic problem involved the satisfaction of the romantic drive for total fulfillment, unattainable as long as the poet remained bound by late romantic indeterminacy and impulses to possess through merger.

"Fergus and the Druid" is another early poem which throws light on these problems and their solution. It, too, deals with the notion of two worlds, here the world of action and the world of knowledge, other faces of the worlds of time and eternity in "Sailing to Byzantium." In it Fergus finds his sovereignty a burden, specifically in his responsibility for making judgments. We are reminded by Yeats's concentration on this aspect of kingship of the difficulty of all exercise of the will in this twilight world where happiness lies in dreaming and words alone are good. Furthermore, this immobilization of will depends in turn on the indeterminate nature of the reality so represented throughout these early poems. The ultimate source of the yearning and weariness is the frustration of the will, all our desires to assert ourselves and feel our own reality in coming up hard against an external world which yields or does not yield to us but a world in which choices count, in which actions have consequences. Here, there is no reality outside us and within us only dreams and vague shifting emotions. Fergus thinks to surrender his sorrow with the responsibility to make judgments, a burden he cannot support. He chooses wisdom rather than power, so he thinks. But just as he has never really experienced power, but found it illusory, so wisdom too, is ultimately elusive and frustrating. The romantic drive for knowledge through direct experience reaches its highest point here in Fergus's transformations into the forms of life he wants to know:

> ... I have been many things—
> A green drop in the surge, a gleam of light
> Upon a sword, a fir-tree on a hill,
> An old slave grinding at a heavy quern,
> A king sitting upon a chair of gold—
> And all these things were wonderful and great;
> But now I have grown nothing, knowing all. (p. 33)

The self that knows is lost in the thing known; that surrender of the responsibility of choice, difficult as it was, and the realm of action for this realm, called wisdom, but conceived of as unreal, entails the loss of self. Some sixty years earlier Emerson was exhilarated and energized by an experience in which he saw everything and was nothing. But Emerson felt the tides of universal being course through him, and he felt himself one with the Self which animated the world. No sorrow that but joy, even if "to the brink of fear," as he put it. That Self no longer lies behind the objects of the world Yeats projects for Fergus. His dilemma is a cruel one. All action in this world is like Cuchulain's fighting in the dark wood, where reality is so hidden he cuts off his own future in the person of his son; and his final battle, ending and epitomizing all the warfare of his life, is against the sea, formless and invulnerable. Fergus was prepared to surrender power for wisdom but finds that he must give up all, his very being, for it. Yet the alternative is also a kind of annihilation. In a sense the end of both action and knowledge is annihilation. The most sought after state is difficult to distinguish from the most feared. The "Far-off, most secret, and inviolate Rose," the mystic salvation whose horn Yeats waits for in "The Secret Rose," will bring a "great wind of love and hate" to blow the stars out of the sky. Yet O'Driscoll's fate in "The Host of the Air," apparently much lamented, is to be kept from his beloved by the dream of a card game with "the host of the air." In both poems, real love remains unfulfilled. The event, whether lamented or celebrated, is fundamentally the same: the hero is either cheated of or delivered from ordinary experience by the unseen powers.

The disappearance of the ordinary world is a source of great disquietude to Yeats. Like Fergus, he is never sure that what he gains is worth what he surrenders. But at this point in his career, his answer to the failure of a sense of reality is a greater unreality, a retreat into mysticism and, structurally, a greater denial of determinate form.

He cannot, however, surrender his notion of two realms, one in which satisfaction eludes him and one in which it is entirely his—one the natural, ordinary world, the other in some way not: whether spiritual, visionary, dream, or imaginary. Just how the gratification and the reality were to be related and the realms fully articulated was by no means clear at this point. Nor in fact was such clarity an aim. He feels his resources emotionally and poetically to be wholly verbal, as he tells us in "The Song of the Happy Shepherd." Just as the world of "great and wonderful objects" is no longer supported by an absolute spiritual reality, so the world of words is no longer supported by the reality of the objective world. The emotions of the poems are almost entirely verbal, generated by language apparently, not experience to which the language refers, precisely because experience *is* no longer real, only language. The insistent anapests of "The White Birds" speak of Swinburne's influence, and we might usefully recall T. S. Eliot's essay on Swinburne, in which he speaks of just this separation of language from reality. Eliot is defending Swinburne against a charge of morbidity, claiming it to be a morbidity of language, not of human feeling. "Language in a healthy state presents the object, is so close to the object that the two are identified. They are identified in the verse of Swinburne solely because . . . language, uprooted, has adapted itself to an independent life of atmospheric nourishment. In Swinburne, for example, we see the word 'weary' flourishing in this way independent of the particular and actual weariness of flesh or spirit."[3] Eliot wrote this, of course, at the end of the second decade of the twentieth century. He was never a poet of the eighties and nineties as Yeats was. He came to the problem of the relationship of the realm of words and the realm of objects, of poetry and experience, of the spiritual and the natural, with the benefit of a Harvard education, several courses with Santayana, and Santayana's criticism of the nineties. By this time Yeats also had emerged from the world where, as Santayana feared in his first sonnet sequence, dream and truth were one.

Three things happen, then, in Yeats's work to transform him from a poet of the *fin de siècle* to the great modernist. The most important was the continuing definition of what a realm of perfection might actually be and what its relationship was to the realm of experience. The act of defining the realm of spirit by no means resulted in a further denigration of the natural realm. On the contrary, it resulted in a clearer, more faithful and fullblooded realization of the natural. Nevertheless, the mutual definitions of the realms also resulted in a turning away from the natural, not only in favor of the realm of spirit but also in favor of the process by which one might pass from the natural to the perfected. For although the spiritual realm was only sometimes conceived of as art, the process of transition was the creative process, the act of imagination, and the act itself, the exercise of symbolic power, was as gratifying as the imagined realm. And it is this exercise of symbolic power which distinguishes modernism.

Necessarily accompanying this definition of realms and their proper relations is the return to language as a carrier of significance, a preference for articulated meanings rather than vague emotional states. Language was linked again to the real world which gave it birth. No longer did Yeats need to rely on lilies, roses, or meteors. His own experience yielded the events, people, and objects to embody the significance of that experience. For he came to see, like Santayana, that this perfect realm was just the significance and meaning which always eluded men in the midst of their lives. The golden bird in Byzantium sings of the world as it is, but from a distance which enables it to comprehend that world entirely. Like Santayana, Yeats conceived of the highest ideality as the comprehension of the real.

For example, in "Easter 1916," the "terrible beauty" (p. 178) is born from the hitherto partial, insignificant, incomplete, or wasted lives of the rebels. Each of the rebels is a kind of failure as he is evoked in the opening sections. The poet has passed them with "polite meaningless words." He has lived with them "where motley is worn"; the "woman's days were spent / In ignorant good-will," and she wasted the beauty of her youth growing shrill in argument. Two others were poets who "might have won fame in the end." The last had seemed "a drunken, vainglorious lout," who had wronged the poet's friends. All of these were actors in "the casual comedy," that is, ordinary, incomplete life. Yet their singleness of purpose "enchanted" their hearts to stone. A crucial word, "enchanted," because Yeats wants a complicated idea in that stone. The death of emotion which turned the heart to stone embodies a certain cruelty and an inhumanity that is necessary for the act of rebellion. But hearts "enchanted" to stone remind us also of magic stones, mystical properties and powers that trouble life as the stone disturbs the "living stream." All ordinary life, "the horse that comes from the road, / The rider, the birds that range," all these change; but the stone does not, yet is "in the midst of all" (p. 179). The stone, which is the transformed heart of the rebel, is magical in that it brings about the event in which the terrible beauty is born. The stone is in the midst of ordinary life as the meaning of these rebels' lives, formerly meaningless, is in their action. The stone is unchanging amid changing forms; the significance of their lives is now unchanging, complete: beautiful even though terrible. The success of the action, whether the deaths were "needless," is beside the point. "That is Heaven's part," Yeats writes, "our part / To murmur name upon name." In fact, the poet clearly indicates the irrationality and failure of the action in itself when he asks: "And what if excess of love / Bewildered them till they died?" The poet is not concerned with the failure and success of action but with the way in which it has made integral and significant these scattered lives. The rebellious death has perfected them. It has not made them good, successful, intelligent, admirable. It has made them fully what they were and enabled us to comprehend them. That is the only kind of fulfillment and perfection Yeats, like Santayana, wishes to ascribe to his second realm. None of the terror of life is denied, but detached from it, understanding it, we have what Santayana calls "a glimpse into the ultimate destinies of our will" (*Interpretations*, p. 281). Like a tragic play, the Easter rebellion has detached passions from "their accidental occasions in our earthly life."

If such transformations are to be the subject of poetry, then the accidental occasions of our lives must be restored to poetry. If the unchanging significance of ever-changing objects is to be poetry's highest revelation, then those objects must be reinstated in poetry and so Yeats's language restores the relation of word and object that was absent in poems like "The Happy Shepherd" and "The White Birds." In "Words," from the 1910 volume, *The Green Helmet*, he shows quite a different attitude from the one which found words the only good:

> I had this thought a while ago,
> "My darling cannot understand
> What I have done, or what would do
> In this blind bitter land."
>
> And I grew weary of the sun
> Until my thoughts cleared up again,
> Remembering that the best I have done
> Was done to make it plain;
>
> That every year I have cried, "At length
> My darling understands it all,
> Because I have come into my strength,
> And words obey my call";
>
> That had she done so who can say
> What would have shaken from the sieve?
> I might have thrown poor words away
> And been content to live. (p. 88)

Here it is perfectly clear to Yeats that his frustrated desire is the source of his achievement—his failure of strength with his love, the origin of his success in poetry: the words, if not the woman, obey his call. But even more than that, words have been a medium of intelligence, carriers of meaning and the meaning of his actions, not simply evocations of emotional states. Thirdly, in that marvelous image of the sieve containing both the idea of straining out what is valuable and the ideas of losing substance and frustration, there is a combination of elements difficult to articulate in discursive writing. It entails the question of whether we want what goes through the sieve or what remains, just as the last two lines play ironically with the question of whether what he has gained in words through frustration is worth what he has lost. At the same time, the image shows already in 1910 the same sense of the relationship between poetry and life as "Easter 1916"; the words are strained out of life running through it as the stone of the later poem remains unchanging in the midst of the stream of ordinary things. What we see here in "Words" is the beginning of that lifelong meditation on the way the second realm emerges from the first. So, in "Vacillation," a still later poem, the Soul says, "Seek out reality, leave things that seem," and the Heart answers, "What, be a singer born and lack a theme?"

The image of the heart "enchanted" into a stone in "Easter 1916" further reflects the changes going on in the poetry. In the early volumes the idea of enchantment is a commonplace. "The host of the air" enchants many, as O'Driscoll is enchanted, with illusions and dreams and cuts them off from ordinary life and possible natural fulfillment. But, as we have seen, the poems are ambivalent toward the realm of these spirits; they also forestall disaster and blot out sorrow. One thing seems sure about them, however. In a world where humans are paralyzed, weary, ineffectual, or defeated, the spirits wield undeniable power. In "Easter 1916" that power has been rescued from faeryland and returned to actuality. Or I might better say that it is bestowed on the creative process. The people in "Easter 1916" cannot be said to be effective agents any more than those in the early poems; their action does not achieve their ends. But in the process by which beauty is born—its emergence as imperfect lives pass into perfected forms—in that process, over which the poet presides, power inheres. And that process, though it culminates in art, originates in experience.

One final aspect of "Easter 1916" which is representative of the kind of change that was accelerated in Yeats's poetry after 1909 is the violence which accompanies the transformation of experience into art. While so much in Yeats's development parallels Santayana's ideas about poetry, this aspect is strikingly dissimilar. In "The Tower," "The Statues," and "Under Ben Bulben," as well as in "Easter 1916," the exercise of the imagination is an exercise of power either associated with or directly analogous to some actual aggressive act. Santayana, as we have seen, wholly denied the rage he experienced in the face of a world so resistant to his desires. He dealt with it by focusing on and confirming the necessity of his own frustrations and affirming the vanity of his desires and the implicit powerlessness of the human condition. Understanding the mechanism of sublimation before Freudian psychology made it generally available, he was aware of his own transfer of energy to the realm of intellect and both exploited and erected into a theory the imaginative act as an act of symbolic power. It is clear from the poems that Yeats understands the imaginative act in the same way, but his temperament and psychic maneuvers are different. His emotions threaten him less, and, far from suppressing them or utterly transforming them he keeps them available and integrates them in the poems so that we are always kept aware of the roots of imagination in human passion in a way that Santayana's elegant and controlled style, although it speaks about it, cannot as forcefully embody. His images, like the one of the poet dipping into the chaos of primary sensation and emotion over which we construct our bridges of useful conventions, are likely to bring us away from experience as quickly as they can to moving and powerful conceptions about it. We never feel in his criticism the violence and threatening disaster that we do in Yeats's poetry.

So, for example, in "The Tower," the poet summons figures from his poetry along with memories and imagined images, among them the "ancient bankrupt master of this house" (p. 194), a man whom nothing could cheer, an avatar of the poet's present mood, depressed and angry at his own aging. The poet summons all to show that he is in fact not bankrupt himself, but has something to leave in the will that he will make later in the poem. They come up the stairs of the tower, all creatures of his earlier days, just as before that ancient master's "ruin came, for centuries / Rough men-at-arms, cross-gartered to the knees / Or shod in iron, climbed the narrow stairs" (p. 194). The poet's imagined figures are like the ancient master's soldiers, creatures of victorious power. Similarly, in "the Statues," the sculptors of Greece who gave form to Pythagoras's numbers "put down / All Asiatic vague immensities, / And not the banks of oars that swam upon / The many-headed foam at Salamis" (p. 322). The conquest of space by form was the true Greek victory. The actual power is here converted into a metaphor and the imaginative act is made the real power. In the last stanza, when Pearse, amid actual violence seeks power, he calls on Cuchulain, a mythic warrior, and summons the intellect, calculation, number, and measurement he symbolizes. And finally, Yeats writes in "Under Ben Bulben":

> Know that when all words are said
> And a man is fighting mad,

Something drops from eyes long blind,
He completes his partial mind,
For an instant stands at ease,
Laughs aloud, his heart at peace.
Even the wisest man grows tense
With some sort of violence
Before he can accomplish fate,
Know his work or choose his mate. (p. 342)

The moment of vision here is also the moment of highest power, when a man acts truly. It is inseparable from rage and violence. These lines speak of the illusion of detachment—even the wisest grow tense. Desire is never really surrendered. Santayana reminds us that even the pursuit of philosophy is never disinterested but meets the needs of the philosopher. Earlier. in "Leda and the Swan," Yeats asked, apparently uncertain, if Leda "put on his knowledge with his power / Before the indifferent beak could let her drop?" In "Under Ben Bulben," knowledge and power *are* one, but in the succeeding stanzas we see again that Yeats is thinking of imaginative power; the "work" is the work of art, for the poem continues:

Poet and sculptor, do the work,
Nor let the modish painter shirk
What his great forefathers did,
Bring the soul of man to God,
Make him fill the cradles right.

And the work is no less than the salvation of both the soul and the body.

There is a violence, then, in the passage from the world of ordinary life to the world of art and knowledge that is absent from Santayana. Nevertheless, the violence speaks for both the initial frustration and sense of constraint and the ultimate inflow of power and gratification by which the passage from one world to the other is marked in both writers. Furthermore, as in Santayana, whatever the awareness, and it was acute, of the importance of the realm of passion and actuality in the imaginative process, it was the product, not the place of origin, that mattered most. In "The Circus Animals' Desertion," the loss of power which the poet's old age means to him is his incapacity to make those "masterful images" which "Grew in pure mind." He remembers his early themes and says that, whatever the realities that gave them birth, "this dream itself had all my thought and love" (p. 336). And here by dream he means the imagined events. "Players and painted stage took all my love, / And not those things that they were emblems of."

Now these images are gone; his ladder is gone. The way up from the "foul rag-and-bone shop of the heart" to the realm of imagination is the ladder of Plato's *Symposium*, the steps by which the lover attains his true desire, which is eternal possession of what he loves. But, unlike the poems in which, lamenting his age, he feels he must begin to school his soul, or to make his soul as he sometimes puts it, he shows here what I think is fundamental to his sense of his poetry. He shows that his imaginative potency is fundamentally implicated in his sexual potency. Now "a broken man," he must be satisfied with his heart, but "Winter and summer till old age began / My circus animals were all on show." The growth of those masterful images in pure mind were another exercise of his potency. The faery bride and the Countess Cathleen have dwindled into the raving slut just because he can no longer possess her.

Yeats's aging was almost always a poetic resource. He seems to have gone from young manhood to old age and is no sooner finished complaining about not getting what he wants than he is complaining about no longer being able to enjoy it. He is decrepit in middle age. We are reminded that Santayana felt all the good things of life were finished at thirty, and that Eliot felt himself "an aged eagle" unseasonably. Just as the weariness of the early poems was symbolic, so is this age. Not that Yeats was not an old man when he wrote "The Circus Animals' Desertion, " but his chronology had merely caught up with his metaphors. He sailed to Byzantium before he was fifty. The physical world was no more a country for young men than for old. The lover, as Plato knew, wants his beloved forever, but in that world all things were transient.

Like the violence associated with imaginative action, the sexuality identified with it is a sign of the degree to which imaginative power both symbolized and contained actual power in Yeats's mind, and the extent to which the energies expended in the poetry are energies withdrawn from actualities. Yeats pursued an unattainable woman throughout his early maturity, and he linked that unsuccessful pursuit with his poetic success, as we have seen. Santayana, we remember, wrote Platonic love poems to an imaginary unattainable lady which he felt to be and which our analysis showed as being a moving away from passion. Similarly, Yeats wrote that in his youth he preferred "the love poetry when one sang at the same moment not the sweetheart but some spiritual principle" and that he wrote love poems which "my fellow countrymen, discerning the presence of some abstraction plainly not 'the finest peasantry above the earth,' found very obscure."[4] In the first draft of his *Autobiography*, we find that when Maud Gonne's defenses were most vulnerable to the persistent Yeats she admitted to a horror of sex and the physical side of love. It was a moment when, nevertheless, she was most likely to yield to him and his offer of marriage. Yet, in spite of Lady Gregory's advice not to leave Maud until she agreed to marry him, Yeats felt that he could not take advantage of her spiritual confusion and also that he himself was too exhausted to pursue his advantage. Such a relationship, maintained over a long period of time, in which gratification is denied must be maintained by both people. That Yeats did sustain it signals some sense in which such frustration was not enough to extinguish his desire, though frustration, if total, might be expected over a long enough time to do so. His frustration, like his aging, was not merely an accident of experience to him. It was wholly significant and fatal: it was what life meant. Frustration and aging were what constituted the "gong-tormented sea," but they were also what drove him to transcend it. Like Santayana's memories of childhood and youth, which made him see ordinary experience as mutilation, they led to the conceptions of perfection and control which both men saw as the essence of art. We ought further to remember that Yeats's weariness preceded the frustration and aging; it was already present in the early poetry. The feelings of incapacity and powerlessness in those poems are cultural, just as the aging and sexual frustration are poetic subjects, symbolic of a view of life, not merely personal emotions.

The "masterful images" he writes of in "Under Ben Bulben" grew in "pure mind." That phrase is almost the same as the one he uses in the early essay, "The Symbolism of Poetry," (1900) where he wrote:

It is the intellect that decides where the reader shall ponder over the procession of the symbols, and if the symbols are merely emotional, he gazes from amid the accidents and destinies of the world; but if the symbols are intellectual too, he becomes himself a part of pure intellect, and he is himself mingled with the procession.[5]

So, while he is still writing poetry whose distinguishing features are powerlessness and indeterminacy, he is searching for a way to go beyond it. Even before that, in 1893, he had come to oppose the intellectual to the emotional and wished to make it a force in poetry. In a book review of Buchanan's *Wandering Jew*, he calls it the "phantasy of an empty day" that "you can separate poetry from philosophy and belief" (quoted in Ellman, p. 41). The wish to emerge from the "merely emotional" and to stand outside "the accidents" of the world emerges along with the desire for determinate form. In 1903 he wrote to George Russell: "The close of the last century was full of a strange desire to get out of form, to get to some kind of disembodied beauty, and now it seems to me the contrary impulse has come."[6] But his earliest symbols were drawn from mysticism and the occult, Swedenborg and the Rosicrucians; these supplied a variety of beliefs and lifted him, as he felt, above mere accidental emotion. In such a poem as "The Secret Rose," the "great wind" will blow away that whole dreaming world he evokes in his poetry at that point. But as Santayana found so distressing in mysticism, the rose brings destruction of that world but cannot build another in its place. It brought Yeats no further along the road to the articulation of the two realms on which the mature poetry is based. Furthermore, the drive to some special knowledge beyond the world, when it meant the complete turning away from the ordinary impulses of life, was insufficient to overcome the sense of powerlessness which so debilitated the poetry. Nor did it arrest the movement away from form since symbols like the rose pointed away from experience to the ineffable while what he needed, as Santayana saw and he was later to understand, were symbols which referred to experience, which typified and made articulate the meaning of emotions and accidents. This he found under Nietzsche's stimulus. Here is one of the annotations he made in a volume of Nietzsche he read in 1902:

	Socrates	
Night		one god—denial of self in the
	Christ	soul turned toward spirit, seeking knowledge
Day	Homer	many gods—affirmation of self, the soul turned from spirit to be its mask and instrument when it seeks life (Ellman, p. 98)

The activity of Night is the same means by which he had hoped to escape the world of "The Happy Shepherd," but the world of Day is new. This little marginal note is packed full of significance on which Ellman does not comment: in it the two worlds are finally seen in their just relations. First of all, the day is associated with Homer, with action and character, which in "Under Ben Bulben" "dominate the present and engross memory." The many gods of Homer, which embody various and conflicting human impulses and passions, are juxtaposed to the one god of Christianity in whom all impulses are surrendered. In the affirmation of self the soul turns away from the spirit to be its mask and instrument. In this we are in the world of Emerson, which came to Santayana directly and to Yeats partly through Blake, whom he edited, partly through Swedenborg, whom Emerson read, and partly, as we see here, through Nietzsche, who read Emerson. The soul here is the disguise and expression of spirit, which we should understand as an undifferentiated universal power. If the soul seeks to lose itself in spirit, then the self is denied, as in the moment of ecstasy in which Emerson or Yeats sees all and is nothing. But just as Emerson saw all the forms of the world as embodiments of spirit and all of material life as the enactment of spirit, so here the soul becomes spirit's form in life. It is spirit's body. But here is an area left productively vague by the syntax of the annotation. This event is in apposition to "affirmation of self." It *is*, then, the affirmation. But the *soul* becomes the spirit's mask and instrument, not the self. How, then, is it an affirmation of *self*? Are the impulses and instincts of that self affirmed in that they are to be acted out and fulfilled? It seems not. It seems that the new life of the soul as a mask is to replace the life of the self, and yet it is to affirm it at the same time. Emerson would have said, and Nietzsche with him, that the truest life of the self is the expression of spirit, that to follow one's instinct most faithfully was to let spirit live through us. But here the self is not to be directly fulfilled but mediated through the soul's activity. And with the notion of mediated fulfillment, Yeats was ready to imagine poetic activity, like every activity, an expressive gesture taking its form from experience but the instrument of and speaking for value and meaning—the life of the soul. His fascination with systems of belief is like Santayana's and has been misunderstood as Santayana's attitude toward Catholicism has been misunderstood. Neither wants to believe, that is, to believe literally. Any system could speak of certain truths of human experience without being true in the usual sense. Furthermore, the energies that were frustrated in attempting direct affirmation were now profitably engaged in the symbolic activity.

Although Yeats never turns away from this mediated affirmation of the self, he turns as fully as Santayana away from direct affirmation. The passions, the impulses, the instincts remain always thereafter only a starting point. The poet looked away from them just as he looked away from spirit to the poetry that mediated between them. Just as Santayana thought of the romantic immersion in emotion and instinct of Whitman or the symbolists as a mysticism that destroyed the self as surely as religious mysticism, so Yeats came to think of the life of the imagination as the maintenance of the self against an attack by indeterminacy on each side. In 1934, Yeats found in Joyce, Woolf, and Pound a surrender to the unconscious that destroyed intelligent structure and compared it to an Indian mysticism in which he saw

mental and physical objects alike material, a deluge of experience breaking over us and within us, melting limits whether of line or tint; man no hard bright mirror dawdling by the dry sticks of a hedge, but a swimmer, or rather the waves themselves. (quoted in Ellman, p. 187)

However, Yeats does not continue to use the terms of his Nietzsche annotation in the same way throughout his poetry. He is likely to use self and soul with their more usual connotations as in "Vacillation," where the self refers to the life of ordinary experience and the soul to the simple transcendence of it, the turning away from self to spirit and knowledge. He is more likely to speak of the soul in its activity as mask and instrument of spirit as an anti-self, as in "Ego Dominus Tuus." This dialogue of Hic and Ille is particularly interesting in the way it brings together the two elements of Yeats's view of poetry that we have been speaking of. Hic wonders at Ille's search for images while Hic prefers to search for himself. But it is precisely this sinking back on the self, this reliance on the slender resources of the self that Yeats rejects, saying "That is our modern hope, and by its light / We have lit upon the gentle, sensitive mind / And lost the old nonchalance of the hand" (p. 158). Ille sees art opposed to action, to love of the world and its prizes; he sees it made out of the poet's fundamental frustration which all would share, even those lovers of the world, would they only awake from the common dream. All action, he says, is "the struggle of the fly in marmalade." The "lecherous" Dante finds justice and purity; the "poor, ailing and ignorant" Keats, "his senses and his heart unsatisfied," made "luxuriant song." Again we are reminded of the *Symposium* where Socrates proves that Eros is not love and beauty, but ugly and full of unsatisfied desire. Those who remain in the self know only the self; "Own nothing but their blind, stupefied hearts" (p. 159). We should be brought up short by the word "own." Up to now Ille has been speaking of not owning. "What portion in the world can the artist have?" he asks. He has nothing, only a vision. But to speak of owning a vision is to reveal how much this knowledge brought by the image of what is not the self brings with it, the imaginative possession of the world it signifies.

In "A Dialogue of Self and Soul," the role of the soul that turns away from spirit to be its mask and instrument is called the self, but we ought not to be misled by this. It is not a self that seeks itself, as Hic does. It is a self transformed by that notion of the not-self to whom human experience is no longer painful, frustrating, and guilt-ridden. Yet it does not lose the world or its identity in the process. The soul in this poem speaks for the night, for the denial of self as a release from a life experienced as "the crime of death and birth" (p. 231). The self is bidden to ascend the stair to where "intellect no longer knows / *Is* from the *Ought*, or *Knower* from the *Known*— / That is to say, ascends to Heaven," but instead the self sits contented with the sword and a remnant of a silken dress, "Emblematical of love and war." These objects, beautifully detailed and realized, embody fundamental human experience to which the self cleaves because they free him from the guilt that drives the soul to Heaven since "Only the dead can be forgiven." But the self has discovered a way to be free of that guilt. Through those objects he holds, he feels he has a "charter to commit the crime once more," the crime of life and death. Those objects signify to him the finished man, as opposed to the pain and clumsiness of the unfinished man. Seeing his own life from their perspective, he can relive his life, as Santayana does in "Above the battlements of heaven rise," without remorse. He is content to live it all again because he lives it as if it were not his own. He is no longer attached to it; he feels no responsibility. His life, like the sword, has lost its actuality to become "Emblematical of love and war."

> I am content to follow to its source
> Every event in action or in thought;
> Measure the lot; forgive myself the lot!
> When such as I cast out remorse
> So great a sweetness flows into the breast
> We must laugh and we must sing,
> We are blest by everything,
> Everything we look upon is blest. (p. 232)

No more than the sword do the circumstances of life have any power to hurt him. They have been removed from the realm of action to the realm of the imagination, where they are now vehicles of meaning, not of will. The experience of release is so great as to approximate a sense of re-entry into paradise. Very early in his career, in a brief essay called "The Moods" (1895), Yeats speaks of "argument, theory, erudition, observation" as "merely . . . illusions of our visible passing life, who must be made to serve the moods, or we have no part in eternity" (*Essays and Introductions*, p. 21). By moods he seems to have meant a feeling state which he conceives of as eternal, as opposed to any particular circumstances of life in which that mood is experienced. This dates of course from a period when visible passing life was mere illusion for Yeats, not yet raised to the importance it would come to have. But in this view, generally representative of the nineties, we see the transformation of all the elements of experience into esthetic materials. "Everything that can be seen, touched, measured, explained, understood, argued over," he goes on in the essay, in short, everything, serves the moods. The idea of the moods appears in this essay in contradistinction to explanation and scientific writing and makes the same kind of discrimination Santayana is making in this period between the instrumental and the imaginative. It shares the references to Olympus and transcendence that mark Santayana's writing. The last clause of the essay, in which the artist is "to discover immortal moods in mortal desires, an undecaying hope in our trivial ambitions, a divine love in sexual passion," might have been written by Santayana himself. This early essay differs from the later "Dialogue of Self and Soul," as Santayana's early sonnets do from the later "Elements and Function of Poetry." It emphasizes transcendence, the extent to which the accidents of life are somehow left behind, while the maturer concept firmly integrates the elements of experience in the esthetic vision. As in the Nietzsche annotation, the poet faces toward life. The sweetness that flows into his breast, the desire to laugh and sing, the feeling of blessedness—these are all signs of what it is like to be "the mask and instrument of spirit."

Similarly, when Yeats writes about the periods, the Great Years, in *A Vision*, he says he regarded them "as stylistic arrangements of experience comparable to the cubes in the drawing of Wyndham Lewis and to the ovoids in the sculpture of Brancusi. They have helped me to hold in a single thought reality and justice."[7] This way of looking at ideas is, of course, precisely the same as his way of looking at other aspects of experience and strikingly shows the effects of regarding all experience as esthetic material only. It returns us to the peculiarity of "belief" for Yeats. The ideas of *A Vision* are no more subjected to criteria of truth and falseness than any "argument, theory, erudition, observation." *They* all served the moods. The Great Years serve the ideas of reality and justice. As a result, however, although Yeats and Santayana both argue for the place of philosophy and belief in poetry, the ultimate fate of all ideas in poetry, intellectual and moral, is a fatal weakening of substance, a degradation to "stylistic arrangements." Such a view leads to the conclusion of the "Dialogue of Self and Soul," a blessed but morally indifferent state. Apparently, it was only on such terms that the life so vividly and terribly imagined in the earlier stanzas could be affirmed. We must sympathize with the bargain, yet we ought to recognize that such moral surrenders create the very circumstance Yeats in other poems so laments: centers cannot hold, and great beasts may be born when we cast out remorse. And sometimes the poet does not himself recognize the beast when it appears. So the vision of art in "Lapis Lazuli" is rich and elevated: the three Chinese with their glittering gay eyes are carved in the stone where every discoloration and every accidental crack or dent is transformed into an esthetic whole. The poet says of them and of all artists whom they typify:

> All things fall and are built again,
> And those that build them again are gay. (p. 292)

Yet this is a perspective in which only "hysterical women" worry about the possible bombing of London and the bombs themselves are reduced to balls pitched in a game by King Billy. Such a view is fully able to communicate the range and depth of esthetic experience; it embodies powerfully what art can mean in human life. But it may be woefully inadequate for other kinds of human experience. The poet himself may be enchanted by this view of life as an esthetic spectacle, as the rebels' hearts were enchanted to a stone in "Easter 1916." The view of art as "character isolated by a deed / To engross the present and dominate memory" gives way to the image of action as dance. Again this is a rich and moving symbol of wholeness and fulfillment, delight and inflooding life. Suzanne Langer has written about dance as virtual power. Through dance we conquer or see conquered all the restriction of gravity or physical limit placed on us. She points out that dance originated in ritual and magic and reflected the belief that it allowed an actual participation in power but that with these beliefs discarded it continued to exercise its ecstatic function.[8] First of all, it allows us to stand outside experience, as in "Among School Children," "where the body is not bruised to pleasure soul, / Nor beauty born out of its own despair, / Nor blear-eyed wisdom out of midnight oil" (p. 214). There is the dance, as it is in Eliot. But again the result: while it makes human suffering bearable, it also makes it indifferent to us. Secondly, it is again to exalt a transethical energy and to place our ideal of wholeness on other than a human basis. It reflects the extent to which energy and power can be imagined only in such terms at this time. And lastly, it shows the extent to which action is no longer real but wholly symbolic. Action as dance is virtual action: it has no real objects, no real goals, and cannot be frustrated. But its achievements are also virtual, not real. It effects no changes and has no consequences. But as a symbol it is superb, combining in one the ideas of freedom, control, and eroticism. But its function is, as Mrs. Langer says of dance, ecstatic. Yet we must remember that this is not the loss of individual consciousness and experience that Yeats criticized in Woolf and Joyce. For the dancer not to be distinguished from the dance is not the same as for the swimmer not to be separable from the wave. The dance is human activity, ideal but human. It is not a loss of self but a complete actualization of the self, all its desire achieved, action and goal one. The self conscious of itself only through its frustration and limitation is transformed into the self potent and free, yet defined by its appropriate activity. To this extent, then, the realm is neither transethical nor inhuman. To the degree that it enacts appropriate human behavior, it continues to make moral distinctions and to rescue from experience that part of it, however small, as Santayana put it, worthy of our love.

In the transformation, then, of Yeats from a poet of the *fin de siècle* to the modernist master, we see the same drive to articulate the worlds of experience and imagination as we saw in Santayana. The discovery of the way in which the imagination could both transform and possess the real and make its components the vehicles of meaning and value was both the energizing force and the subject of Yeats's greatest poetry, as it was the subject of Santayana's esthetic theory and criticism. The myth it created to sustain society that Santayana called for turned out to be a myth consisting wholly of the liberating and gratifying experience of art—not a myth which was much use to men in the difficult choices of action but a myth which affirmed the indifference of choices and the uniform failure of every kind of action, while it exalted as the only power men possessed the capacity to convert reality into symbol. If we compare this with Henry James's notion of the triumphant imagination, we can see how the moral component has dropped out. In James the action was likely to be, as Lambert Strether's was, for example, noble, to speak for a generosity and largeness of spirit that went with the imaginative capacity . In Yeats, however, it is the energy of spirit that is uppermost, and the qualities of the heart are as likely to suffer as not.

NOTES

1. William Butler Yeats, *The Collected Poems* (New York: Macmillan, 1952), p. 7.
2. Richard Ellman, *The Identity of Yeats,* 2nd ed. (reprinted New York: Oxford, 1968), p. xxv.
3. T. S. Eliot, *The Sacred Wood*, 3rd. ed. (London: Methuen, 1932), p. 149.
4. From unpublished draft of *Autobiography*, quoted Ellman, p. 72.
5. Yeats, *Essays and Introductions* (New York: Macmillan, 1961), p. 161.
6. Yeats, *Letters*, ed. Allen Wade (New York: Macmillan, 1955), p. 402.
7. Yeats, *A Vision* (New York: Macmillan, 1956), p. 25.
8. Suzanne Langer, chapters I and II, *Feeling and Form* (New York: Scribners, 1953).

Eliot's Refining Fire

When we turn to T. S. Eliot and Wallace Stevens, the two major voices of modernist poetry who were both students of Santayana at Harvard, we see the development of two fundamental strains of Santayana's intellectual synthesis. Stevens' work emphasizes the death of religion and our descent into the earthly garden and makes explicit the conviction that nature has made us all poets as a condition of knowledge. He is the modernist most at peace with the naturalist basis of value and the one who most exalts the unsupported power of what Eliot might see as merely human knowledge. Eliot, on the other hand, strives to fulfill roles vital to the poet as Santayana conceived him. He assumes a public voice and takes positions as the enunciator of ideals that will restore a center to the society which had lost its traditional centers, for it would be a mistake to view Eliot's Christianity as a mere refurbishment of traditional religion. Furthermore, he self-consciously assumes a position at the outset of his career as an heir of Matthew Arnold. More than either Stevens or Yeats, Eliot felt, as Santayana did, how necessary tradition was to the emergence of values, to ease the burden of the single psyche knowing otherwise only its own desire, the prison of the self as he conceived of it in the last section of *The Waste Land*, "I have heard the key / Turn in the door once and turn once only / We think of the key, each in his prison / Thinking of the key, each confirms a prison."[1] The use of tradition was the first theme in the meditation which was to bring Eliot to the articulation of the poetic imagination as the mediator between the two realms of experience and value.

Tradition was the opening wedge in his long effort, so much a continuation of Santayana's, to separate art and experience, knowledge and action, insight and energy, poetry and mere personal emotion. Tradition began by freeing us from personality, which was a prison, but it freed us also from the senseless repetitions of the past, as Santayana saw. It gave us the present. In "The Possibility of a Poetic Drama," he wrote, "By losing tradition, we lose our hold on the present." And in a review of Pound's *Quia Pauper Amavi*, he said, "Mr. Pound proceeds by acquiring the entire past, and when the entire past is acquired, the constituents fall into place and the present is revealed." Yet his sense of tradition and the past is curiously ahistorical. We remember that when Santayana wrote of the development of morality he began by conceiving of it in an historical way. Prerational, rational, and post-rational morality emerged from and were features of specific cultural contexts. Yet, no sooner had he worked out their sequence than he abolished their historicity. They became instead recurrent possibilities, not only during the life of a single culture but within a single person. Similarly, Eliot's discussion of the historical sense consists largely of the denial of history:

> ... the historical sense compels a man to write not merely with his own generation in his bones, but with a feeling that the whole of the literature of Europe from Homer and within it the whole of the literature of his own country has a simultaneous existence and composes a simultaneous order. This historical sense, which is a sense of the timeless as well as of the temporal and of the timeless and of the temporal together, is what makes a writer traditional. And it is at the same time what makes a writer most acutely conscious of his place in time, of his contemporaneity. (*The Sacred Wood*, p. 49)

Eliot doesn't care here about evolution, development, sources, influences, debts, or even what we might most obviously expect, continuities. He evokes the whole of European literature so that we imagine it in simultaneous existence with a simultaneous order, the word repeated twice as if to erase historicity effectively. And "within it" lies the present moment in literature. Not as its outcome, its issue, its development, its culmination; not as its end or any other most outlying point, however conceived, but "within it." The phrase intensifies both our sense of the present supported and held firm by the past and our sense of the whole of literature as a contained and self-sustaining order, wholly apart from the political, social, and intellectual network we call society, wholly apart from what Eliot summarily dismisses in "The Possibility of a Poetic Drama" as "conditions."

Such an order Eliot felt to be the true ground and assurance of the individual talent, not his own time, or his own emotions, or personality, or experience. The problem with romanticism, he says in "Imperfect Critics," is that it leads its disciples only back upon themselves, repeating Yeats's and Santayana's diagnosis. And in the essay on Blake in *The Sacred Wood*, he comments on the provincialism of Blake's ideas, suffering as he did, through lack of education, exclusion from the literary tradition. In "Tradition and the Individual Talent" he finds the poet's continuing development of the consciousness of the past to be a "continual surrender of himself as he is at the moment to something which is more valuable" (pp. 52-3). The distinction central to this famous and enormously influential essay is the one central to modernist poetics: the distinction between the moment and the something more valuable, between the individual and the vision of self-contained order, between the two realms of experience and art. The difference between art and the event, he tells us, is absolute. The poet is the medium by which the latter is transformed into the former. The entire second part of the essay is a restatement of the ideas we found set forth partially in *The Sense of Beauty* and then fully in "The Elements and Function of Poetry." The poet cannot be said to express anything. He is not telling us of his own life or his own emotions. In his mind combine aspects of experience to make some new event wholly poetic. Like Santayana, he wishes to show that the effect comes from many objects and details brought together and that the effect does not exist in the poet's mind, then to be expressed, but comes to exist there in the poem for the first time. "For it is neither emotion, nor recollection, nor, without distortion of meaning, tranquillity. It is a concentration ... of a very great number of experiences which to the practical and active person would not seem to be experiences at all ..." (p. 58). Nor need he seek to experience new emotions, for he can use emotions he has never experienced. Eliot makes some distinction between feeling and emotion which never becomes clear. At this point he speaks of "feelings which are not in actual emotions at all." Earlier he says, "Or great poetry may be made without the direct use of any emotion whatever: composed out of feelings solely" (p. 54). Again, he says of a passage of poetry, "But the whole effect, the dominant tone, is due to the fact that a number of floating feelings, having an affinity to this emotion by no means superficially evident, have combined with it to give us a new art emotion" (p. 57). I cannot make any consistent sense out of this usage, but on the whole he seems to want to distinguish between feelings attached to particular objects, events, images, words in the poetry, and emotions as states of mind experienced by the poet. The distinction between the two is important to him because, far more than Yeats, he wishes the poet to disown the emotion of the poetry. While one of the great subjects of Yeats's poetry was how the transformation of experience into poetry worked for the poet, Eliot focuses on the transformation itself and the disjunction between the end result and its origin. He wants to make the point *The Sense of Beauty* makes, that poetry does not "express" a poet's emotions, that it is an "expression of *significant* emotion, emotion that has its life in the poem and not in the history of the poet." The use of the word "significant" without any explanation of what it might mean speaks again for ideas incompletely articulated in the essay. He may very well mean only emotion which has its life in the poem and not in the history of the poet counts for us or should count for us. But why this should be so he does not tell us. We generally assume it means emotion that has meaning, that is representative, symbolic, but we assume this on grounds other than the essay.

What I find most striking in this essay is its narrow focus. Eliot uses Santayana's important distinction between the poet's emotion and the emotion of the poem only to emphasize the impersonality of poetry. What this might mean for the reader or for the function of poetry is left unexplored. The essay concludes with a bringing together of its two major ideas:

The emotion of art is impersonal. And the poet cannot reach this impersonality without surrendering himself wholly to the work to be done. And he is not likely to know what is to be done unless he lives in what is not merely the present, but the present moment of the past, unless he is conscious, not of what is dead, but of what is already living. (p. 59)

The purpose of tradition for the poet is to show him what work needs to be done, thus enabling him to reach the impersonality of art. The tradition, then, defines possibilities and aims, and the poet responds to it, rather than to his passions or his social experience. We must look elsewhere in *The Sacred Wood*, Eliot's first book of essays, in which "Tradition and the Individual Talent" appears, in order to appreciate the extent to which this invocation of tradition follows Santayana's, in its effort to widen poetic scope and to free poetic energies. The narrow focus of this essay speaks for the extent to which it is a reaction to the subjective world of the eighties and nineties, the world of Yeats's "Song of the Happy Shepherd" and "The White Birds," where the poet attends only to his own emotions, yet finds even these weak and attenuated, and where, turning his back on the world, he yet cannot be said to experience a self, perhaps because he turned toward it alone. This is the world that provokes Eliot's comment, "But, of course, only those who have personality and emotion know what it means to want to escape from these things" (p. 58).

We must turn to the essay on Dante to appreciate what tradition restores to an increasingly narrow poetic kingdom. There he begins by taking Paul Valéry to task for insisting on the separation of philosophy and poetry. Valéry finds philosophical poetry anomalous because philosophy seeks to create power and an instrument of power, while poetry seeks to create in us a state. Following the Santayana of *Three Philosophical Poets*, Eliot looks to Lucretius and Dante as models for philosophic poetry. His essential point about them is that they "realize" ideas in poetry; they turn theory into perception. In a vision of human life, which is what poetry should be, philosophic ideas must hold an important place since they are an important part of experience. The state of mind induced in the reader is merely his "mode of perceiving what the poet has caught in words." The poetic aim is not the state of mind but the capturing of the vision. Lucretius's shortcomings arise, not from his method, in Eliot's view, but from the fact that his philosophy was not various enough to supply material for his poetry. Dante's philosophy was. It permitted him "the most comprehensive and the most *ordered* presentation of emotions that has ever been made" (p. 168). Eliot contrasts him, interestingly, with Shakespeare, who subjects the emotions to such criticism that they are "perhaps destroyed in the process." Dante, on the other hand, does not analyze so much as show the relations among emotions. Shakespeare appears elsewhere in *The Sacred Wood* as a negative example. In the famous essay on Hamlet, Shakespeare exemplifies the failure to find the concrete objective embodiment for emotion, which is the poet's first business. In a recasting of that section in "The Elements and Function of Poetry" where Santayana describes the poet's method as the creation of a theater of the emotions, of finding or making up correlative objects for the emotions, Eliot criticizes *Hamlet* because it contains no objective correlative, as he rephrases it, for its hero's feelings. This, however, is just what Dante's allegorical method permits him triumphantly to accomplish. The devaluation of Shakespeare relative to Dante was a feature of Santayana's view of literature as well. His criticism of Shakespeare's plays lay also in their failure to achieve a philosophic synthesis, content, as he saw them, to rest in individual characters and passions. We remember that for Yeats, too, Dante was an exemplary poet and, of course, for Ezra Pound. The rediscovery of Dante and his appearance around the turn of the century in a small cheap edition was one of the many fruits of romanticism to be turned against itself. He exemplified for the younger poets what he had exemplified for Santayana, a comprehensive vision of human life in a cosmos wholly defined, its moral ends and fate understood, where nothing was accidental, lost, or wasted. Yet, with all that, his was a world not abstract or theoretical, but concrete, various, full of all aspects of life in all its possible relations. But none of those aspects and relations were treated in or for themselves but as part of a great, orderly universe.

At the same time, we can see the extent to which Eliot and his modernist generation, like Santayana, remained in Yeats's early world, "where words alone are certain good." Surely Valéry is right to say that philosophy aims to create an instrument of power while poetry hasn't to do with power. Eliot, of course, agrees that poetry hasn't to do with actual power. Eliot's own scholarship forces him to acknowledge that Dante did not conceive of his poetry as either Valéry or Eliot did. It forces him to quote Dante's claim in the *Convivio* that his design is "to lead men to knowledge and virtue." For Dante poetry could be an instrument of power. Eliot deals with this by hurrying past it and turning our attention to what, from his point of view, is really important, the way in which the episodes in the *Commedia* contain in their events the emotional significance inseparable from the allegorical and the didactic, and inseparable from the poem as a whole. Dante's allegory works for Eliot because the episodes are such realized examples of ideas wholly embodied in correlative objects. Once the philosophy is turned into something perceived, it is no longer in the realm of power but in the realm of art. Philosophy as argument, as something that might really lead men to virtue, has disappeared in Eliot's reading of Dante. He says "we accept the allegory," but not on Dante's terms; only, as Eliot calls it, as a framework. This is just what Yeats felt about his Great Years, we remember, that they were stylistic arrangements of material which permitted him to hold reality and justice in a single thought. Just so, Eliot sees Dante's allegory as an esthetic, not a moral, method. He values it because it leads to order, to wholeness. Again we hear the voice of Santayana saying in his essay on Shakespeare that "what is required for theoretic wholeness is not this system or that system but some system. Its value is not the value of truth, but that of victorious imagination" (p. 164). Philosophy is admitted into poetry on terms which Valéry would, of course, accept, in spite of the argument Eliot appears to pick with him; it is no longer an instrument of will but one of the materials of poetry. Furthermore, the use of the word "framework" highlights for us the fact that, more even than Yeats and Santayana, Eliot emphasizes the craft aspect of this use of philosophy and does so without the unction of the vocabulary of "reality and justice," which was so much a part of both Yeats's and Santayana's view of poetry.

This is consonant with the kind of poetry Eliot was writing up to the 1920s. In it questions of tone, diction, image, and rhythm are paramount, even exclusive. The effect is wholly critical and analytic. The characters and actions chosen for the two most important dramatic monologues, "Prufrock" and "Portrait of a Lady," are from a wholly private world. The characters suffer from their own heightened sensibilities and the verbal facility of their social milieu. Attention to fine distinctions, sensitivity to nuance, appreciation of the sensuous and esthetic aspects of life, an exaggerated respect for the fruits of friendship, sentimental and otherwise— all of these elements that were the very foundation of one kind of literary life of the nineties are now seen in Eliot's poetry as psychically disabling. These elements are, of course, the results, rather than the cause of the felt loss of power, arising in fact as a refuge from it, but now felt as a burden rather than a support. They remain a refuge for at least one literary circle of Eliot's generation with which he has personal ties, the Blooms- bury group, as well as the basis for at least one fully achieved though attenuated body of work, Virginia Woolf's. The difficulty of making poetry wholly without any resource but the individual sensibility is the first thing Eliot becomes self-conscious about, but following closely and inevitably, so closely are they linked, is his awareness of the more insup- portable burden of life lived under those circumstances.

So that while Eliot's initial debt to Dante is the realization of the formal uses of ideas, his ultimate debt is one of subject matter. The tradi- tion gives him first a way to speak, a way to approach his craft, but it un- covers to him, in his craftsman's phrase, the work he is to do—in the broadest sense. In *Poems 1920* we begin to see the uses of literature, the widening of the cityscape in "Gerontion" to include medieval Europe, the broadening of memory to include Thermopylae. The individual sensibility gives way to history. But the uses are random; they chiefly point to the ironic distance between our own and a more heroic civilization. In *The Waste Land*, however, the image of Dante's refining fire makes the first of repeated appearances in the poetry, signifying important changes. From being merely analytical, merely concerned with failures of individual passions or even social futilities, the poetry passes into an attempt to capture a vision of human experience, its hysterias and vulgarities sus- tained formally and philosophically by ideas of damnation and purgation. Frazer and Jessie Weston were more important at that moment for Eliot structurally, but Dante's fire speaks for Eliot's discovery of the reason for all the human failures that are his subject in the poem. In an important sense the Fisher King myth is misleading—it is a central image for all the infertilities and impotencies of the poem, but in itself it is inadequate to sustain the vision of the poem because the vision does not permit, as the myth of the Fisher King does, the restoration of potency. The vision allows only for the surrender of will and desire. The wound is neither social nor personal; it is the wound Santayana writes about in his memoirs; it is the mutilation of experience itself.

What many readers have been most struck by in *The Waste Land* is the difference in tone between the great loves of the past and the loves of the present. Out of our own romantic regard for Tristan, Cleopatra, and Dido, we see them evoked for ironic contrast with the typist. The deter- minedly deflating presentation of contemporary love is in sharp contrast to the grand rhetoric at the opening of "A Game of Chess." What we have not been quick enough to remark on is the way the juxtaposition throws light both ways. If we read "good night, sweet ladies" after Lil only as a mockery, a comment on a dwindling dignity, we are missing a vital, if not the most vital, aspect of the poem. Compassion enters the poem in this allusion as well as the sense of the unity and fundamental continuity of human experience. Yes, the river on which Elizabeth and Leicester floated in a gilded shell now "sweats / oil and tar," but the refrain of the Rhine Maidens appears in both moments. Similarly, the seduction of the poor Thames maiden from Highbury occurs in the language of the *Purgatorio*. We have been ready enough to see, perhaps because Eliot calls our attention to it in the notes, how he regards the hanged god of Frazer, the merchant from the east, the man with the pack from the Tarot deck, Christ, and the third man hallucinated by the polar explorers as not merely alluding to each other but as manifestations of the same person. This is also clearly true in the case of all the lovers in the poem. It is not merely London that is falling, but Vienna, Athens, and Jerusalem as well. All these great loves are stories of failures, losses, deaths, separations, and ultimate frustrations. From the sea which is wide and empty between Tristan and Isolde to the Thames maiden, who can "connect / Nothing with nothing," there are only men and women burning as Augustine burned with lust in Carthage. The failure of love in the poem is not merely the decadence of our civilization. The empty chapel is balanced by the agony in Gethsemane. There is nowhere in the poem a moment where human love does not fail. The opening lines of "A Game of Chess" are rich and full, the senses are fed, prepared for an erotic encounter that turns out to be the rape of Philomela. We are reminded that she sings with "inviolable voice" but it is to dirty ears, while her picture and others on the wall are "withered stumps of time." The waste land stretches back through western civilization to some common Indo-European source, but even there rain has not yet come.

The burning in the last moments of the poem is the fire from the Fire Sermon which Eliot read at Harvard. The Sermon tells us that all things are on fire, forms, sensations, everything received by the eye:

And with what are these on fire?
With the fire of passion, say I, with the fire of hatred, with the fire of infatuation; with birth, old age, death, sorrow, lamentation, misery, grief and despair are they on fire . . . .[2]

All human emotion, then, is what we are on fire with, life itself. It is a lust of the eye we burn with, to possess what we see. That is the fire that needs to be put out if the heart is to respond "gaily . . . beating obedient / To controlling hands." This compounding of attachment, lust, and the eye is also a less obvious but fundamental connection between this Buddhist material and Dante. Arnaut Daniel, who undergoes the purging fire in the quotation from the *Purgatorio* in *The Waste Land*, and Dante himself are poets in the Platonic love poetry tradition, which has been of such interest to Santayana and Yeats and continues to live for Eliot through the Provencal poets Pound introduced him to and through the *Commedia*, which was the greatest issue of the tradition. There the fire which entered the lover's being through the eye became the highest transforming agent, the fire of love became the "foco che gli affina," the flame that refines them in the *Purgatorio*, which is alluded to again in "Ash Wednesday" and the *Four Quartets*.

What Eliot found so congenial in Buddhism reinforced the lesson of Dante. Both speak for the turning away from experience for its own sake. In this sense Dante's lesson is both methodological and philosophical. On the one hand, it showed how the acting out of human desires and ambitions for their own sake was in their obsessive repetition hell itself. This was the lesson of the Fire Sermon as well: all human desire tied one to the wheel of life and rebirth from which only detachment could liberate. The effect of both medieval allegory and the Buddhist notion of eternal repetition is to reduce the importance of any single human action in itself and to underscore its importance as a type of human experience. These two ways of thinking both reflected and encouraged in Eliot the shift from interest in experience for its excitement, its success or failure, its energy or its color, to an interest in its significance. Santayana searched western literary tradition for the moment when events in it ceased to have reference to some system of values transcending the events. Similarly, in his criticism Eliot sought the moment in English literature when things perceived had inherent emotional and philosophic significance. They are talking about the same thing. Santayana wanted the poet so to dispose of the world in his poetry, so to reorganize it, that is, concretely through events, objects, character, that it would mean. The poet would not tell us what this world meant; the world would speak its own meaning. That was what Eliot looked for in a sensibility not dissociated—not a poet telling us about the meaning of a thing, but the thing speaking its own meaning. Henry James's world and things did that; that is why Eliot said he had a mind so fine that no idea could violate it. It was his highest praise. No ideas but in things, the imagist said. And Pound, perceiving that things were too limited, added characters and events in history. He gave up the image for the vortex because the single image could not mean enough. What he really wanted was a world, as Dante had made a world, and he hoped by capturing significant events in their imagined occurrence he could mean the world without depicting all of it, or at least mean the most valuable part of the world. His use of the vortex in the *Cantos*, in which he "rhymes" events, as Hugh Kenner puts it, that is, juxtaposes one moment in history, imagined or real, with another which it resembles in its vital features, attempts so to strike one incandescent moment of experience against another as finally to let shine forth the light of the world as Dante had. The *Cantos* fail to shed that ultimate saving and binding light, but not for methodological reasons. The method is inspired and worthy of the great number of brilliantly conceived and exquisitely executed individual moments in the poem, but it fails because, while Pound's ideas of what was right with experience could be largely shared and understood, the dark areas which would properly set them off and ultimately allow them to show their congruence and noble patterning were so narrowly and eccentrically conceived as to deny the reader's consent.

But the idea of a poetry of crucial moments, of the quintessential event or image through which the meaning of life, if not life itself, streams into our possession, is at the center of modernist literature. In Eliot it emerges in special purity. The sense of the waste time before and after these epiphanies, as Joyce called them, was so enveloping, the absence of order and the accompanying sense of weariness and impotence so pervasive, he surrendered the attempt to embody their force and significance in secular terms. In his view, the emptiness and sense of failure could be understood finally only through religious symbols; their depth is the depth of damnation felt as distance from God and obsessive repetition of inherently unsatisfying actions. Eliot came to feel, like Yeats and Santayana, that the proper human aim was to still desire and hope, which would be hope for the wrong thing, though unlike them he returned to Christian symbols and indeed, more striking still, to Christian belief. In Eliot the experience of disorder and loss is so overwhelming and the moment of order and gratification so brief, though full and powerful—and experienced so totally as given rather than achieved—that the presentation of it in the poetry as a moment of Christian ecstasy is a beautiful example of a wholly successful correlative object. It goes a long way towards explaining the astonishing influence and success of a Christian poetry in a literary culture profoundly devoted to finding non-Christian bases for values. The experience Eliot wished to capture and the view of experience he wished to embody are patently similar to the one we have been tracing in Santayana and Yeats and the one we shall trace in Stevens, though the temperament and emotional range of the poetry are quite different. A literary culture with an attitude toward belief like Yeats's toward his Great Years could understand a Christian poetry in the same way—the precise way Santayana himself understood Christian symbolism—wholly on an esthetic and structural basis. Of course, Eliot's Christianity involves a taking up of strands of Christianity, such as those of Saint John of the Cross and other mystics, which were not a part of the attenuated Christian culture of the nineteenth century. However, most important is the fact that a non-Christian audience could accept Eliot's Christian poetry in the way that Eliot accepted Dante's allegory before his own conversion. As Santayana predicted, the modernist view of poetry more or less self-consciously assumes the function of religion while at the same time exploiting a symbolic method that was itself used in religious revelation and sacrament. The poetry of the crucial moment can easily return to the poetry of the cross, the moment of the intersection of time and eternity, or revert to the intrusion of the divine into the secular; the transfiguration of experience into reality can become again the redemption of time. In fact, one pair hardly seems more Christian than another to anyone familiar with the criticism of the period, which abounds in the appropriation of religious terminology by the profane.

Eliot writes of his ecstatic moment in these terms:

> The inner freedom from the practical desire,
> The release from action and suffering, release from the inner
> And the outer compulsion, yet surrounded
> By a grace of sense, a white light still and moving,
> *Erhebung* without motion, concentration
> Without elimination, both a new world
> And the old made explicit, understood
> In the completion of its partial ecstasy,
> The resolution of its partial horror.[3]

There are emotional, sensuous, and intellectual components in the moment. Emotionally, it means a sensation of liberation, withdrawal both of desire and inhibition, of internal and external drive or constraint; sensuous delight is present through the light, but not through forms, which we remember from the Fire Sermon are on fire with lust. Finally, the ideal of this poetry, "concentration without elimination," is the seeming paradox which underlies the esthetic of the symbol, the image and the vortex—the significant form which opens out finally to include the world. A new world—the world of the ecstatic moment—combines with "the old made explicit," that is, all its meanings said, understood, its horrors and ecstasies both worked out to their end, as Santayana asked of poetry. The two worlds are really one—as in Yeats and Santayana—the second being a clarification and perfection of the first. How easily this moment of grace translates into the literary moment as Santayana defined it and Yeats enacted it! It translates easily because the equivalency exists in Eliot's mind, because the *Four Quartets* are not only about religious experience, but also about esthetic awareness. After telling us what the experience of the still point, the moment of consciousness, is like, Eliot specifically reminds us that it is what Emily Dickinson would have called a "compound moment":

> Yet the enchainment of past and future
> Woven in the weakness of the changing body,
> Protects mankind from heaven and damnation
> Which flesh cannot endure. (p. 5)

He reminds us of our bodies; what enchains us and is our weakness is also our protection. Our biology, then, threatening to be the source of our deepest sorrow and loss, is converted to the source of a kind of redemption, but without the specifically Christian categories of Heaven and Hell. If we could be outside our biological selves, if, that is, "all time is eternally present," then time is unredeemable. If, as *The Waste Land* threatened, there were no real history, only endlessly repeated desires and frustrations, then experience is loss. But although the moments of fulfillment are brief and transcend time,

> . . . only in time can the moment in the rose-garden,
> The moment in the arbour where the rain beat,
> The moment in the draughty church at smokefall
> Be remembered; involved with past and future.
> Only through time time is conquered. (p. 5)

Through the reminder of the "changing body," which cannot sustain the experience of the still point, Eliot returns us to time, and through a pun on time he looks forward to the last section of "Burnt Norton," which is about art. There time appears to refer only to human memory, which possesses those moments of consciousness and thus compounds them with the biological self who is time's creature, thus conquering its own limitations. Here is a new version of the fortunate fall. If by our natures we were not forced to return to our ordinary experience, we would not be able to "involve" that extraordinary moment of consciousness in our lives, and our ordinary experience would remain lost to us—"unredeemed." Furthermore, the word "time" looks forward to the world of music and poetry in section V:

> Words move, music moves
> Only in time; but that which is only living
> Can only die. Words, after speech, reach
> Into the silence. Only by the form, the pattern,
> Can words or music reach
> The stillness, as a Chinese jar still
> Moves perpetually in its stillness. (p. 7)

Words and music, like our changing bodies, move in time. In their actual sound they live and die. But through their form, which is an order, not an existence, they can persist; they overcome their utterance in time and reach into the stillness of eternity—to the "still point of the turning world."

Nevertheless, it is not only the stillness Eliot wants, not only transcendence. It is the world, too—the coexistence of the world and the transcendent which sustains the world. Yet there remains a murky area here. "Or say," "Burnt Norton" goes on, "that the end precedes the beginning, / And the end and the beginning were always there / Before the beginning and after the end. / And all is always now." But if all is always now, "If all time is eternally present" as the poem begins, then "All time is unredeemable." What becomes, then, of the idea that through time, time is conquered? It is no wonder that "Words strain, / Crack and sometimes break" under the burden of articulating the two realms in such a way that experience will be repossessed, neither lost nor utterly surrendered in an absorption in the transcendent but repossessed through art.

In "The Dry Salvages," he speaks of the "moment in and out of time" as Incarnation, "an impossible union / Of spheres of existence":

> Here the past and future
> Are conquered, and reconciled,
> Where action were otherwise movement
> Of that which is only moved
> And has in it no source of movement—
> Driven by daemonic, chthonic
> Powers. And right action is freedom
> From past and future also. (pp. 27-28)

In this Incarnation, for which "Burnt Norton" tells us art is an analogue, time is conquered—and again he uses "conquered," not "redeemed"; at the end of "Little Gidding," he will speak of *people* being "redeemed from time," but time itself is conquered, not redeemed. I think this distinction is an attempt to work out the contradiction in the notion that, if all is now, time is not redeemable and the notion that it is just when we are free of past and future that we are redeemed. The problem originates in Eliot's use of both Christian and Buddhist notions about time, which are at odds. The Christian scheme of the fall, the crucifixion, and the last judgment is fundamentally historical. It assumes the reality of time. The Buddhist scheme does not. Furthermore, when the Buddhist surrenders self and desire, he does it, as Eliot does at the end of the *Four Quartets*, without reference to God, but out of the realization that the idea of a self that has continuity and independent existence is an illusion. When a Christian surrenders his will, it is specifically in favor of God's will. His insight is into his own essential impotence, not into his illusory existence. Eliot may have become Christian, but God is surprisingly absent from his poetry.

In any case, his moment in and out of time not only conquers time but also restores power and autonomy. In ordinary experience we do not truly act, we are acted upon, Eliot feels, driven by our appetites and instincts, concerned with possessions and satisfactions, fearful of consequences, preoccupied with success and failure. But the lesson of the Lord Krishna is to act without regard to the fruits of action; then we are free from the wheel of rebirth, from past and future. We act but we are not attached to our action. Only when our action is no longer in the service of our will is it right action. Those lines which characterize wrong action as "that which is only moved / and has in it no source of movement" remind us that that which is not moved but is the source of movement is God. Here, scarcely covered, is the gigantic drive to mastery which the poetry, in all its surrenders, entails. It is no surprise, then, that "For most of us, this is the aim / Never here to be realized," yet we are to continue striving. Both the model and vehicle of our effort is the "use of memory."

> History may be servitude,
> History may be freedom. See, how they vanish,
> The faces and places, with the self which, as it could, loved them,
> To become renewed, transfigured, in another pattern. (p. 36)

We die to our ordinary selves and our ordinary sense of experience and live again as in "Burnt Norton," "the boarhound and the boar / Pursue their pattern as before / But reconciled among the stars." The *Four Quartets*, through "Dry Salvages," leave us with a sense of the enormous striving toward transcendence, toward the moment of Incarnation, away from the voices of temptation, the twittering world. Then in "Little Gidding," the lesson of Krishna is integrated and we are returned to the ordinary world, now transfigured, where "all manner of thing shall be well." The fire that burns there, the first fire of lust, then the second fire of purgation, are in fact one, both further united with the rose as symbol of perfection and salvation. History, then, is conceived of not simply as experience, what happens to us, but our memory of experience. History is "a pattern / Of timeless moments." But experience is so conceived of, is so transfigured, only at the cost of experience itself. As in Santayana's earliest view of this liberated state, our life is no longer our own. Tradition freed the poet from himself early in Eliot's career, before his conversion, in exactly the way memory now frees the poet spiritually. The work to be done, which tradition was to show the poet, turns out in "Little Gidding" to be this discovery of "that which was the beginning"—the "condition of complete simplicity." When the work is done right, whether in life or in poetry, then the fire and the rose are one, the moment of the rose and the moment of the yew-tree are of equal duration—we have a moment of Incarnation. Every poem is an epitaph summing up the significance of life. "We die with the dying . . . We are born with the dead." Our experience dies into its memory, into a pattern of itself. Nor is this to be confused with the idea of gaining knowledge from experience. In "East Coker," Eliot says,

> There is, it seems to us,
> At best, only a limited value
> In the knowledge derived from experience.
> The knowledge imposes a pattern, and falsifies,
> For the pattern is new in every moment
> And every moment is a new and shocking
> Valuation of all we have been. We are only undeceived
> Of that which, deceiving, could no longer harm. (p. 13)

Old age does not bring wisdom. Our moments are not cumulative. They are radically discontinuous. That is why, in "Dry Salvages," we who disembark are not those who began the journey. That is why we cannot fare well but can only fare forward. Our memory saves us from the hell of these radical disjunctions by seeing the past under the form of repeated moments of Incarnation, like Pound's rhymed vortices. So at Little Gidding, in the chapel, "History is now and England." The fate of the king who was dethroned and came in the night to Little Gidding is the fate of all of us. The politics of that event, the struggles for power of the time are resolved and abolished in these lines:

> These men, and those who opposed them
> And those whom they opposed
> Accept the constitution of silence
> And are folded in a single party. (p. 37)

They leave us "A symbol perfected in death" as Yeats's Irish revolutionaries' actions did, which transcends the actions, abolishes categories of right and wrong, and leaves us only the esthetic category of the beauty of the perfected moment. So the English factions are transcended as they submit to a constitution of silence and a single party. But the meaning of the symbol they leave us is not only the strife that united as it divided them but the ending of that strife in silence and wholeness. Just as the disorder and fragmentation of the Irish rebels are changed into order and integrity, so does death transfigure the disorder of the English. But we have also left behind here categories of good and bad. Just as poetry and music and the Chinese jar reach into the silence, so these men's actions through our memory, which conceives of their actions as symbols, reach into the silence. But in just the same way the divisions and failures of our own lives are to be transformed. Our lives, too, can reach into the silence; we can transcend the categories of right and wrong and the categories of loss and gain when we die to our own lives. When we give up all our claims, "then all manner of thing shall be well." Then history, art, and life become one order of being. Ordinary experience, in which "From wrong to wrong the exasperated spirit / Proceeds," is utterly transfigured. Spiritual salvation, like the poetic salvation explored in "Tradition and the Individual Talent," comes through history, abolition of the self, and the surrender of private emotion. Eliot's writing of this very impressive religious poetry in an essentially irreligious age is not the eccentricity it might appear. It was made possible precisely by the transfer of religious energies and functions to poetry, as well as by the exploitation of the symbolic aspect of religious dogma. The close association of poetic with spiritual strivings throughout the *Four Quartets* and with poetic and spiritual achievement—the movements in measure, the reaching into silence, the keeping time, the image of the dance—these are all applied to both poetic and spiritual order. They speak for this as well as for the enormous spiritual burden now specifically assigned to poetry. Poetry redeems time. Without it, our moment at the still point would remain outside of time. Nevertheless, the sphere of time, of our ordinary experience, suffers in this poetry. There is an abstractness to it as it figures in the poetry after *The Waste Land*. It does indeed have the summary quality of the epitaph. We get only glimpses, as through the turret windows of "Ash Wednesday," of the actual sources of Eliot's despair. "The hawthorne blossom," the "broadbacked figure drest in blue and green," the "lost lilac," the "lost sea smell," the cry of quail and the whirling plover are all equally allegorical notations, but the lilac, the quail, the sea, and the plover are not meant to be of the same order of experience as the professedly allegorical hawthorne and the figure in blue and green. Nevertheless, already like them, at two removes from actuality, they are more like the star and falling meteors of Yeats's early "The White Birds" than like the sword and the brocade of "Dialogue of Self and Soul." They depend on previously accrued associations, which we are not sure we share except in the most general way. The context does not control the reader's associations. We are not at all sure what satisfactions or frustrations inhere in those quail and plover. Yet they and what they are meant to embody are what we are giving up when we arrive at the "condition of complete simplicity / (Costing not less than everything)," which Eliot tells us is our goal. But then the force of that line is very much diminished because the price remains uncertain.

One of the things this reflects about the sources of energy of Eliot's poetry is that the sense of loss, of impotence, of failure, of sexual disgust is prior to any experience the poet cares to describe as its cause. We might say at this point, however, that the burden of meaning of the later poetry is that in ordinary experience itself, of whatever kind, the very forms of life frustrate us, make us fail, cause us suffering. That is the meaning of the Fire Sermon and of Krishna's advice to Lord Arjuna, which carry us from the Waste Land to Little Gidding. It is not any particular desire, but desire itself, which causes our suffering. It is not a particular lust we must purge in the refining fire but the general lust which is our attachment to life. But Dante's sinners, Arnaut Daniel, for example, whose fire recurs in Eliot, burn with and for a particular love. We are never, after all, attached to life but to some particular things and persons. Supported by the examples of Santayana and Yeats, we ought to see in this not so much a reticence about his private life, or an inability to come to grips with the personal sources of his suffering, but rather an attempt to find a correlative object for the radical sense of loss that experience engendered and the sense of incapacity with which he feels himself always to have faced it, quite apart from any particular experienced failure or suffering. Such were the conditions under which these men lived, the terms in which they saw and felt their lives. Their lives as writers were given over to restoring through imaginative effort the fullness and wholeness that experience denied them. And this effort in all three men was explicit and conscious, not implicit or underlying; it was, in fact, their subject both poetic and critical.

Nevertheless, while all three deal with the liberating and enabling effects of recognizing the inherently frustrating nature of experience and the necessity of the surrender of claims to life, in the imagined reconstitution of the world to which they then have entire claim to, Yeats far more than Eliot makes us feel the force of both realms and, ultimately, the way in which the second realm is a perfected and transfigured version of the first. Eliot's energies are much more directed to the second realm and to the difficulty of reaching it, both spiritually and poetically. Nor is the relationship of the two realms quite clear. It is too easy to feel that we are leaving experience behind in Eliot, although we are told the boar and the boarhound pursue their pattern as before, but reconciled, and that all manner of things shall be well, that is, that it is ordinary experience transfigured that is the second realm; any moment detached from human will and aims can be a timeless moment like the one in the chapel at Little Gidding. This is obscured by another conceptualization of the achieved second realm as a discovery of the beginning in the end:

> At the source of the longest river
> The voice of the hidden waterfall
> And the children in the apple-tree
> Not known, because not looked for
> But heard, half-heard, in the stillness
> Between two waves of the sea. (p. 39)

This appears to be something quite different from the timeless moment, entirely apart from any actual experience, however conceived. Similarly, how is the still point of the turning world— how is that related to the rose and to the fire which is one with the rose? The fire which refines, which purges us of our desire, is, then, salvation itself; that involves a certain way of living and viewing our life. It is also a way of saying that our death is our new life—our eternal life. But the corruptible flesh shall put on incorruptibility; that is the ultimate promise. Once we die to the flesh, Christianity promises, we shall rise in the flesh, just as the first realm surrendered is repossessed as the second. But the condition of utmost simplicity at our source, which we gain at the price of everything, seems to be a state that precedes ordinary experience. Perhaps it is a way of characterizing the entire wholeness and freshness of the new state of the self, an echo of the Christian admonition that we must become as little children, an evocation of the primitive peace of Eden before ordinary consciousness, which must always spring from deprivation. It is a way of saying what Santayana meant when he talked of there being no reason in Eden where there were no needs. In any case, the effect of it in the poetry is to point away from experience rather than to experience transfigured.

Furthermore, before the refining fire appears in the final lines of "Little Gidding" as the crowned knot of fire that is one with the rose, it appears in the fire of the bombing of London in World War II. It lends a frightening note of apocalypse, of cleansing destruction, to the last image of perfection, which is reminiscent of the beautiful but appalling lines on pity in Pound's *Cantos*:

> Pity befouleth April,
> Pity is the root and the spring.
> Now if no fayre creature followeth me
> It is on account of Pity,
> It is on account that Pity forbideth them slaye.
> All things are made foul in this season,
> This is the reason, none may seek purity
> Having for foulnesse pity

And things growne awry;
No more do my shaftes fly
To slay. Nothing is now clean slayne
But rotteth away.[4]

There is a ruthlessness in Eliot toward ordinary experience that is not to be found in Dante in spite of the horrors to which he consigns his lost souls. When temporal life so disgusts him, it is disingenuous to pretend that it costs him anything to leave it. It also makes it all the more difficult to believe that all manner of things shall be well except through their destruction. But a world so emptied of particularity, so divested of human aims and frustrations and converted into timeless moments, is all the more easily sacrificed to that ultimate flame. So, while Eliot strives in some moments to make his poetry the instrument by which the world is fed by the word made flesh, there is a countervailing drive to make his poetry an altar on which the world endures self-immolation, which makes his work narrow but exceedingly powerful.

NOTES

1. T. S. Eliot, *Collected Poems, 1909-1935* (New York: Harcourt, Brace, 1936), p. 89.
2. "The Fire Sermon," *Buddhism in Translation*, ed. and trans. Henry C. Warren, quoted in Herbert Howarth, *Notes on Some Figures Behind T. S. Eliot* (Boston: Houghton, Mifflin, 1964), p. 204.
3. T. S. Eliot, *Four Quartets* (New York: Harcourt, Brace, 1943), p. 5.
4. Ezra Pound, *Selected Poems* (New York: New Directions n.d.), pp. 125-26.

Stevens and the Sufficiency of Reality

Like Yeats and Eliot, Wallace Stevens put an enormous burden on the imagination and received commensurate returns. For him, as for them, the imagination was to construct a world in which loss and striving would be comprehended and transformed and all mortality's bitter violence reconciled so that harmony might be brought, in Santayana's figure, to the perturbed kingdom of the self. As in Yeats and Eliot, we have the sense of Stevens inhabiting two worlds whose definition and relations are the chief subject of his poetry. In fact, both the demands and the rewards are greater because they are made in a solitude and poverty rivaling that of the most obedient monastic soul. Stevens' work most closely embodies the view of the constructive imagination as Santayana conceived it, and creates a body of poetry on its basis. Older than Eliot, Stevens knew at first hand the estheticism of the end of the century at Harvard and was a student when Santayana published *The Sense of Beauty* and was writing the essays that were to comprise *Interpretations of Poetry and Religion*. He was a close reader of the French symbolists against whom he turned, like Santayana and for the same reasons, the better to feel his different and separate self, and justly so in spite of his debt. Although his poetry appropriates and transforms two key images of Platonism and Christianity, the sun of intelligence and the rock of faith, he reaches past them through his naturalism to create the myths that will embody and dramatize naturalism's view of the world; to create, as Santayana called on the poet to do, the "religion of disillusion" wholly in terms of his natural experience. The cold, stillness, emptiness, whiteness of winter; the color, sound, movement, warmth, and multiplying forms of summer—these were the sources of his mythic representations of the foundations and possibilities of our lives.

On their firm base he could stand in the natural moment which has neither tradition nor community, and nevertheless be sure of speaking to an audience who shared that experience and who would be made into a community through the poetry he gave them. Whereas Joyce tried to make our ordinary lives vibrate with the meaning and energy of older myths, Stevens seems to have taken very seriously Santayana's warning not to take words for things and to make the basis for values the place where values originate, our primary sensations and desires. Yet what Joyce was looking for in that most particular of Dublin days in *Ulysses* was a shared life which a reader feeling the disintegrating fabric of his community might cling to. As the parody and painstaking details through which Joyce tries to recreate a story the ancients told themselves fade for us, we are compelled still by the figures of Bloom and Molly, who live for us through their primary sensations and desires. For all his literary baggage, Joyce was driven at the last in *Finnegan's Wake* to the place where Stevens began, to the fundamental poles of experience, night and day, waking and dreaming. These remained ways of organizing experience in a period when no action as it was traditionally understood, with a protagonist, a goal, an antagonist, a defined setting and an end, no matter how tragic, could be taken as representatively human.

If Stevens was to be what Santayana called Wordsworth, a herald of a religion he thought to be possible, then he would celebrate the action which typified human destiny, and, following Santayana, he found it to be the imaginative act. I think it is Stevens—with all his richness, grandeur, celebration, and successful embodiment of a sense of power, with the uncomplaining rigor of his naturalism untainted by the least nostalgia for God and dogma—who makes us most feel the strong shock of the descent to earth, the dissolution of traditional authority, the surrender of those ideas which supported community in western society. He makes us feel it because in his career we see enormous energy, wit, originality of language and image, all devoted to the most fundamental aspects of our existence, to an explanation of the emergence of the very forms and colors of our lives, how we come to know and what we come to know in our ordinary existence. Questions of right action, personal aspiration or conflict, spiritual adventure or psychological revelation: none of these appear in their accustomed forms. All our admiration for human heroism and pathos is elicited for the single heroism of accepting our humanity. The simple terms of our existence, which had always been taken for granted, now seem to become the major business of our lives, along with the surrender of all the disguised notions of divinity that the romantics adhered to in their terror of their own solitude.

The burden of Stevens' work is twofold. On the one hand, it strives to make us aware that reality is enough, and by reality he means our ordinary experience. And, simultaneously, it wants to make us realize how that reality is a poetic image. As Santayana said, nature made us poets as a condition of our knowing her. Stevens wants us to feel the bareness and intractability of the world we inhabit, its hard and impenetrable core, the irreversibility of the fate it imposes on us, and, at the same time, the green world we turn it into by directing our human gaze upon it. Although the poetic act is his subject repeatedly, he escapes a narrow self-absorbed estheticism, as Santayana does, by making that act a figure for human consciousness. He may thereby suffer, particularly in the later poems, as Santayana does, from an abstractness, a superabundance of concept, and an insufficiency of particular concrete detail, but he projects a strength, a range and depth of comprehension, and a broad compassion and serenity unsurpassed in modernist poetry.

In speaking of poetry, of what the poet does, Stevens repeatedly proceeds in terms of what effect the poet has on reality itself, and on the relationship of imagination to fact. Speaking of art in an age of disbelief, he says in *The Necessary Angel*:

Men feel that the imagination is the next greatest power to fact: the reigning prince. Consequently their interest in the imagination and its work is to be regarded not as a phase of humanism but as a vital self-assertion in a world in which nothing but the self remains, if that remains. So regarded, the study of the imagination and the study of reality come to appear to be purified, aggrandized, fateful. How much stature, even vatic stature, this conception gives the poet![1]

Even more than a vital self-assertion, poetry is, he says elsewhere, an internal violence opposing the violence of reality as it presses on us. And we see here the violence we found in Yeats. The energies which might be acted out in actual confrontations are wholly directed to symbolic self-assertions so that the study of the imagination and the study of reality, that which might be thought of as subsidiary to action, become instead the central activity of life, through which we are fulfilled and know our destiny. He calls our attention to the prophetic stature this gives the poet. Similarly, when he wants to define the experience of a poet writing "a poem that completely accomplishes the purpose of the poet" (p. 50), he uses the language of sainthood: aspiration, liberation, justification, and purification. Then he goes on to show that what might be thought of as a mere esthetic satisfaction is really something else:

... if we say that the idea of God is merely a poetic idea, even if the supreme poetic idea, and that our notions of heaven and hell are merely poetry not so called, even if poetry that involves us vitally, the feeling of deliverance, of a release, of a perfection touched, of a vocation so that all men may know the truth and that the truth may set them free—if we say these things and if we are able to see the poet who achieved God and placed Him in His seat in heaven in all His glory, the poet himself, still in the ecstasy of the poem that completely accomplished his purpose, would have seemed, whether young or old, whether in rags or ceremonial robe, a man who needed what he had created, uttering the lyrics of joy that followed his creation. (p. 51)

First, we see here a version of the last part of Santayana's essay on the function of poetry, in which religion is seen as a form of poetry and the poet takes on the function of the priest. It is furthermore an exaltation of the poetic process not at the expense of the religious. The religious impulse is not degraded or debunked, or its fruits devalued. That is why to speak of this merely as humanism is misleading. There is something about this experience of the poet that is not part of the world of ordinary men. Stevens is speaking of ecstasy, of transfiguration. The poet, he tells us, lives apart from politics, from the world of action, in a world "radiant and productive" and the pleasure he has is the pleasure of "agreement" with that world. But he must use religious terminology to explain fully the poetic experience, to make us understand it as equally transforming, but one in which the "revelations are not the revelations of belief, but the precious portents of our own powers" (p. 175). But only, as in Santayana and Yeats and Eliot, *imaginative* powers in this world apart from politics. Again, we see how all our claims to potency, to satisfaction, to assertion against our environment are to rest on what we can see, not on what we can do; in some way the world, which is so resistant to us, will remain as it is and yet seen by us in a particular way will be the source of everything we need. For, as Stevens says in "Of Modern Poetry," the poet seeks above all to find "what will suffice."[2]

In order to find what will suffice, Stevens makes certain distinctions that we found in Santayana and Yeats. He distinguishes between the imagination that works on reality for its destruction and for the poet's own use and the imagination that is associated with good sense and civilization. Like Eliot, he saw Paul Valéry as an antagonist. He associated with Valéry a theory of the imagination that sees a poet's imagination as not wholly his own but part of a "much larger, much more potent imagination which it is his affair to try to get at" and therefore living "on the verge of consciousness," producing a "marginal, subliminal" poetry (p. 115). Following Santayana, Stevens turns away from the use of forms to get beyond forms, the exploitation of indeterminacy, the use of the world and its objects and events to figure forth some other, supposedly better reality, rather than to embody and convey the significant value of the world itself.

161

Against this rejected view Stevens sets the notion of a "central poetry." Such a poetry comes from a theory of the imagination which sees it as a power within the poet to have "such insights into reality as will make it possible for him to be sufficient as a poet in the very center of consciousness" (p. 115). This central poetry is related to philosophy and good sense and civilization, towards which the central poetry presses and away from mysticism. And we are reminded of the lines in which Yeats tells us that Greek sculptors and their measure defeated Asia, not Greek sailors. But we have found all of this in Yeats and Eliot, and in Santayana before them: the reintroduction of philosophy into poetry, the reaction against mere mysticism, the compounding of real and imaginative power, the turning away from the merely personal and the romantic.

At the same time that this theory turns away from the romantic plasticity of reality which so appalled Santayana in Emerson and denies to the imagination a reified existence outside of man, it seeks to conflate poetry and reality while still holding them apart: the double effort at the heart of the modernist imagination. For Stevens' argument proceeds in this way. First, he reminds us of the analogy between nature and the imagination. Here again we see the debt of modernist poetics to Emerson, although it is important to remember that the debt, like Marx's to Hegel, involves standing Emerson on his head. For Stevens, as for Santayana, the imagination is born of nature; it is not the final issue of a force of which our imagination partakes. Stevens never forgets that analogy maintains difference, not identity, and he speaks of the "parallel" of nature and the imagination, again emphasizing their distinctness. However, he goes on to say: " . . . possibly poetry is merely the strange rhetoric of that parallel: a rhetoric in which the feeling of one man is communicated to another in words of an exquisite appositeness which takes away all their verbality" (p. 118). The poetry in its justness of analogy loses its "verbality," the quality that marks it as artificial, made, different from the emotion which is its subject. Is it, then, made a part of the world of emotion which is the natural world? Not exactly, but something like it. The poetry comes to be seen to reside in the change of emotion in the audience, and Stevens calls it the metamorphosis brought about by one imagination working on another through a figure of speech. In this very way Whitman could feel that he reached out and touched his reader: the words somehow cease to exist. "Is and as are one," as Stevens says. Or, as in "Peter Quince at the Clavier," the sounds of the music "On my spirit make a music, too. / Music is feeling, then, not sound" (p. 8). And the poem can continue by turning desire into music and conclude by claiming, "Beauty is momentary in the mind— / The fitful tracing of a portal; / But in the flesh it is immortal." The process of metamorphosis, of transformation, then, is the essence of poetry, so that he can speak of something he sees as moving *as if* it had been transformed, that is, an accident of nature affected him as if it were poetry. At the same time he can speak of "the morality of the poet's radiant and productive atmosphere" as being "the morality of the right sensation" (*Necessary Angel*, p. 58). For as much as his work, especially the earlier poetry, calls attention to the texture of the verse, to the functioning wit of the poet, the ultimate aim, as in the figure of the poet as the glass man, is to locate the result of the creative process, like its provocation, in the physical world. His preference for the word "metamorphosis" over the word "metaphor" shows us again how imaginative power and real power are brought so closely together in Stevens as to be two aspects of the same thing.

What we see in Stevens is what we found, as he did, in Santayana: the dual appreciation of the quite different properties and necessary linkage of the physical and imaginative realms. All force and energy reside in the former, the ultimate object and field of all our strivings as biological beings; yet, in itself, it is unknowable, dumb, intractable, the rock over which the green leaves proliferate. Our imaginations, separate, yet springing out of our physical selves that live in that physical world, speak to us of what we need that world to mean but keep always within the bounds of our experience of that world. That world presses in upon us with a violence to which poetry, which finds what will suffice, is a counterviolence. The realm of the imagination must be distinguished from that reality: Stevens' words are invisible, significant, abstract, fictional; he calls that realm major and central. And it is major and central precisely because, although it is what the actual world is not, poetic truth is the truth of fact, and "absolute fact [like Santayana's realm of essence] includes everything that the imagination includes" (p. 60). The truth of the imagination is like light, "it adds nothing, except itself" (p. 62). Stevens finds fault with the romantic imagination for the same reason Santayana does; it does not extricate itself from experience to arrive at the significance of experience. Stevens finds that the romantic belittles the imagination; he ascribes to it a failure of the imagination whose greatest achievement lies in abstraction, of which the romantic is incapable, achieving only what Stevens calls "minor wish-fulfillments" (p. 139).

Furthermore, like Santayana, Stevens wishes to transcend any dichotomy between the imagination and reason. As Santayana did in the essay on the understanding, the imagination, and mysticism, Stevens sees the function of the mind as unitary but essentially under the dominance of the imagination, an imagination conceived of as the great sane central force of our lives. It is to the imagination, not common sense, or understanding, or reason that we owe our concepts of normality and structure. Writers like

Rimbaud and Kafka, who exploit the abnormality of imagination rather than extending its normative function, he feels, merely abuse it. Imagination, Stevens tells us, establishes normality; reason is simply its methodizer. By the normal he means "the instinctive integrations which are the reason for living." What value, a Kafka might ask, is such an imagination to those who live in "solitude, misery and terror?" Like Santayana, who early came to feel so much of experience as ashes in the mouth and only imagination as rising above that desolation, Stevens answers: "Of what value is anything to the solitary and those that live in misery and terror except the imagination?" (p. 155).

Concept, abstraction, central, normal, major, invisible, significant, integrating: these are the terms in which Stevens describes the characteristic fruits of the imagination. In "Notes toward a Supreme Fiction," one of his three injunctions is, "It must be abstract." All these terms seem to take us far from our ordinary experience, seem to describe a realm of the imagination as removed from our common life as William James mistakenly supposed Santayana's similar notions about value and experience. Actually, in both the criticism and poetry, these terms are the means by which we are enabled to affirm our ordinary lives and see their meaning. These concepts are the means by which we recognize the ordinary as the source of everything we value in those lives, just as in "Notes toward a Supreme Fiction," it is of "the man / in that old coat, those sagging pantaloons" that the aspiring poet is "to confect / The final elegance" (p. 215).

However, notice that the idea of metamorphosis contained in these lines is somewhat at variance with the image of the imagination, which like light adds nothing but itself, and the image of the poet as a glass man who, as in "Asides on the Oboe," is "the transparence of the place in which / He is" (p. 187). The transformation of the man in the old coat seems to involve as well an idea of clothing, of decoration. In "An Ordinary Evening in New Haven," the poet seeks the object

> At the exactest point at which it is itself,
> Transfixing by being purely what it is,
> A view of New Haven, say, through the certain eye,
>
> The eye made clear of uncertainty, with the sight
> Of simple seeing, without reflection. (p. 336)

Yet in "Credences of Summer," he writes of the sun seen without evasion:

> Look at it in its essential barrenness
> And say this, this is the centre that I seek.
> Fix it in an eternal foliage

> And fill the foliage with arrested peace,
> Joy of such permanence, right ignorance
> Of change still possible. (p. 288)

On the one hand, the poet is simply to show us reality, and, on the other, he is to make us experience as he does, its sufficiency. The decoration, what the poet adds to the old man or to the essential barrenness, the "eternal foliage," is the conviction of its sufficiency. The joy is born of the conviction. At the same time the poet wishes to see himself as he truly is: "I have not but I am and as I am, I am" he says in "Notes toward a Supreme Fiction." He tells us repeatedly that the poet's subject is "things as they are" ("The Man with the Blue Guitar"), and that "to impose is not / To discover" ("Notes toward a Supreme Fiction"). That poem has a particularly moving section in which the Canon's sister holds her daughters "closelier to her by rejecting dreams":

> She had two daughters, one
> Of four, and one of seven, whom she dressed
> The way a painter of pauvred color paints.
>
> But still she painted them appropriate to
> Their poverty, a gray-blue yellowed out
> With ribbon, a rigid statement of them, white,
>
> With Sunday pearls, the widow's gayety.
> She hid them under simple names. She held
> Them closelier to her by rejecting dreams.
>
> The words they spoke were voices that she heard.
> She looked at them and saw them as they were
> And what she felt fought off the barest phrase. (p. 228)

Reality is sufficient and it is faithful. Our mind is "not imprisoned" but "resides" in a permanence composed of impermanence. The sun goes, the sun returns. Poetry, then, is simple seeing, "Ourselves in the tune as if in space / Yet nothing changed, except the place / Of things as they are, and only the place." This reality discovered, this simple reappearance of things as they are in the song, "for a moment final," is a paradox repeated throughout the poetry, like the permanence composed of impermanence, like the fiat of the Emperor of Ice Cream, "Let be be finale of seem," and "is and as are one," and "to seem—it is to be." In all of these the momentary and the eternal are one; the partial is the absolute. This bringing together of what we have talked of as the two realms of experience—the ordinary, fragmentary, frustrating and the full and perfected—is the reason that "in his poems we find peace." Is this not, however, a kind of sensory mysticism? To see "with the sight of simple seeing, without reflection"—we have met that before in American poetry, most powerfully in the concluding passages of "Crossing Brooklyn Ferry," where Whitman apprehends the world with "free sense" and experiences the momentary as the eternal. Experience on that level is full, complete. No demands are made that cannot be met. The world can withhold meaning from our reflection, it can deny gratification to our impulses, but how can it frustrate our senses? Such an experience, as Whitman movingly attests, is liberating and healing of the terrible separation he feels between himself and the world. But such an overcoming of separation and distinction as Whitman achieves by planting the world within himself is not at all what Stevens is after. "That I may reduce the monster to / Myself, and then may be myself / In face of the monster, be more than part / Of it . . ." sings the man with the blue guitar. Though the beginning of poetic process may be to reduce the monster reality to the dimensions of the human, the end of it is not unity but confrontation, not loss of self but definition of self. No reader of such a representative text as *The Education of Henry Adams* can fail to feel the full force of the threat to the sense of self the naturalist world of forces and sensations could be to those who just entered it. Not only could it mean, as it did for Santayana, an incapacity to distinguish dream from reality, but also self from other. For Stevens, then, poetry had this double task of discrimination. That moment of peace the poet brings is precisely the moment of potential torment seen from a new transforming perspective: the moment when we realize our permanence is impermanence, our being, seeming and *find it sufficient*; the moment when we realize that we live in concepts of the imagination for which reason is only the methodizer; the moment when we demand no absolute but fiction. Like Santayana, Stevens turns Lucifer's terror that he will be lost if once he believes in the world which is his own making into delight. The web in which Lucifer feels "imprisoned" is the home in which Stevens "resides."

This transformation can occur because, once again following Santayana, Stevens sees the mind as a poet and our poems as the only way nature permits us to know her. The fact among appearances that Stevens and Santayana would reveal to us is that ultimately appearance is fact. Thus Stevens writes in *The Necessary Angel*:

Take the case of a man for whom reality is enough, as, at the end of his life, he returns to it like a man returning from Nowhere to his village and to everything there that is tangible and visible, which he has come to cherish and wants to be near. He sees without images. But is he not seeing a clarified reality of his own? Does he not dwell in an analogy? His imageless world is, after all, of the same sort as a world full of the obvious analogies of happiness or unhappiness, innocence or tragedy, thoughtlessness or the heaviness of the mind. In any case, these are the pictorializations of men, for whom the world exists as a world and for whom life exists as life, the objects of their passions, the objects before which they come and speak, with intense choosing, words that we remember and make our own. Their words have made a world that transcends the world and a life livable in that transcendence. It is a transcendence achieved by means of the minor effects of figurations and the major effects of the poet's sense of the world and the motive music of his poems and it is the imaginative dynamism of all these analogies together. Thus poetry becomes and is a transcendent analogue composed of the particulars of reality, created by the poet's sense of the world, that is to say, his attitude, as he intervenes and interposes the appearances of that sense. (pp. 129-30)

This superb passage, which moves us as much by its sense of life as by its sense of poetry, by its tenderness as by its eloquence, brings together strikingly the attitudes that produce the double perspective of poetry as transparence and poetry as artifice. The man for whom reality is enough sees without images. Then he has achieved in his life what Stevens tells us the poet achieves for us in his poetry. But he dwells in an analogy. His village, everything that is tangible and visible, is as much analogy as the pictorialization of the poet. This is so because the imageless world of the man returning to his village is a world full of meaning for him. The man is at the end of his life, a form close to completion, and reality gratifies him because it sums up everything he knows, very like "Little Gidding," where poetry is epitaph. In another essay, Stevens makes a distinction between what he calls "reality in its most individual aspect" and "isolated fact," the first embodied in Marianne Moore's ostrich and the second in the *Encyclopedia Britannica*'s ostrich. Moore's reality, Stevens tells us, using Santayana's word for the world of art, is "significant." So is the man's village. The poet, then, makes a clarified reality as real and as free of "images" as the man's, composing it just as the man does of the particulars of reality and working through his own sense of the world. The poem, which is the transcendent analogue of reality, is no more an analogy and no less a reality than the man's village, but it is no less an analogy and no more a reality than that village either. Both are mediated visions of the world.

A further important feature of this passage is that it is in part an elaboration of an idea stated earlier in Stevens' essay, that the poet's sense of the world, so important in making his poetry, is the result of his personality and temperament over which, as Santayana and, before him, Emerson pointed out, he has no control. Such a view of the nature of the poet's sense of the world has an effect like that of the exquisite appositeness of analogy, which banishes verbality and allows one man's emotion to work directly on another, an effect like the preference for the term metamorphosis over metaphor. That effect, namely, is to return poetry to the natural world from which its character of transcendent analogue has separated it.

Now the notion of the man for whom reality is enough implies the man for whom reality is not enough. In another discussion of reality and imagination, Stevens tells about being in a cemetery in an old churchyard in Pennsylvania. He has already said that time and experience in the artist, rather than the artist himself, create or reveal (this is his own characteristic conflation) reality. The cemetery is depressing and empty:

There could not be any effective diversion from the reality that time and experience had created here, the desolation that penetrated one like something final. (*Necessary Angel*, p. 100)

Time and experience, like a poet, had created an analogy in what was at the same time an imageless reality, an analogy of the ultimate desolation of human life. But then Stevens goes to the Morgan Library to see an exhibit of graphic art:

The brilliant pages from Poland, France, Finland and so on, books of tales, of poetry, of folk-lore, were as if the barren reality that I had just experienced had suddenly taken color, become alive and from a single thing become many things and people, vivid, active, intently trying out a thousand characters and illuminations. (p. 102)

And the passage ends as a masterly summary of Stevens' view of the relation of reality and imagination, in which reality, like any picture, is created, and in which the art is merely reality itself become alive, differentiating and discriminating itself, peopling itself. At the same time, time and experience made the cemetery and the graphic art both, so that art is neither more nor less natural than reality, more nor less man's product. Just as the illuminations of the manuscripts are the artists' variations in another mode of the meaning in the text, so the manuscripts themselves are a version of the reality embodied in the cemetery.

The illuminated manuscripts enrich the reality of the cemetery as "one day enriches a year" in "Credences of Summer," "not as embellishment. / Stripped of remembrance, it displays its strength— / The youth, the vital son, the heroic power." The essay is later than "Credences." In the poem, Stevens celebrates the moment "stripped of remembrance," that is, of the thought of any other moment. The rock of summer is the rock of his church. "It is the truth"—it is the visible and the audible. It is one of the limits of reality, absolutely reliable, as summer is one of the limits of the year, and its parallel in poetry is the full apprehension of the object which the "thrice concentrated self . . . grips . . . in savage scrutiny, . . . Fully made, fully apparent, fully found." What the essay does instead is to possess the moment of summer while remembering the moment of winter. When we are in a summer moment, we are likely to feel the great celebration of the given sensuous world, the world of forms, what Stevens calls the near world, full of color, movement and warmth; then, the task of the poet appears to be to become the transparence of the place. But when memory enters, the poet becomes aware of the other pole of reality: cold, distant, formless, motionless. How is that winter experience, that other limit of reality, to be integrated into a unitary vision?

Throughout the poems the distant, icy pole is the place of the mythic, the abstract, the absolute, the supreme fiction which the poet creates. It is out of the mythic cold that the warm particulars of the earth seem eventually to come. They are related as the base of the rock of summer itself, green and blooming, is to its upper half, "luminous . . . in the extremest light / Of sapphires flashing from the central sky." The base is green and natural; the upper part with its light and precious jewels and centrality speaks of the presence of the poet's imagination. They pass one into the other but not of themselves, only through time and experience working in the poet.

In "The Rock," also later than "Credences," human experience and his own life seem to the remembering poet not to be believed, an illusion,

> As if nothingness contained a métier,
> A vital assumption, an impermanence
> In its permanent cold, an illusion so desired
>
> That the green leaves came and covered the high rock,
> That the lilacs came and bloomed, like a blindness cleaned,
> Exclaiming bright sight, as it was satisfied,
>
> In a birth of sight. The glooming and the musk
> Were being alive, an incessant being alive,
> A particular of being, that gross universe. (p. 363)

In "Credences," the rock covered with bloom is a given—it needs only to be grasped, conquered by the thrice concentrated self—although, to be sure, the desperate repetitions of that grasping which grips the object in "savage scrutiny, / Once to make captive, once to proclaim / The meaning of the capture, this hard prize" subverts the force of "given" and "only to be grasped." The violence and desperation of that grasping speak of the difficulty of fully living in that summer moment, and the celebration in the poem is not only of the day but of the difficult task of the singers who "sang desiring an object that was near, / In face of which desire no longer moved, / Nor made of itself that which it could not find" (p. 291). This is a moment of surrender of self equal to Santayana's in the early sonnets and to Eliot's and Yeats's, while the tower of part III of "Credences," "the point of survey, green's green apogee," is another version of Santayana's point "high above the battlements of heaven." In "The Rock," however, the rock blooms *through* human desire; it is an illusion; the leaves come to cover the rock through the illusion that is also a vital assumption, a métier and an impermanence in the permanent of cold of nothingness. Because reality is unstable, because we do suffer desire, because we can have no certain knowledge—all the conditions of life we lament—because of them the rock blooms. But in this poem, the greening of the rock is the birth of sight, no longer the green object given and grasped. Now the blooming rock is something that has happened, like Rilke's unicorn, the beast that doesn't exist but can come into existence if we give it room; in any case, we love it. That is, his subject is not beauty as something possessed by an object but the sense of beauty as Santayana found it to be, an experience occurring in the perturbed kingdom of the self.

Furthermore, it is no longer enough to fix a barren center in an eternal foliage as it was in "Credences." Stevens asks here for a "cure" of the rock through a "cure of the ground / Or a cure of ourselves, that is equal to a cure / Of the ground, a cure beyond forgetfulness." He imagines a modern version of the sacrament in which, "if we ate the incipient colorings / Of their fresh culls," it might be a cure. The subjugation of the object by the grasping imagination was insufficient to cure us of our desire after all. The language removes us still further into an esthetic realm, away from the palpable, substantial world. We are invited to eat the colorings of the culls and thereby to become one with their fleshlessness. Or so we might assume if we are partaking of a coloring, especially only an incipient coloring. But Stevens' sacrament is no consubstantial compromise; the blood and the flesh are there. In the next image, the leaves that cover the barren rock quicken man's body and cause his mind to root. As Stevens wrote in *The Necessary Angel*, the purpose of the analogy is to banish verbality: to make the vehicular words transparent and return us to the actual world.

> They bear their fruit so that the year is known,
>
> As if its understanding was brown skin,
> The honey in its pulp, the final found,
> The plenty of the year and of the world. (p. 364)

There is no getting away from the natural world in Stevens, from sense and flesh, as there is in Eliot. While Eliot's strivings bring us to the edge of apocalypse, Stevens reaches toward perspectives which breed creation. Stevens' utmost effort transforms the entire world from its mere self into an analogy. Then it is flesh and fleshless at once. The experience becomes the meaning of the experience, as the skin of the fruit is its understanding. The rock, the permanent cold, the barren which lies at the foundation of that experience is turned into meanings, and the meanings are those of the leaves which cover it, which are both the real leaves bringing us the plenty of the year and of the world, and the poems which do the same. The rock, the poem concludes, is the "grey particular of man's life, / The stone from which he rises . . . " (p. 364).

In "Notes toward a Supreme Fiction," Stevens is even more specific about the grey particular of man's life, and he is most explicit about the conditions from which poetry springs: ". . . that we live in a place / That is not our own and, much more, not ourselves / And hard it is in spite of blazoned days." Poems are made because we cannot live only in summer, "in blazoned days." We are always aware of those great empty spaces which it is the poet's task to fill with his supreme fictions, for "The air is not a mirror but a bare board." We sense always those cold distances from which we cannot always avert our glance to focus on the near. Stevens' serpent of "The Auroras of Autumn,"—"form gulping after formlessness"—inhabits Eden and drives us continuously forth. And when driven forth into the great spaces:

> These external regions, what do we fill them with
> Except reflections, the escapades of death,
> Cinderella fulfilling herself beneath the roof? (p. 231)

Yet, as Santayana believed, the substances of these fulfillments are not fantasy but involve the possibilities of the actual world. "We are the mimics," Stevens writes. "Clouds are pedagogues." If we go to school closely enough to nature, she will cure us of herself. We take in her colorings without her substance as the clouds figure forth her forms without her substance; this the poet does in his poems until we live in a clarified reality, composed of our ordinary experience whose shape we then wholly understand and therefore wholly possess, and we all become men for whom reality is enough. Because, of course, underlying Stevens' work as it does Yeats's, Eliot's, and Santayana's is the profound conviction that reality as we ordinarily experience it—trivial, shapeless, irrational, obsessive, uncontrollable—is not enough.

But both the nature that schools us, like the clouds, and the response we are taught to make in the face of our expulsion from Eden, which Stevens calls "the first idea," are hardly what we think of as natural:

> The lion roars at the enraging desert,
> Reddens the sand with his red-colored noise,
> Defies red emptiness to evolve his match . . . . (p. 210)

That is Stevens' nature, wholly theatrical and decorative. The world belongs to that lion, so conceived, not to us. Poets are the "heroic children whom time breeds / Against the first idea—to lash the lion, / Caparison elephants, teach bears to juggle" (p. 211). Like Yeats, Stevens thinks of the poet as making circus acts of the beasts who threaten him. Both by this image of the world and by this image of our response to the world, we are again reminded of the artificial, theatrical, and fictive nature of our lives as well as our poetry. This gaiety and theatricality are there in the word "confect," which Stevens uses in the lines where the poet must confect "the final elegance" out of the man in baggy pantaloons. The poet will "confect" the ideas that will make reality sufficient out of the "grey particulars" of our lives.

The credences of summer themselves, then, are fictions in which our imaginations clothe the grey particular world. Therefore, when the poet performs his function of being the transparency of the place he is in, he is also, at the same time, revealing the power of his imagination and of ours, the shared human power to create this green world. In the world of Stevens' poetry, as in Santayana, we never know the world in itself but only the world we make of it. Furthermore, the world we did not make also exists for us through our ideas of it, as in the lions in the red desert and the expulsion from Eden. We can know even our passions and our sufferings only mediately, not directly. Stevens' poetry is the most comprehensive embodiment of Santayana's poetics and his epistemology as well, for what we see happening throughout both men's writings is the compounding of poetics and epistemology just as the real and the imagined, and reason and imagination are compounded.

We have traced in Stevens, as in Yeats and Eliot, the view of the imagination which made such a compounding possible, the view which we watched emerge in Santayana's poetry and criticism at the turn of the century out of the pressure of his private needs on the quite public and shared intellectual interests of his period. It was a view that responded to the extraordinary loss of satisfaction in the ordinary paths of action open to us. Rooted in an overwhelming sense of the insufficiency of experience, responding to a devastating feeling of futility, it raised the expectation of the failure of every human action to a first principle. Santayana's personal sense of the inherently inevitable mutilations of experience was shared by these poets, and such a view of their necessity was as liberating for them as for him. It was the source of the idea of the imagination creating a poetic world which was the world of experience but perfected and understood and therefore wholly possessed. In Yeats, the worlds were most wholly distinct. We feel in his work most forcefully the passionate frustrations of experience and see most clearly the emergence of the second world and its relation to the first. In Eliot, the second world is the first world seen through the eyes of a saint. In Stevens, the second world is also the first world properly seen, but his vision is further complicated by the belief that the first world, too, even when it is miscellaneous and random, is a world our imagination makes.

All three men share with Santayana the rejection of the imaginative act as an expression of poetic personality. All find a major theme in the creation of order and of determinate form as opposed to the celebration of the abnormal or the unique and the evocation of the infinite. All are absorbed in the relationship of the imagined and the experienced, and in all the imagined *is* the experienced emptied of personal desire and exercise of the will and filled with meaning.

In a moving tribute to the dying Santayana, "To an Old Philosopher in Rome," Stevens makes Santayana the man for whom reality is enough. At the end of his life, he is in the poet's representative position, at the "extreme of the known in the presence of the unknown." Santayana is on the threshold of "the total edifice" of reality, a moment when the actual poor Rome he inhabits is one with the rich, imperial Rome of the imagination. Stevens imagines Santayana's life as transfigured by the impending transition, made immensely full and powerful, yet remaining no more than his simple life, just as his room, which has the "total grandeur of a total edifice," is an immense theater, yet remains "No more than a bed, a chair and moving nuns." This Santayana lives in an analogy. More than any other modernist poet, Stevens realized in his work Santayana's idea of poetry as a world made by the poet from the basic components of actuality but given the shape and clarity which he conceived to be the heart's deepest desire, a shape and clarity which would bring peace, no matter how tragic the import so shaped and clarified. Santayana in Rome, as poor and powerless as any actual monastic, sitting as still as Eliot might pray to sit, typifies his own and Stevens' sense of man's condition. Stevens imagines for him in this poem what Santayana imagined for himself when he was thirty years old, that once he gave up claim to every particular thing in the world, he might nevertheless possess the entire world in idea.

For strikingly, in all these men, the discipline of poetry was also the way to live and be reconciled to life. The discipline involved a glorification of the poetic act which granted the poet his one great transforming power in place of all the actual power it denied him in the world of action. This, along with the discrimination of form, the impersonality, the striving for the normative and communal, was as Santayana envisioned and hoped for. What he did not foresee but what was implicit in his concept of the imagination was the way in which all of life became merely the material of art. It is not a minor art compounded of design and color only, but an art of scope and depth, seeking to understand the foundations of our lives and the terms on which we may accept human limits; yet it is art and art that powerfully invites us to a view of life which values knowledge over action. In fact, more than that, it absolutely separates knowledge from action. In this view the choices and consequences of our active lives are not of the highest importance; whether we achieve our goals or whether in fact our goals are worthy of our desire are not questions to which our attention is directed. The conflicts of our emotional lives, coming as they do from our pursuit of goals, tend to be scanted, with so much of the energy of the poetry committed to the transcendence of those conflicts. We are all asked, in a sense, to make that renunciation Santayana called his metanoia. The inevitable frustrations of action, the imperfection of every satisfaction, the radical ignorance and blindness of human passions, these could all be transcended in the imaginative moment free of time and desire— the moment in which we might be willing with Yeats to live it all again, or with Eliot to affirm that all manner of things were well, or with Stevens to find that reality is enough. When such a mode of experience is one among several, then it is illuminating, liberating, and comforting. When it becomes the primary mode of experience, it is dangerously weakening to vital human claims. For, as Santayana spent so much energy reminding us, desire is the source not merely of our suffering but of all our values, and as Stevens and Yeats saw more clearly than Eliot, of all our art. Nevertheless, for a long time modernist poetry did indeed perform for a large segment of its culture the function Santayana assigned to it: it did create a myth to embody that culture's understanding of its limits and powers. Santayana's own drive to mastery was re-enacted on a broad social stage. As modernist claims for the imagination become a part of literary history, they perforce lose some of their strength and inevitability. We are more aware of what remains intractable to the imagination and what such a solution to a culture's view of the futility of action costs. But it was a solution, and it did salvage, as Santayana hoped it would, at least a portion of that part of experience worth saving from a blind world of force and instinct that seemed at the time the only alternative.

STEVENS AND THE SUFFICIENCY OF REALITY

NOTES

1. Wallace Stevens, *The Necessary Angel: Essays on Reality and Imagination* (New York: Knopf, 1951), pp. 170-71.
2. Wallace Stevens, *The Palm at the End of the Mind*, ed. Holly Stevens (New York: Knopf, 1971), p. 174.

Index

Ambassadors, The, 18
Animal faith, 5, 109
Aristotle, 36, 85
Arnold, Matthew, 3, 35, 42, 50, 86, 89-90, 92-93, 100
Art, Santayana's theory of, 43-44, 48-49, 54-87; barbarism in, 82, 86, 90, 103, 109; the beautiful in, 56-58, 85; expression in, 83; form in, 72-73, 77-78, 80; the ideal in, 73, 75, 86; morality in, 93; poetic creation in, 111-12; religion and, 113; sexuality in, 61; the sublime in, 84-85; symbolism in, 69-70, 113-14; the tragic in, 83-84; visual element in, 62, 68-69. See also Imagination; Religion: as imaginative form; Santayana: concept of value in; spiritual crisis (metanoia) in; and Eliot; and Stevens; and Yeats
Awkward Age, The, 62

Blackmur, R. P., 70
Blake, William, 132, 140
Boas, George, 59
Brooks, Cleanth, 70
Browning, 23, 35, 63, 82, 103, 107, 109
Burke, Kenneth, 70
Byron, 45-48

Christianity: Santayana's view of, 7, 11, 15, 23, 40-41, 43, 49, 51, 90, 100-02; Eliot's view of, 139, 148-51, 154, 156; Stevens' view of, 158. See also Religion; Arnold, Matthew

Classicism in Santayana, 24, 52, 90, 93, 95-96
Commedia, 144
Conrad, 45, 49, 50, 63, 86
Convivio, 144
Cory, Daniel, 15, 28
"Crossing Brooklyn Ferry," 166

Dante, 25, 42, 105-06, 143-47, 155, 157
Decadence in art, 63, 76, 107-08

Eliot, T. S., 69, 78, 124, 137, 139-57; and Buddhism, 146-47, 151, 152, 155; and Christianity, 139, 148-51, 154, 156; expression in, 143-44; and history, 140, 145, 152; and Santayana, vii, 124, 139, 141-43, 149, 152, 172-74; symbolic power in, 174
Eliot, T. S., Works: "Ash Wednesday," 154; "Burnt Norton," 149-50; "Dry Salvages, The," 151; "East Coker," 153; *Four Quartets,* 149-50, 151-52; "Imperfect Critics," 142; "Little Gidding," 152-53, 156; "Love Song of J. Alfred Prufrock, The," 144; *Poems 1920,* 145; "Possibility of a Poetic Drama, The," 140; "Portrait of a Lady," 144; *Sacred Wood, The,* 140-44; "Tradition and the Individual Talent," 140-42; *Waste Land, The,* 139, 145-46, 150
Ellman, Richard, 118, 132
Emerson, 23, 63, 69, 77, 89, 90-91, 93, 98-99, 101-02, 109, 123, 132-33

Estheticism, 23-24, 75-77. See also
    Decadence in art
Essence, 17, 48

Faust, 104
Feeling and Form, 70, 137
Finnegan's Wake, 159
Fire Sermon, The, 146-47, 155
Frazer, James George, 100-01
Freud, 24, 28, 61, 107-08

Goethe, 17, 21
Gonne, Maude, 130-31
Golden Bowl, The, 63
Greek civilization. See Classicism
Guido Cavalcanti, 25, 27

Harvard, Santayana at, 16, 46, 59, 60,
    75
Harvard Monthly, 17, 36, 63
Hobbes, 67, 76
Howgate, George, 27

Idealism, 54
Identity of Yeats, The, 118, 132
Imagination: Santayana's concept of, ix,
    68-70, 89-114; Stevens' concept of,
    161-72. See also Art, Santayana's
    theory of
Interpretation of Dreams, The, 107-08

James, Henry, 18, 62, 63, 86, 93
James, William, 5, 28, 54, 59, 60,
    95-97
Joyce, James, 112, 133, 159
Jung, 112

Kenner, Hugh, 147
Kris, Ernst, 11
Krishna, 152, 155

Lahor, Jean, 91
Langer, Suzanne, 70, 137
Le Gallienne, Richard, 63, 107-08
Lucretius, 110, 143

Manfred, 45-48
Modernism, vii-ix, 45, 55, 69-70, 74, 105,
    148; in poetry, 87, 114, 116, 124-25,
    137-38, 141, 172-74. See also
    Imagination
Montaigne, 70
Moore, Marianne, 167
Morality, 51-52
Munro, Thomas, 74
Mysticism: Santayana's criticism of, 94,

97-99, 107, 123; Yeat's criticism of,
    123, 133

Naturalism: in Santayana, viii, 19-20,
    23-24, 40-41, 47-48, 51, 100, 105;
    in Stevens, 139, 159
Nature, 91, 98, 123
Nietzsche, 35, 65, 132-33, 153
Nigger of the Narcissus, The, 63, 86

Pater, Walter, 23
Phelps, William Lyon, 4
Platonic love, 25-33, 40, 78
Poetics. See Art, Santayana's theory of;
    Imagination; Modernism
Potter, Warwick, 16
Pound, Ezra, 133, 140, 147-48,
    156-57
Pre-Raphaelites, 63, 65
Purgatorio, 146-47

Reason, Santayana's concept of, 44,
    51-52
Religion: as imaginative form, 44, 83,
    89-93, 100, 102, 110; post-
    rational, 94; Arnold's view of, 92,
    93, 100; Santayana's view of, 4,
    7; Stevens' view of, 158-61. See
    also Christianity; Imagination
Romanticism: Santayana's criticism of,
    35, 43-44, 47, 52-54, 69, 104;
    Stevens' criticism of, 159, 162
Rossetti, 63
Royce, 35, 54, 60
Ruskin, 23, 75
Russell, George, 131

Santayana, George, 3-115; abandonment
    of poetry by, 80-82; at Harvard, 16,
    46, 59, 60, 75; architectural interest
    of, 64-65; childhood of, 3, 13, 64,
    69; concept of value in, 50, 55-56,
    75, 82; father of, 15-16, 47, 58,
    65-68, 76; first sonnet sequence of,
    4-23; mother of, 10- 47, 66, 67;
    hlaf-sister of, 7, 14-16, 28, 46-47;
    homosexual feelings of, 27-28, 46;
    second sonnet sequence of, 24-34;
    spiritual crisis (metanoia) in, viii-ix,
    11, 14-18, 24-25, 34, 43-44, 46,
    48, 174; theory of knowledge in,
    50, 79-80, 105; and Eliot, vii, 124,
    139, 141-43, 149, 152, 172-74; and
    Stevens, vii, 158-61, 163, 166,
    171, 172-74. See also Art, Santay-
    ana's theory of; Classicism;

Christianity; Imagination; Modernism; Naturalism; Religion; Romanticism

Santayana, George, Works: "Although I decked a chamber for my bride," 30; "Among the myriad voices of the spring," 29; "Apologia Pro Mente Sua," 36, 52, 81; "As in the midst of battle there is room," 30-31; "Blaspheme not love, ye lovers, nor dispraise," 20; "But is this love that in my hollow breast," 30; "Deem not because you see me in the press," 9; "Heaven it is to be at peace with things," 33; "I sought on earth a garden of delight," 6; "I would I might forget that I am I," 9; *Interpretations of Poetry and Religion*, 17, 27, 33, 37, 43-44, 70, 89-114, 126; "Let my lips touch thy lips and my desire," 32; *Letters*, 4-5, 23-24, 27-28, 64, 74; *Life of Reason, The*, 27, 37, 49, 52, 58; *Lucifer: A Theological Tragedy*, 20, 33, 35-53, 166; *My Host the World*, 14-18, 24-26; "Mutability of Aesthetic Categories, The," 57; *Persons and Places*, 10-13, 16, 64; "Poetry of Barbarism, The," 94; "A perfect love is nourished by despair," 26, 28, 33; "Out of the brackish dust the queen of roses springs," 31-32; "O world thou choosest not the better part," 4; *Realms of Being*, 27, 52, 62; *Reason in Art*, 56, 68, 71, 81-82; *Reason in Science*, 51-52, 94; *Scepticism and Animal Faith*, 79, 109-10; *Sense of Beauty, The*, 21, 33, 42, 52, 54-87; 94, 118; "Sleep hath composed the anguish of my brain," 32; "Sweet are the days we wander with no hope," 18; "Soul is not on earth an alien thing, The," 31-32; "There may be chaos still around the world," 18; "There was a time when in the teeth of fate," 19; "These strewn thoughts by the mountain pathway spring," 22; *Three Philosophical Poets*, 46, 71, 94, 104-05, 142; "Thousand beauties that have never been, A," 20; "'Tis a sad love like an eternal prayer," 117

Schopenhauer, 56
Shakespeare, 90, 102-03
"Song of Myself," 63

Stevens, Wallace, 36, 139, 158-74; concept of imagination in, 161-73; naturalism in, 139, 159; religion in, 158-61; and Santayana, vii, 159, 160-63, 166, 171-74

Stevens, Wallace, Works: "An Ordinary Evening in New Haven," 164; "Asides on the Oboe," 164; "Auroras of Autumn, The," 171; "Credences of Summer," 164, 168; "Man With the Blue Guitar, The," 165-66; *Necessary Angel, The*, 160-64, 166-68, 170; "Notes Toward a Supreme Fiction," 164-65, 171-72; "Of Modern Poetry," 161; "Peter Quince at the Clavier," 162; "Rock, The," 169-71; "To an Old Philosopher in Rome," 173

Swinburne, 124
Symbolists, 97, 99, 158
Symposium, 134

Tennyson, 23

Ulysses, 159

Valéry, Paul, 142-43, 161
Victorians, 23, 24, 74

Well Wrought Urn, The, 70
Whitman, 63, 106-07, 109, 166
Wilde, Oscar, 76-77
Woolf, Virginia, 133, 145
Wordsworth, 110

Yeats, William Butler, 30, 45, 116-38; mysticism in, 122-23, 133; poetic development of, 118-27, 131-33; and Santayana, ix-x, 116-18, 121, 125, 127-28, 130-32, 135-38, 172-74; symbolic power in, 124-25, 127-30, 134-37, 174

Yeats, William Butler, Works: "Among School Children," 137; *Autobiography*, 130; "Circus Animals' Desertion, The," 129-30; *Crossways*, 116; "Dialogue of Self and Soul, A," 134-35, 154; "Easter 1916," 125-27; "Ego Dominus Tuus," 134; "Fergus and the Druid," 122; *Green Helmet, The*, 126; "Host of the Air," 123; "Lapis Lazuli," 136; "Leda and the Swan," 129; "Moods, The," 135; "Sailing to Byzantium," 118, 120-21; "Secret Rose, The," 123; "Song of the Happy Shepherd," 116;

"Statues, The," 127-28; "Symbolism of Poetry, The," 131; "Under Ben Bulben," 127-28, 131; "Tower, The," 127-28; "Vacillation," 127, 134; *Vision, A,* 136; "White Birds, The," 118-20, 154; "Words," 126

Saint Peter's University Library
Withdrawn